weightwatchers

what to cook now

300 Recipes for Every Kitchen

ST. MARTIN'S GRIFFIN ⚞ NEW YORK

WEIGHT WATCHERS WHAT TO COOK NOW. Copyright © 2014 by Weight Watchers International, Inc. All rights reserved. Printed in the United States of America. For information, address St. Martin's Press, 175 Fifth Avenue, New York, N.Y. 10010.

On the front cover, clockwise, from top left:
Warm Mozzarella and Tomato Flatbreads, 233; Chocolate Cupcakes with Peanut Butter Frosting, 337; Spaghetti with Mussels, Clams, and Shrimp, 201; Grilled Sirloin with Coffee-Molasses Barbeque Sauce, 111.

On the back cover, from top:
Grilled Salmon with Honey-Lime Fruit Salad, 176; Filet Mignon with Arugula and
Maple-Balsamic Glaze, 240; Chocolate Brownie Ice Cream Sandwiches, 361.

www.stmartins.com

Editorial and art produced by W/W Twentyfirst Corp., 675 Avenue of the Americas, New York NY 10010.

WEIGHT WATCHERS is a trademark of Weight Watchers International, Inc. Printed in the USA

Library of Congress Cataloging-in-Publication Data
   Weight watchers what to cook now : 300 recipes for every kitchen / by Weight Watchers. —First U.S. edition.
      pages   cm
      ISBN 978-1-250-04454-9 (paper over board)
      ISBN 978-1-4668-4292-2 (e-book)
      1. Reducing diets—Recipes.   2. Weight loss.   I. Weight Watchers International.
   RM222.2.W32842   2014
   613.2'5—dc23   2013032284

St. Martin's Griffin books may be purchased for educational, business, or promotional use. For information on bulk purchases, please contact Macmillan Corporate and Premium Sales Department at 1-800-221-7945, extension 5442, or write specialmarkets@macmillan.com.

First Edition: January 2014

10 9 8 7 6 5 4 3 2 1

about weight watchers

Weight Watchers International, Inc. is the world's leading provider of weight-management services, operating globally through a network of company-owned and franchise operations. Weight Watchers holds nearly 45,000 meetings each week worldwide, at which members receive group support and education about healthful eating patterns, behavior modification, and physical activity. Weight-loss and weight-management results vary by individual. We recommend that you attend Weight Watchers meetings to benefit from the supportive environment and follow the comprehensive Weight Watchers program, which includes a food plan, an activity plan, and a behavioral component. **WeightWatchers.com** provides subscription weight-management products, such as eTools and Weight Watchers Mobile, and is the leading Internet-based weight-management provider in the world. In addition, Weight Watchers offers a wide range of products, publications (including **Weight Watchers Magazine**, which is available on newsstands and in Weight Watchers meeting rooms), and programs for people interested in weight loss and control. For the Weight Watchers meeting nearest you, call **1-800-651-6000**. For information about bringing Weight Watchers to your workplace, call **1-800-8AT-WORK**.

WEIGHT WATCHERS PUBLISHING GROUP

VP, Editorial Director
Nancy Gagliardi

Creative Director
Ed Melnitsky

Photo Director
Deborah Hardt

Managing Editor
Diane Pavia

Assistant Editor
Katerina Gkionis

Food Editor
Eileen Runyan

Editor
Jackie Mills, R.D.N.

Nutrition Consultant
U. Beate Krinke

Photographers
Iain Bagwell
Kate Sears
Rita Maas

Food Stylists
Adrienne Anderson
Sally Jo O'Brien
Lori Powell

Prop Stylists
Dani Fisher
Paige Hicks
Pam Morris

foreword

It's an understatement to say that the way Americans think about food has changed. In the last decade, dramatic shifts in food production and distribution have raised countless new issues (in terms of the environment and consumption) resulting in numerous well-intentioned organizations and people with just as many agendas. What is the implication of all these changes? What you choose to consume says a great deal about who you are, as well as what you believe. Pretty heady stuff, yet the fact remains: Everyone eats, and whether the food choices you make are politically motivated or not, eating is intensely personal.

The reality is that if you're trying to eat in a more healthful way, you are making a statement given that the foods that will help you lose weight—fresh fruits and vegetables, lean meats and whole grains—are often at the very heart of the food discussion. Wholesome foods, such as these, with minimal processing also often require a bit more effort and TLC—in terms of choosing, as well as preparing or cooking. Think about it: A tomato is something to toss into a salad, unless you know that choosing a fully ripe beauty and seasoning it with a sprinkle of salt and pepper and a drizzle of olive oil can transform it into something truly delicious.

If this is how you want to (or do!) think about food, this cookbook will help. Guiding you through all the steps of preparing healthy fare that is satisfying without being labor-intensive is the goal and modern approach of *What to Cook Now*. This complete guide provides you with all the tools you need for getting flavorful meals on the table without spending hours in the kitchen. It's an all-encompassing compendium that includes more than 300 recipes—everything from the basics like stocks and sauces made easier, speedy weeknight dinners, meals and menus ideal for entertaining, and luscious sweets for every season. Also, each dish includes complete nutrition information and clever tips to boost your kitchen and cooking prowess.

In addition to recipes, there are sections on the new, user-friendly kitchen tools (like an immersion blender) and must-have pantry basics (such as intensely flavored pastes or condiments borrowing from cuisines around the globe); the latest thinking on food safety; new information on mastering basic cooking techniques; fresh ideas on amping up the forgotten meals, breakfast and lunch; choosing the best cuts of meat; plus a complete produce primer for helping the health-conscious cook choose and prepare veggie-and-fruit based dishes; and much more.

With everything in one place, *What to Cook Now* is destined to become your go-to cookbook, a classic you'll reference again and again.

—Nancy Gagliardi
VP, Editorial Director

contents

weight watchers and simple start

Weight Watchers is with you—and for you—all the way to your weight goal. Our meetings provide support, motivation, and accountability. Our digital tools—the tools on **WeightWatchers .com** and a robust suite of apps for smartphones and for iPad—provide our biggest database of foods and their *PointsPlus*® values; a barcode scanner; great community features; thousands of recipes and articles; and more. All these products are designed to help you toward your goal.

Our newest plan is Simple Start. It will get you off to a great beginning. See opposite for a list of recipes built from good-for-you foods that work with Simple Start. From there, either keep going with our Simply Filling technique (which is what Simple Start is based on), or try tracking against your personalized daily *PointsPlus* Target.

recipes that work with simple start

about our recipes

While losing weight isn't only about what you eat, Weight Watchers realizes the critical role it plays in your success and overall good health. That's why our philosophy is to offer great-tasting, easy recipes that are nutritious as well as delicious. We make every attempt to use wholesome ingredients and to ensure that our recipes fall within the recommendations of the U.S. Dietary Guidelines for Americans for a diet that promotes health and reduces the risk for disease. If you have special dietary needs, consult with your health-care professional for advice on a diet that is best for you, then adapt these recipes to meet your specific nutritional needs. To achieve these good-health goals and get the maximum satisfaction from the foods you eat, we suggest you keep the following information in mind while preparing our recipes:

getting started, keeping going, and good nutrition

- Recipes in this book have been developed for Weight Watchers members who are just getting started (with Simple Start) and for members who are further along toward their goals, including those who are using our *PointsPlus* plan, as well as anyone interested in smart weight loss in general.
- *PointsPlus* values are given for each recipe. They're assigned based on the amount of protein, carbohydrates, fat, and fiber contained in a single serving of a recipe.
- Recipes include approximate nutritional information: they are analyzed for Calories (Cal), Total Fat, Saturated Fat (Sat Fat), Trans Fat, Cholesterol (Chol), Sodium (Sod), Carbohydrates (Carb), Dietary Fiber (Fib), Protein (Prot), and

Calcium (Calc). The nutritional values are calculated by registered dietitians, using nutrition analysis software.

- Substitutions made to the ingredients will alter the per-serving nutritional information and may affect the *PointsPlus* value.
- Our recipes meet Weight Watchers Good Health Guidelines for eating lean proteins and fiber-rich whole grains and for having at least five servings of vegetables and fruits and two servings of low-fat or fat-free dairy products a day, while limiting your intake of saturated fat, sugar, and sodium.
- Cook's Note suggestions for making a meal have a *PointsPlus* value of *0* unless otherwise stated.
- Health agencies recommend limiting sodium intake. To stay in line with this recommendation, we keep sodium levels in our recipes reasonably low; to boost flavor, we often include fresh herbs or a squeeze of citrus instead of salt. If you don't have to restrict your sodium, feel free to add a touch more salt as desired.
- Recipes that work with Simple Start are listed on page vi. Find more details about Simple Start at a Weight Watchers meeting.
- For information about the science behind lasting weight loss and more, please visit **WeightWatchers.com/science**.

calculations not what you expected?

- You might expect some of the *PointsPlus* values in this book to be lower when some of the foods they're made from, such as fruits and vegetables, have no **PointsPlus** values. Most fruits and veggies have no **PointsPlus** values when served as a snack or part of a meal, like a cup of berries with a sandwich. But if these foods are part of a recipe, their fiber and nutrient content are incorporated into the recipe calculations. These nutrients can affect the **PointsPlus** value.

- Alcohol is included in our **PointsPlus** calculations. Because alcohol information is generally not included on nutrition labels, it's not an option to include when using the hand calculator or the online calculator. But since we include alcohol information that we get from our nutritionists, you might notice discrepancies between the **PointsPlus** values you see in our recipes, and the values you get using the calculator. The **PointsPlus** values listed for our recipes are the most accurate values.

shopping for ingredients

As you learn to eat healthier, remember these tips for choosing foods wisely:

lean meats and poultry

Purchase lean meats and poultry, and trim them of all visible fat before cooking. When poultry is cooked with the skin on, we recommend removing the skin before eating. Nutritional information for recipes that include meat, poultry, and fish is based on cooked, skinless boneless portions (unless otherwise stated), with the fat trimmed.

seafood

Whenever possible, our recipes call for seafood that is sustainable and deemed the most healthful for human consumption so that your choice of seafood is not only good for the oceans but also good for you. For more information about the best seafood choices, and to download a pocket guide, go to environmentaldefensefund.org or montereybayaquarium.org. For information about mercury and seafood go to weightwatchers.com.

produce

For best flavor, maximum nutrient content, and the lowest prices, buy fresh local produce, such as vegetables, leafy greens, and fruits, in season. Rinse them thoroughly before using, and keep a supply of cut-up vegetables and fruits in your refrigerator for convenient healthy snacks.

whole grains

Explore your market for whole grain products, such as whole wheat and whole grain breads and pastas, brown rice, bulgur, barley, cornmeal, whole wheat couscous, oats, and quinoa, to enjoy with your meals.

preparation and measuring

Before you start cooking any recipe, consider the following.

read the recipe

Take a couple of minutes to read through the ingredients and directions before you start to prepare a recipe. This will prevent you from discovering midway through that you don't have an important ingredient or that a recipe requires several hours of marinating. And it's also a good idea to assemble all ingredients and utensils within easy reach before you begin a recipe.

weighing and measuring

The success of any recipe depends on accurate weighing and measuring. The effectiveness of the Weight Watchers Program and the accuracy of the nutritional analysis depend on correct measuring as well.

the essential pantry

Everyone's got pantry basics on hand, but when you're committed to cooking quick healthy meals, it's critical to have the right stuff on hand.

smart seasonings

With these ingredients on hand, you can add instant flavor to everything you cook.

ASIAN CONDIMENTS AND SEASONINGS

Hoisin sauce, oyster sauce, fish sauce, miso, and Thai curry pastes punch up the flavor of everything from stir-fries to soups, from meat loaf to marinades.

CANNED ANCHOVY FILLETS

Mince a couple of these salty little fish and add them to a hearty soup or stew, pasta sauce, or salad dressing for a mysterious flavor dimension that's not at all fishy. No one will guess your secret ingredient.

CANNED CHIPOTLES EN ADOBO

Just a teaspoon of these fiery chiles add spice—and smoky flavor—to any dish.

HERB AND SPICE BLENDS

Check the spice section of your supermarket and add a few new flavors to your cooking. Get Cajun seasoning for spicy dishes, garam masala for Indian recipes, and Mexican seasoning for easy chilis, fajitas, and tacos.

REFRIGERATED PESTO

Stir it into cooked pasta, rice, or couscous to make a flavorful side dish; add a spoonful to vegetable or tomato soup to pump up the flavor; or add it to a marinade for chicken or seafood.

WHOLE GRAIN MUSTARD

Whisk it into a salad dressing, slather it on pork chops, or smear it on a sandwich for pungent flavor.

quick-cooking ingredients

There's never an excuse not to make a homemade meal when your kitchen is stocked with foods, such as the following that you can cook in just a few minutes. For convenience, stock up when

you shop and wrap meats, poultry, and seafood in individual portions, then freeze them. When you're ready for dinner in a hurry, thaw them in the microwave just before cooking.

- Flank steak or top sirloin steak
- Center-cut pork loin chops
- Pork tenderloin
- Skinless, boneless chicken breasts
- Turkey breast cutlets
- Fish fillets
- Shrimp
- Eggs
- Fresh whole wheat pasta
- Whole wheat couscous
- Whole wheat orzo
- Canned beans
- Plain frozen vegetables

long-lasting fresh fruits and vegetables

When you shop for produce, always buy a few fruits and vegetables that are "keepers"—varieties that will stay fresh for a week or longer. You can turn these into a quick side dish for dinner, or enjoy them for a snack without another trip to the grocery store. These are some of the longest-lasting fruits and vegetables to have on hand.

- Apples
- Broccoli
- Cabbage
- Carrots
- Cauliflower
- Celery
- Citrus fruits
- Potatoes
- Radishes
- Romaine lettuce
- Sweet potatoes
- Winter squash

whole grain goodness

Whole grains, with their big measure of fiber and nutrients, are a must-have pantry staple for healthy eating. Here's what to keep in your pantry for wholesome everyday meals and snacks.

- Barley
- Brown rice, wild rice
- Bulgur
- Dried whole wheat pasta
- Oats
- 100 percent whole wheat bread
- Polenta
- Popcorn
- Quinoa
- Whole grain crackers

the new pantry

If you're looking to take flavor to the next level, consider these essential staples used in Asian cooking. Though once considered unusual, they're readily available in most supermarkets today.

Asian Fish Sauce   This pungent, salty condiment is derived from salted fermented fish. It's known as *nam pla* in Thailand and *nuoc nam* in Vietnam.

Black Bean Sauce   This ready-to-use sauce is made from fermented black beans. It's intensely flavorful and quite salty, so use it sparingly.

Chili-Garlic Sauce   A thick, paste-like condiment made from hot peppers, garlic, and salt. It's excellent for quickly adding heat and flavor to dishes. It can also be used as a table condiment so that spice-loving diners can add more to their food if they wish.

Chinese Rice Wine   Also known as Shaoxing wine, this amber wine is usually aged at least 10 years. It has a deep, rich flavor similar to dry sherry. Both sherry and Japanese sake are good substitutes. Those who prefer to cook without alcohol can use apple juice instead.

Cinnamon Sticks   Cinnamon is a classic spice in many savory Indian dishes, and sticks (as opposed to the ground spice) deliver mild, fresh flavor and aroma without overwhelming the other seasonings in recipes. In a pinch, substitute 1/8 teaspoon ground cinnamon for each stick.

Coconut Milk   Rich, naturally sweet coconut milk is a staple ingredient in many Southeast Asian soups and curries. Using light (reduced-

fat) coconut milk instead of regular coconut milk will deliver good flavor and creaminess while trimming the number of fat grams in your recipes.

Garam Masala This ubiquitous blend of ground dry-roasted spices may include cloves, coriander, cumin, cardamom, fennel, black pepper, cinnamon, and more. It's available in the spice section of most supermarkets or at specialty stores.

Hoisin Sauce Sweet and tangy hoisin sauce is made from a mixture of soy beans, vinegar, sugar, salt, and chiles. It's extremely versatile: use it for everything from marinating meats to glazing roasted or grilled foods to imparting flavor to stir-fries.

Indian Chile Powder Made from ground dried red chiles, this fiery powder is the top choice for adding instant heat to your Indian dishes. You can purchase it at Indian grocery stores or online from spice specialists. Cayenne is a good substitute and packs a similar punch of heat.

Lemongrass Look for fresh lemongrass in the produce section of your supermarket or in Asian specialty stores. To prepare it, peel off the green, fibrous husk of the stalks and finely chop the pale core. If you can't find lemongrass, you can substitute a mixture of equal parts of grated lemon and lime zest.

Oyster Sauce This rich dark condiment is made from a combination of oyster extract and soy sauce and brings deep, smoky flavor to dishes. A version made with mushrooms instead of oysters is commonly available if you prefer not to consume shellfish, or you can substitute hoisin sauce.

Sambal Olek A fiery blend of ground chiles, vinegar, and salt, sambal olek is used throughout Southeast Asia as both a cooking ingredient and a table condiment. You can use Sriracha or other chili sauces as a substitute.

Sesame Oil Rich, aromatic sesame oil adds a distinctive nutty flavor to many Chinese dishes. Asian (dark) sesame oil and toasted sesame oils are usually "unrefined" and not recommended for high-heat cooking like stir-frying. Sesame oils labeled "refined" are suitable for stir-frying.

Sriracha This Thai-style chili sauce is available in most supermarkets and is a good all-purpose hot sauce to use in Southeast Asian dishes. The most popular brand is sold in convenient squeeze bottles with a white rooster on the label.

Tandoori Spice A.k.a. tandoori masala, this mixture of dried spices and aromatics is blended specifically to be mixed with yogurt and used as a marinade. Blends vary from brand to brand but typically include chiles, garlic, cayenne, cumin, cloves, coriander, and more. Large supermarkets and Asian grocery stores usually carry at least one brand of tandoori spice.

Thai Chile Peppers A.k.a. bird chiles, these tiny, super-spicy peppers are the standard chiles for Southeast Asian cooking. If you prefer, you can substitute milder serrano or jalapeño peppers.

Thai Curry Paste Small jars of thick, pungent concentrated Thai-style curry pastes are available in most large supermarkets. Red and green varieties are the most popular.

great flavor—fast

Keep these flavor-boosting ingredients on hand for quick, delicious meals.

VINEGARS

Think beyond salad dressings when using flavor-enhancing vinegars. Slightly sweet balsamic vinegar is delicious in sauces and gravies, sprinkled over roasted meats, or drizzled on strawberries. Tart white-wine vinegar perks up the flavor of cantaloupe or honeydew, fresh vegetable salsas, and marinades. Fruity raspberry vinegar is great for cooked veggies or in marinades for grilled chicken or shrimp.

FRESH HERBS

Hands down, fresh herbs are the quickest, easiest way to add flavor to almost any dish. Here, we've included our picks for the top herbs with intense flavor. Try one of these ideas and you'll see why:

- **Basil:** Toss whole leaves into green salad, stir it into vegetable soup just before serving, add it to sautéed vegetables, or toss it with roasted red bell peppers.

- **Chervil:** Whisk into salad dressing, sprinkle it over steamed vegetables, or fold it into a cheese omelette.

- **Chives:** Sprinkle over pasta salad or egg salad, stir into vegetable dips, or use as a peppery garnish for soups.

- **Lavender:** Add fresh lavender to a spice rub for meat or poultry, toss it with roasted potatoes, or stir it into a fruit compote.

- **Mint:** Use in cucumber salad, chilled soups, or fresh tomato sauce; sprinkle over roasted beets or steamed peas; or toss it with fresh fruit.

- **Rosemary:** Try in meat and poultry marinades, sprinkled on lamb before roasting or grilling, or in potato salad.

- **Thyme:** Incorporate into marinades for meats or chicken, tuck small sprigs under the skin of chicken before roasting, add it to beef barley soup or minestrone, or sprinkle it over roasted pears.

If you're looking for more foods with a big flavor payoff, consider the following:

FRESH FENNEL

Use chopped fennel bulb to add anise flavor and crispy crunch to tuna, egg, or pasta salads;

grill or roast the bulb to serve as a side dish; add the chopped feathery green fronds to egg dishes, salad dressings, or marinades for seafood or chicken.

FRESH HORSERADISH

Peel this slender root, then finely grate it and swirl it into sauces or dressings, mix it into potato salad or coleslaw, or stir it into fat-free sour cream and drizzle over a baked potato.

LEMON ZEST

Grate the outermost skin layer of a lemon to remove the zest to add flavor to broiled fish fillets, sautéed shrimp, steamed veggies, cooked rice or pasta, or fruit salads.

LEMONGRASS

Remove the tough outer leaves from the cream-colored base and finely chop to add flavor to stir-fries, chicken soup, seafood marinades, or shrimp salad.

OLIVES

Add bold-flavored olives to pasta sauces, salads, or vegetable dips, sprinkle them into a cheese sandwich, or stir them into a rice pilaf just before serving.

PARMIGIANO-REGGIANO

A kitchen essential, this handmade cheese from the Emilia-Romagna region of Italy adds complex flavor to pasta, risotto, polenta, vegetable soup, or Caesar salad.

PROSCIUTTO

Pair this salt-cured Italian ham with sweet cantaloupe or peaches, sprinkle thin strips over a cheese pizza before baking, add chopped prosciutto to omelettes, or wrap it around thin breadsticks for a chic and easy hors d'oeuvre.

the 9 best tools

Today's modern cook requires a few essential cooking tools to help cook fast, healthy and flavorful meals with ease.

BROILING PAN
These pans have a perforated rack that fits inside a pan where fat drips away. Broiling is ideal for cooking steaks, chicken, pork chops, or shrimp in minutes.

FAT SEPARATOR
With a sharply angled spout at the base, this tool lets you easily pour off the flavorful fat-free broths and pan juices.

GRILL PAN
A cast-iron grill pan will give you that outdoor flavor in the middle of winter, or when you just don't want to go to the trouble to fire up the outdoor grill. It's perfect for quickly cooking steaks, chops, chicken breasts, shrimp, and veggies.

HANDHELD GRATER
A small handheld grater, such as the Microplane grater, makes it easy to add a bit of finely grated cheese to pastas, salads, or soups.

IMMERSION BLENDER
Puree soups right in the pot, make salad dressings and smoothies, and whip egg whites with this lightweight appliance.

KITCHEN SCALE
For ensuring correct portion sizes and for weighing ingredients such as meats, cheeses, and vegetables, a kitchen scale is indispensable.

KNIVES
A paring knife for small jobs, a chef's knife for chopping and slicing, and a serrated knife for cutting bread are all you need.

NONSTICK SKILLETS
These skillets are essential for cooking with very little fat and to keep food from sticking. A 6-inch pan is perfect for cooking eggs or reheating single servings of foods. A 10- to 12-inch skillet is handy for cooking larger servings, making stir-fries, or sautéing chicken breasts.

STEAMER
Perfect for cooking vegetables and seafood with no added fat.

play it safe

With these simple tips, you'll keep you and your family safe from food-borne illness.

keep it clean

- Always wash your hands thoroughly before beginning any food preparation.

- Wash all fresh produce—even if the label says "prewashed"—before eating. Place greens in a large bowl of cold water and lift them out to drain in a colander. Place vegetables, such as broccoli, cauliflower, green beans, and baby carrots, in a colander and rinse under cold running water. Scrub sturdy produce, such as apples, potatoes, and celery with a brush.

- Use hot soapy water and a dishcloth to clean kitchen countertops and appliances. Wash dishcloths and towels often in the washing machine using hot water.

don't cross contaminate

- Place meats, poultry, and seafood inside plastic bags from the produce department before adding them to your cart. This prevents juices from dripping onto other foods and spreading bacteria.

- Keep two cutting boards: one for meats, poultry, and seafood and one for produce. Either wood or plastic cutting boards are acceptable to use. Wash them in hot soapy water after each use and dry thoroughly. To sanitize cutting boards, wash them with a solution of 1 tablespoon bleach in 1 gallon of water.

- Use a clean plate for cooked food—never place it back on the same plate that previously held raw food.

chill out

- Keep your refrigerator at 40°F or below and your freezer at 0°F or below.

- Cook or freeze raw poultry, fish, and ground meats within 2 days of purchase. Beef, lamb, or pork can be refrigerated 3 to 5 days.

- Store leftovers in the refrigerator and use them in 3 to 4 days or freeze them up to 3 months.

- Thawing in the refrigerator is the safest method of defrosting foods. Count on about 12 hours to thaw 1 pound of steak, ground beef, pork chops, chicken, or shrimp.

- Always marinate foods in the refrigerator. If you use the marinade to make a sauce, you must boil it first.

cook it safe

Use this chart as a guide to ensure that you cook all foods to a safe temperature.

- Use an instant-read thermometer to ensure that cooked foods are at a safe temperature.

- Insert the thermometer into the center of the food (without touching a bone in roasts, chops, or poultry) to get an accurate reading.

- Wash the stem of the thermometer with hot soapy water after each use.

Type of Food	Minimum Safe Temperature
Ground beef, pork, and lamb	160°F
Beef, pork, and lamb steaks, chops, or roasts	145°F and allow to rest for at least 3 minutes
Fresh ham	145°F and allow to rest for at least 3 minutes
Fully cooked ham (to reheat)	140°F
Chicken or turkey, whole, parts, or ground	165°F
Egg dishes	160°F
Leftovers and casseroles	165°F

produce primer

fruits

Sweet and flavorful nutrient-packed fruits are healthy foods that everyone loves to eat. And no matter what the season, there's always a bumper crop of something fresh and delicious at the market. Use our tips for incorporating fresh fruits into everyday meals and check out the health benefits, too.

berries

Blackberries, blueberries, strawberries, and raspberries

- Berries are easy to add to cereal, granola, or oatmeal at breakfast.
- Revitalize yourself with a smoothie made with fresh berries, plain fat-free yogurt, and ice cubes.
- To make your own fruit-flavored no-sugar-added yogurt, mash fresh berries with a fork, then swirl the fruit into plain fat-free yogurt.
- For a healthy ice-pop treat, puree fresh berries with a little water, then freeze in small paper drink cups.
- Blueberries are one of the most antioxidant-rich foods and they're an excellent source of fiber and vitamins A and C.
- Raspberries are one of the highest fiber fruits with 8 grams of fiber in 1 cup.

tree fruits

Apples, apricots, bananas, cherries, kiwifruit, nectarines, peaches, and pears

- Keep fruit in sight. A bowl of apples and pears on your desk or countertop will remind you to eat them.
- Tree fruits are the ultimate in portable snacking—keep them in your purse, at your desk, and in the car.
- Fruits are not just for sweet dishes. Make a peach salsa for fish or add sliced apples to a green salad.
- Bananas, as well as most other fruits, are a good source of potassium, which helps maintain healthy blood pressure.
- Eat apples with the peel; it provides a large part of the fiber and antioxidants.
- Consuming cherries may help relieve the pain of arthritis and gout.
- One kiwifruit has all the vitamin C you need in a day.

citrus fruits

Oranges, grapefruit, tangerines, and clementines

- Separate oranges into segments and carry them in a resealable plastic bag for easy eating during your commute.
- Section pink grapefruit and serve with thinly sliced avocado for a colorful and delicious salad.
- Add orange segments to a spinach salad, or serve them alongside broiled salmon to add sweet citrus flavor.
- Replacing high-calorie snacks like cookies and chips with fruits like oranges or tangerines can help you consume fewer calories and more nutrients.
- Red and pink grapefruit are an excellent source of vitamin A.
- Oranges are a good source of folate, fiber, and antioxidants.

melons

Watermelons, cantaloupes, and honeydews

- With their refreshing taste and high water content, melons are a great after-workout treat.

- Honeydew is the sweetest of the melons, making it the perfect summer dessert.

- To make a melon salsa to serve with fish or shrimp, stir together diced melon, minced jalapeño, diced red onion, chopped cilantro, and a squeeze of lime.

- Make a refreshing summer salad with cubed melon and peeled and sliced cucumber tossed with lime juice and sprinkled with crumbled reduced-fat feta.

- Watermelon and cantaloupe are good sources of vitamin C, vitamin A, and potassium.

- Melons and other fruits do contain natural sugars, but because they also have fiber and a wide array of other nutrients, they are a healthier choice than a sugary dessert.

vegetables

Eat your vegetables! If you have trouble taking this age-old advice, see our tips for healthy ways to add more veggies to every meal. We offer nutritional highlights, too, to make indulging in naturally delicious vegetables even more appealing.

leafy greens

Arugula, kale, lettuces, mustard, spinach, Swiss chard, turnip greens, and watercress

- Buy prewashed salad greens or wash a big batch at home to make it effortless to have a salad with dinner every day.

- Have a side salad instead of French fries when you eat fast food.

- Sturdy greens, such as Swiss chard or kale, are delicious when simply steamed or, if thinly sliced, they can be enjoyed raw.

- Most greens are excellent sources of vitamin A.

- Peppery-tasting arugula is an excellent source of vitamin K, which is essential for bone health.

- Salad greens, such as romaine, red and green leaf lettuce, and Bibb lettuce, are all good sources of vitamins A and K and the antioxidant lutein, which is good for eye health.

green vegetables

Artichokes, asparagus, green bell peppers, broccoli, green beans, and zucchini

- Start early in the day by adding diced bell peppers, zucchini, and onions to omelettes, frittatas, or scrambled eggs.

- Make canned soup healthier. Add a cup of quick-cooking small broccoli florets, chopped zucchini, or thinly sliced asparagus when you heat the soup.

- When eating pizza, sandwiches, pasta dishes, or stir-fries in a restaurant, choose options with the most veggies.

- Asparagus is one of the best vegetable sources of folate.

- Broccoli has one of the highest amounts of calcium found in any vegetable and also contains phytochemicals that can protect against cancer.

- Green beans are a great source of fiber, vitamin C, and vitamin K.

colorful vegetables

Beets, carrots, eggplant, radishes, red and yellow peppers, tomatoes, and winter squash

- Craving crunch? Opt for baby carrots and radishes instead of chips or crackers.

- Double up. Instead of a single vegetable at dinner, eat two.

- Use the microwave to make quick work of preparing long-cooking vegetables such as winter squash or beets.

- Bell peppers and tomatoes are good sources of vitamin C.

- Just one medium carrot contains more than twice the amount of vitamin A you need in a day.

- Eggplant, especially the peel, contains a

powerful phytonutrient, which prevents free radical formation that can damage cells.

Potatoes

White potatoes and sweet potatoes

- Make mashed potatoes with the skin on for added fiber, and with fat-free milk or broth to add minimum calories.

- Thin-sliced potatoes tossed with a bit of olive oil and then roasted will satisfy your potato chip craving without deep-frying.

- When baking any entrée for 45 minutes to 1 hour, put a few sweet potatoes in the oven. They make an effortless side dish and need no added fat or sugar.

- White potatoes and sweet potatoes are excellent sources of potassium, which may help to maintain healthy blood pressure.

- Sweet potatoes are one of the best sources of vitamin A; ½ cup provides nearly 4 times what you need in a day.

- The peel of white potatoes contains up to 20 times more of the antioxidant chlorogenic acid than the flesh of the potato.

fruit and veggie FAQ

What's the best apple for baking? For snacking?

A baked apple, whether baked on its own or in a pie, should hold its shape after it's baked. Great choices are Granny Smith, Rome, Jonagold, Pippin, Fuji, and Pink Lady.

For snacking, if you prefer a tart apple, choose Granny Smith, Braeburn, or Cortland. If you like

a sweeter apple, look for Honeycrisp, Golden Delicious, Gala, or Crispin.

Which produce should I buy organic? And which are okay to buy conventionally grown?

The Environmental Working Group, a nonprofit advocacy group that works to promote a cleaner environment, studies the amount of pesticides in fresh fruits and vegetables and offers a list of the most and least contaminated.

The twelve most pesticide-contaminated fruits and vegetables that you should buy organic are apples, celery, bell peppers, peaches, strawberries, imported nectarines, grapes, spinach, lettuce, cucumbers, domestic blueberries, and potatoes.

The fifteen vegetables with the least amount of pesticide residues that are okay to buy conventionally grown are onions, corn, pineapples, avocados, cabbage, sweet peas, asparagus, mangoes, eggplant, kiwifruit , domestic cantaloupe, sweet potatoes, grapefruit, watermelon, and mushrooms.

Do I have to peel cucumbers?

It's not harmful to eat the skin of cucumbers, but the skin can be quite bitter, especially with traditional cucumbers. If you want to leave the skin on, look for long English (seedless) cucumbers or the shorter Lebanese cucumbers, which have a thinner and less-bitter skin.

How do I choose the juiciest citrus fruit?

When you're selecting citrus, pick up four or five oranges or grapefruits one at a time. You'll notice that some weigh more than others. The heaviest ones contain the most juice.

Which fruits should I store at room temperature, and which ones do I refrigerate?

Fruits such as peaches, nectarines, plums, avocados, cantaloupe, honeydew, pears, pineapple, and bananas will continue to ripen if stored at room temperature. Once these fruits reach their peak of ripeness, you can refrigerate them for a day or two to prolong freshness. The skin of bananas will turn dark in the refrigerator,

but the flesh will still be fine to eat. Berries, cherries, grapes, and figs should always be stored in the refrigerator.

Can I store onions and potatoes together?

It's best not to if you're storing them for longer than a week. Potatoes and onions both give off gases that cause spoilage, so keep them in separate containers in a cool place.

How can I make bananas ripen fast?

If they're in a plastic bag from the supermarket, remove them from the plastic and put them in a brown paper bag with an apple or a tomato. The apple or tomato will give off ethylene gas, which will help the bananas ripen quicker.

How do I keep the unused part of an avocado from turning brown?

Sprinkle it with lemon or lime juice or vinegar, wrap in plastic wrap, and refrigerate. If an avocado does turn brown, just cut away a thin layer to expose the bright green flesh underneath.

How do I cook cabbage or Brussels sprouts without having them taste cabbagey?

Choose steaming or sautéing for cooking cabbage and steaming or roasting for Brussels sprouts. And cook them just until crisp-tender to minimize the offensive sulfurous odors.

Do I have to salt eggplant before cooking?

Salting eggplant was once considered essential for removing the bitter juices before cooking. You're not likely to find a bitter eggplant unless it's past its prime. Choose eggplants with taut, glossy skin and no brown spots and you can skip the salting step.

Savory Swiss Chard and Feta Tart, page 9

breakfasts and brunches

poached eggs with green chile–tomato sauce

Serves 4 • Vegetarian

½ teaspoon olive oil
1 onion, halved lengthwise and sliced
1 green bell pepper, thinly sliced
1 jalapeño pepper, seeded and minced
1 garlic clove, minced
1 (14½-ounce) can diced tomatoes with green chiles
1 (8-ounce) can tomato sauce

¼ teaspoon salt
¼ cup chopped fresh cilantro
4 large eggs
½ cup shredded reduced-fat Monterey Jack cheese
2 whole wheat English muffins, split and toasted

1. Heat oil in medium nonstick skillet over medium heat. Add onion, bell pepper, and jalapeño and cook, stirring occasionally, until vegetables are tender, about 5 minutes. Add garlic and cook, stirring constantly, until fragrant, 30 seconds.

2. Stir in tomatoes, tomato sauce, and salt. Reduce heat and simmer, stirring occasionally, until sauce is slightly thickened, about 10 minutes. Stir in cilantro.

3. With back of spoon, make four wells in sauce and carefully break 1 egg into each. Cover and simmer until whites are opaque and yolks are set, 5–6 minutes. Sprinkle with cheese. Cover and simmer until cheese melts, about 1 minute.

4. Place a muffin half on each of 4 plates; top each with an egg and spoon sauce evenly around muffins.

PER SERVING (1 egg with sauce and ½ muffin): 238 Cal, 10 g Total Fat, 4 g Sat Fat, 0 g Trans Fat, 220 mg Chol, 914 mg Sod, 26 g Carb, 5 g Fib, 14 g Prot, 249 mg Calc.
PointsPlus value: **6.**

cook's note

If breakfast time is too early in the day for you to enjoy spicy foods, skip the jalapeño and use regular canned diced tomatoes in this recipe.

cremini, spinach, and goat cheese frittata

Serves 4 • Vegetarian • Ready in 20 minutes or less

4 large eggs
4 large egg whites
½ teaspoon salt
¼ teaspoon black pepper

8 ounces cremini mushrooms, sliced
1 (6-ounce) bag baby spinach
1 cup cherry tomatoes, halved
2 ounces goat cheese, crumbled

1. Whisk together eggs, egg whites, ¼ teaspoon salt, and pepper in large bowl.

2. Spray 10-inch nonstick ovenproof skillet with nonstick spray and set over medium heat. Add mushrooms and remaining ¼ teaspoon salt and cook, stirring occasionally, until lightly browned and most of liquid evaporates, about 8 minutes. Add spinach, in batches if necessary, and cook, stirring constantly, until wilted and most of liquid evaporates, about 2 minutes.

3. Preheat broiler.

4. Pour egg mixture evenly over vegetables. Reduce heat and cook until eggs are set, 7–8 minutes (but do not stir).

5. Top eggs evenly with tomatoes; sprinkle with cheese. Place skillet under broiler and broil frittata 5 inches from heat until top is lightly browned, about 2 minutes. Cut into 4 wedges.

PER SERVING (1 wedge): 164 Cal, 9 g Total Fat, 4 g Sat Fat, 0 g Trans Fat, 193 mg Chol, 504 mg Sod, 7 g Carb, 2 g Fib, 15 g Prot, 105 mg Calc.

PointsPlus value: **4.**

cook's note

This colorful frittata, packed with fresh veggies, is perfect for a casual brunch or lunch. It's as delicious at room temperature as it is hot, so you can even make it ahead.

To cook food quickly in a skillet over medium-high heat in a small amount of oil.

what you need

- A large heavy-bottomed nonstick skillet big enough to hold the food you are cooking in a single layer.
- Plastic-tipped tongs, wooden spoon, or silicone spatula for turning or stirring the food without harming the surface of the skillet.

how it's done

Heat small amount of oil in the skillet over medium heat (2 teaspoons of oil is enough for a 12-inch skillet). Season meats or seafood or dredge in seasoned flour and add to the skillet. For vegetables, just add them to skillet. Wait 1 to 2 minutes to turn or stir. Meats and seafood should develop a brown crust before turning.

Turn meats several times (fish is the exception; since it is delicate, turn it only once) and stir vegetables often until they reach the desired degree of doneness.

sausage and pepper breakfast wraps

Serves 2 • Ready in 20 minutes or less

4 frozen fully cooked turkey breakfast sausage links (3 ounces), thawed and sliced
½ cup diced red onion
½ cup diced red bell pepper
2 large eggs
2 large egg whites
¼ teaspoon black pepper
Pinch salt
2 (8-inch) whole-grain tortillas, warmed
⅓ cup shredded fat-free Cheddar cheese

1. Spray medium nonstick skillet with nonstick spray and set over medium heat. Add sausage, onion, and bell pepper to skillet and cook, stirring occasionally, until vegetables are tender, about 5 minutes.

2. Meanwhile, whisk together eggs, egg whites, black pepper, and salt in small bowl. Pour evenly over sausage mixture. Reduce heat to medium-low; cook until eggs begin to set, about 1½ minutes, pushing egg mixture toward center of skillet to form large, soft curds. Continue cooking until eggs are just set, about 3 minutes longer.

3. Spoon half of egg mixture along center of each tortilla; top evenly with cheese. Roll up each tortilla and cut in half.

PER SERVING (1 wrap): 324 Cal, 12 g Total Fat, 3 g Sat Fat, 0 g Trans Fat, 229 mg Chol, 792 mg Sod, 27 g Carb, 4 g Fib, 28 g Prot, 183 mg Calc.

PointsPlus value: **8.**

smoky sweet potato, canadian bacon, and corn hash

Serves 6

3 medium sweet potatoes (about 2 pounds)
1 medium onion, chopped
1 red bell pepper, diced
1 green bell pepper, diced
1 teaspoon minced chipotle en adobo

¼ teaspoon salt
4 slices Canadian bacon, diced
1 cup frozen corn kernels, thawed
2 scallions, thinly sliced

1. Pierce potatoes in several places with fork. Place potatoes in microwavable dish. Cover with wax paper and microwave on high until potatoes feel soft when pressed, but are not fully cooked, about 10 minutes. Carefully transfer potatoes to cutting board, cut in half lengthwise, and let cool.

2. Meanwhile, spray large nonstick skillet with nonstick spray and set over medium heat. Add onion and bell pepper and cook, stirring often, until tender and lightly browned, about 10 minutes.

3. Peel and chop potatoes and add to skillet. Stir in chipotle and salt. Cook, stirring occasionally, until potatoes are tender and golden, about 8 minutes. Stir in Canadian bacon and corn and cook to heat through, about 2 minutes. Stir in scallions and cook 1 minute more.

PER SERVING (generous 1 cup): 122 Cal, 2 g Total Fat, 0 g Sat Fat, 0 g Trans Fat, 8 mg Chol, 362 mg Sod, 23 g Carb, 4 g Fib, 6 g Prot, 33 mg Calc.

PointsPlus value: *3.*

cook's note
Serve each portion of the hash topped with a poached egg (1 egg will increase the per-serving *PointsPlus* value by *2*).

italian baked egg and vegetable ramekins

Serves 4 • Vegetarian

1 pound plum tomatoes, cut into 1-inch
   chunks
1 red bell pepper, cut into ¾-inch pieces
1 zucchini, quartered lengthwise and cut
   crosswise into ¾-inch chunks
1 onion, halved lengthwise and sliced

2 large garlic cloves, minced
½ teaspoon dried basil
½ teaspoon salt
¼ teaspoon black pepper
4 large eggs
¼ cup grated fat-free Parmesan cheese

1 Preheat oven to 400°F and spray a large shallow roasting pan with nonstick spray.

2 Put tomatoes, bell pepper, zucchini, onion, garlic, basil, salt, and pepper in pan and spray with nonstick spray; toss to coat. Roast, stirring occasionally, until vegetables are browned and crisp-tender, about 30 minutes.

3 Spray four 8- or 10-ounce ramekins or custard cups with nonstick spray. Divide vegetables evenly among cups. Make well in center of vegetables and carefully break 1 egg into each cup. Sprinkle with Parmesan. Place cups on baking sheet and bake until eggs are just set, 20–25 minutes.

PER SERVING (1 ramekin): 157 Cal, 6 g Total Fat, 2 g Sat Fat, 0 g Trans Fat, 191 mg Chol, 455 mg Sod, 15 g Carb, 3 g Fib, 12 g Prot, 142 mg Calc.
PointsPlus value: *4.*

cook's note
To make it a meal, serve the baked eggs with reduced-calorie whole-wheat toast (1 slice of reduced-calorie whole-wheat toast per serving will increase the *PointsPlus* value by *1*).

Italian Baked Egg and
Vegetable Ramekins

wake-up call

Even though eating breakfast has long been linked to good health and a nutritious diet, skipping the morning meal may seem like an easy way to cut calories when trying to lose weight.

Yet breakfast eaters tend to weigh less than breakfast skippers and some studies have even found that skippers can end up eating more calories through the course of the day compared to those who have an a.m. meal. If you're missing out on breakfast, stop: you're more likely to be famished by lunch and end up eating too much.

Eating breakfast is one of the key strategies for maintaining lost pounds. It can also help to reduce hunger later in the day, as well as provide key nutrients that may enhance physical activity, another key strategy for maintaining weight loss.

The bottom line: Making breakfast part of your daily routine can help you achieve long-term, sustainable weight loss. An ideal breakfast is a combination of protein (which slows digestion) and carbohydrates (which deliver a quick shot of energy). Here are some good choices:

- low-fat cheese and tomato slices on a whole-wheat English muffin
- high-fiber cereal with fat-free or low-fat milk and dried or fresh fruit
- peanut butter and jelly on multigrain or whole wheat bread
- hard-boiled or scrambled eggs (or egg whites) with a slice of whole-wheat toast
- low-fat yogurt and a grain-rich cereal bar
- a banana and a small handful of peanuts or almonds

five easy breakfasts that follow Simple Start

1 cup plain fat-free Greek yogurt topped with ½ cup sliced fresh strawberries
and 1 slice reduced-calorie rye toast
   PointsPlus value: **5**

2 slices reduced-calorie whole-wheat toast topped with ½ cup fat-free ricotta cheese
and ½ cup fresh raspberries
   PointsPlus value: **5**

1 cup unsweetened oatmeal (cooked in water) and topped with ½ cup fresh blueberries
   PointsPlus value: **5**

½ cup Fiber One Original Bran with ¾ cup fat-free milk and ½ of a sliced banana
   PointsPlus value: **5**

2 poached eggs with 1 slice reduced-calorie whole-wheat toast and ½ cup cherry tomatoes
   PointsPlus value: **5**

savory swiss chard and feta tart

Serves 12 • Vegetarian

1 cup whole wheat pastry flour
1 cup all-purpose flour
½ teaspoon salt
¼ cup olive oil
4–5 tablespoons cold water
1½ pounds Swiss chard, stems and leaves
    separated and each coarsely chopped
3 garlic cloves, minced

½ cup reduced-sodium vegetable broth
1 cup part-skim ricotta cheese
1 large egg
2 large egg whites
¼ cup crumbled reduced-fat feta cheese
8 oil-cured black olives, pitted and chopped
1 teaspoon chopped fresh thyme
1 tablespoon toasted pine nuts

1 Preheat oven to 400°F.

2 To make crust, put whole wheat flour, all-purpose flour, and salt in food processor; pulse until blended. Pour oil through feed tube and pulse until mixture resembles coarse crumbs. Pour water, 1 tablespoon at a time, through feed tube and pulse until dough forms. Turn dough onto lightly floured surface; roll out to 13-inch circle and ease it into 11-inch tart pan with removable bottom, pressing dough evenly onto bottom and up sides of pan. Prick dough all over with fork. Roll rolling pin over rim of pan to cut off overhanging dough.

3 Line tart shell with foil; fill with pie weights or dried beans. Bake until dough looks dried around edges, about 20 minutes; remove foil and weights. Return tart shell to oven and continue to bake just until crust is golden, 10–12 minutes longer. Cool crust in pan on rack 10 minutes.

4 Meanwhile, to make filling, spray large nonstick skillet with nonstick spray and set over medium heat. Add Swiss chard stems and cook, stirring occasionally, until tender, about 10 minutes. Add garlic and cook 2 minutes. Add Swiss chard leaves and broth; bring to boil. Reduce heat and simmer, covered, stirring occasionally, until stems and leaves are very tender, 10–12 minutes. Pour mixture into large sieve set over bowl; let drain 10 minutes.

5 Whisk together ricotta, egg, and egg whites in large bowl. Stir in feta, olives, and thyme. Stir in chard mixture. Spoon filling into cooled crust and sprinkle with pine nuts. Bake until top is browned and puffed, about 30 minutes. Let cool at least 10 minutes. Remove tart ring and cut tart into 12 slices. Serve warm or at room temperature.

PER SERVING (1 slice): 170 Cal, 8 g Total Fat, 2 g Sat Fat, 0 g Trans Fat, 25 mg Chol, 321 mg Sod, 18 g Carb, 2 g Fib, 7 g Prot, 109 mg Calc.

PointsPlus value: **4.**

Coconut-Almond French Toast with Tropical Fruit

coconut-almond french toast with tropical fruit

Serves 8 • Vegetarian

1¼ cups almond milk
1 cup fat-free egg substitute
4 tablespoons packed light brown sugar
¼ teaspoon almond extract
8 slices whole wheat sandwich bread
⅓ cup flaked sweetened coconut
2 large bananas, halved lengthwise and
   sliced

1 mango, peeled, pitted, and diced
½ pineapple, peeled, cored, and diced
½ (1-pound) container strawberries, hulled
   and diced
1 tablespoon lime juice
1 tablespoon confectioners' sugar

1 Whisk together almond milk, egg substitute, 2 tablespoons brown sugar, and almond extract in large shallow bowl or pie plate. Dip bread into egg mixture, one slice at a time, until evenly soaked. Sprinkle evenly with coconut.

2 Spray large nonstick skillet with nonstick spray; set over medium heat. Add soaked bread to skillet in batches; cook until browned, 2 minutes on each side.

3 Meanwhile, stir together remaining 2 tablespoons brown sugar, bananas, mango, pineapple, strawberries, and lime juice. Divide French toast among 8 plates; top evenly with fruit. Sprinkle with confectioners' sugar.

PER SERVING (1 slice French toast with ½ cup fruit): 231 Cal, 3 g Total Fat, 1 g Sat Fat, 0 g Trans Fat, 0 mg Chol, 235 mg Sod, 46 g Carb, 5 g Fib, 8 g Prot, 136 mg Calc.

PointsPlus value: **6.**

cook's note

You can use any fruit to make the fruit topping for the French toast, depending on what you have on hand. Try blueberries, raspberries, grapes, or orange segments.

corn and gruyère spoonbread

Serves 6 • Vegetarian

2 cups fat-free milk
1 tablespoon olive oil
½ teaspoon salt
½ cup cornmeal
1 (10-ounce) package frozen corn kernels, thawed
4 scallions, thinly sliced

½ cup shredded Gruyère cheese
½ red bell pepper, minced
1 jalapeño pepper, seeded and minced
2 large egg yolks
4 large egg whites
¼ teaspoon cream of tartar

1 Bring milk, oil, and salt to boil in large saucepan over medium-high heat. Very slowly whisk in cornmeal. Reduce heat, switch to wooden spoon, and cook, stirring, until mixture is thickened and smooth, about 5 minutes. Remove pan from heat and stir in corn, scallions, cheese, bell pepper, and jalapeño. Stir egg yolks in one at a time, stirring until blended. Transfer mixture to large bowl and let cool slightly.

2 Preheat oven to 375°F. Spray 8-inch-square baking dish with nonstick spray.

3 With electric mixer on high speed, beat egg whites until foamy; add cream of tartar and beat until soft peaks form. Stir one fourth of egg whites into cornmeal mixture. Fold in remaining egg whites with rubber spatula. Scrape mixture into baking dish; level top. Bake until puffed and cooked through, about 30 minutes.

PER SERVING (generous ¾ cup): 207 Cal, 7 g Total Fat, 3 g Sat Fat, 0 g Trans Fat, 72 mg Chol, 304 mg Sod, 25 g Carb, 2 g Fib, 11 g Prot, 209 mg Calc.
PointsPlus value: **5.**

cook's note

Spoonbread is almost like a soufflé, achieving its light texture and puffy appearance from beaten egg whites. It's an ideal dish for brunch, or you can serve it as many Southerners do, as a dinnertime side dish.

baked skillet pancake with peach-blueberry compote

Serves 4 • Vegetarian

3 large eggs
1 large egg white
¾ cup fat-free milk
1 teaspoon vanilla extract
½ cup white whole wheat flour
2 tablespoons plus ¼ cup sugar
¼ teaspoon ground cinnamon

¼ teaspoon salt
2 teaspoons unsalted butter
3 tablespoons water
1 tablespoon lemon juice
3 peaches or nectarines, peeled and thinly sliced
1½ cups blueberries

1. Preheat oven to 425°F. Place 10-inch ovenproof skillet in oven to heat for 5 minutes.

2. Whisk together eggs, egg white, milk, vanilla extract, flour, 2 tablespoons sugar, cinnamon, and salt in large bowl until smooth.

3. Remove skillet from oven, add butter, and swirl so that butter covers skillet. Pour in batter. Bake until puffed and browned at edges, about 20 minutes.

4. Meanwhile, to make compote, stir together remaining ¼ cup sugar, water, and lemon juice in a medium saucepan. Set over medium-high heat and bring to boil, stirring until the sugar is dissolved. Reduce heat and simmer 1 minute. Add peaches and blueberries and simmer, stirring occasionally, until fruit is warm, about 4 minutes.

5. Cut pancake into 4 wedges and serve at once with compote.

PER SERVING (¼ of pancake with 1 cup compote): 298 Cal, 7 g Total Fat, 3 g Sat Fat, 0 g Trans Fat, 146 mg Chol, 245 mg Sod, 52 g Carb, 5 g Fib, 11 g Prot, 94 mg Calc.
***PointsPlus* value: 8.**

cook's note

A cast-iron skillet works best for baking the pancake, but any heavy ovenproof skillet will do. Serve the pancake immediately when it comes out of the oven, since it rapidly deflates as it cools.

apple-cinnamon dutch baby

Serves 6 • Vegetarian

1 teaspoon canola oil
2 Golden Delicious apples, peeled, cored,
   and cut into thin wedges
3 tablespoons apple juice or cider
½ teaspoon ground cinnamon
Pinch grated nutmeg
2 tablespoons granulated sugar

¾ cup fat-free milk
1 large egg
1 large egg white
2 teaspoons unsalted butter, melted
¼ teaspoon salt
½ cup all-purpose flour
1 tablespoon confectioners' sugar

1 Heat oil in medium ovenproof skillet over medium heat. Add apples, apple juice, cinnamon, nutmeg, and 1 tablespoon granulated sugar. Cook, uncovered, stirring occasionally, until apples are tender and most liquid has evaporated, about 10 minutes.

2 Meanwhile, preheat oven to 400°F. Whisk together milk, egg, egg white, melted butter, salt, and remaining 1 tablespoon granulated sugar in medium bowl. Gradually whisk in flour, whisking until smooth. Pour batter over hot apple mixture. Transfer to oven and bake 20 minutes.

3 Reduce oven temperature to 350°F and continue to bake until pancake is puffed and golden, 15–20 minutes longer. Cool pancake in skillet on rack 10 minutes. Sprinkle top lightly with confectioners' sugar and cut into 6 wedges. Serve warm or at room temperature.

PER SERVING (1 wedge): 135 Cal, 3 g Total Fat, 1 g Sat Fat, 0 g Trans Fat, 39 mg Chol, 133 mg Sod, 23 g Carb, 1 g Fib, 4 g Prot, 49 mg Calc.

PointsPlus value: **4.**

cook's note

This big pancake makes an easy, simple dessert, too. To dress it up a bit, you can serve each slice topped with light vanilla ice cream (a ¼-cup scoop of light vanilla ice cream will increase the per-serving *PointsPlus* value by *1*).

Lemon–Poppy Seed Flax Muffins, Page 25, and Apple-Cinnamon Dutch Baby

all about yogurt

Yogurt can be a healthy, high protein breakfast if you choose a good variety and enjoy a sensible portion. Check the chart below to see how your favorite yogurt fares in **PointsPlus** values.

Yogurt is made by fermenting milk using healthful bacteria. The fermentation process thickens the milk, gives it a creamy texture, and adds a tangy flavor. Yogurt is a great source of protein, calcium, and B vitamins.

Fat-free, low-fat (or "light"), and regular (or "whole milk") yogurts are all available in plain and flavored varieties.

Greek yogurt is yogurt which has had the liquid whey strained off, making it thick and creamy. It is also available in fat-free, low-fat, and regular versions and comes plain and flavored.

To get more protein, choose Greek yogurt, since it has about twice the amount of protein as other yogurt. Enjoy it with fresh fruit and a sprinkle of low-fat granola for a healthy protein-packed breakfast.

Use protein-rich Greek yogurt where you would ordinarily use light sour cream: in baking cakes and muffins; for topping baked potatoes, nachos, or chili; for making chilled soups; or use it for half of the mayonnaise in creamy salad dressing recipes.

If you like flavored yogurt, choose varieties that are artificially sweetened to cut back on added sugars. Better yet, buy plain yogurt and stir in your own fresh fruit to add flavor and sweetness.

Add yogurt to breakfast smoothies, top pancakes or waffles with a dollop of fruity yogurt, or make a parfait with layers of yogurt and fresh fruit.

Although it's a better deal to buy yogurt in large containers, the convenience of single-serving yogurt for on-the-go breakfasts and snacks make them worth the price.

Type of yogurt (½ cup)	PointsPlus value
Plain low-fat yogurt	2
Plain fat-free yogurt	2
Artificially sweetened low-fat yogurt	2
Sugar-sweetened flavored (vanilla, coffee, lemon) fat-free yogurt	2
Sugar-sweetened fat-free fruit-flavored yogurt	3
Plain low-fat Greek yogurt	2
Plain fat-free Greek yogurt	1

cinnamon-raisin granola with sunflower seeds

Serves 8 • Vegetarian

3 cups old-fashioned rolled oats
½ cup raw sunflower seeds
3 tablespoons wheat germ
½ teaspoon cinnamon

¼ cup honey
¼ cup pure maple syrup
¾ cup golden raisins

1. Preheat oven to 300°F. Spray 10×15-inch rimmed baking sheet with nonstick spray.

2. Stir together oats, sunflower seeds, wheat germ, and cinnamon in large bowl. Add honey and maple syrup and stir to coat. Spoon mixture onto baking sheet and spread evenly.

3. Bake, stirring occasionally, until oats and sunflower seeds are golden brown, about 35 minutes. Cool completely and stir in raisins.

PER SERVING (about ½ cup): 276 Cal, 7 g Total Fat, 1 g Sat Fat, 0 g Trans Fat, 0 mg Chol, 6 mg Sod, 50 g Carb, 5 g Fib, 7 g Prot, 43 mg Calc.

PointsPlus value: **7.**

cook's note

If you and your family enjoy granola often—it's fantastic sprinkled over fresh fruit or plain yogurt for an afternoon snack—make a double batch. The granola can be stored in an airtight container up to 1 month.

maple-spice fruit compote

Serves 8 • Vegetarian

2 navel oranges
2 cups apple cider or unsweetened apple
    juice
3 tablespoons maple syrup
1 (3-inch) cinnamon stick

1 whole star anise
1 (7-ounce) bag mixed dried fruit (such as
    apples, pears, apricots, and dried plums)
½ cup dried cranberries
½ teaspoon vanilla extract

1 With vegetable peeler, remove 4 strips of orange peel, each about 1 inch wide and 3 inches long. Set aside oranges. Combine orange peel, apple cider, maple syrup, cinnamon stick, and star anise in medium saucepan. Set over medium-high heat and bring to boil, stirring until sugar is dissolved. Reduce heat and simmer 5 minutes.

2 Add mixed dried fruit and cranberries and simmer, covered, until fruit softens, about 5 minutes. Stir in vanilla extract. Pour fruit mixture into bowl and let cool to room temperature.

3 Remove and discard cinnamon stick and star anise. Cut oranges into sections; gently stir into fruit mixture. Cover and refrigerate overnight.

PER SERVING (½ cup fruit with juices): 148 Cal, 0 g Total Fat, 0 g Sat Fat, 0 g Trans Fat, 0 mg Chol, 8 mg Sod, 38 g Carb, 3 g Fib, 1 g Prot, 36 mg Calc.
PointsPlus value: **4.**

cook's note

Enjoy this compote along with plain fat-free Greek yogurt for a healthful breakfast (½ cup plain fat-free Greek yogurt will increase the per-serving *PointsPlus* value by *1*).

walnut-pear coffeecake

Serves 12 • Vegetarian

STREUSEL

⅓ cup walnuts, chopped
3 tablespoons white whole wheat flour
3 tablespoons packed light brown sugar
1 tablespoon canola oil
¾ teaspoon cinnamon

CAKE

2 cups white whole wheat flour
½ cup granulated sugar
2 teaspoons baking powder
½ teaspoon baking soda
½ teaspoon cinnamon
¼ teaspoon salt
1 (6-ounce) container plain fat-free yogurt
½ cup unsweetened applesauce
2 tablespoons butter, melted
2 tablespoons canola oil
1 large egg
1 ripe pear, peeled, cored, and diced

1. Preheat oven to 375°F. Spray 9-inch square baking pan with nonstick spray.

2. To make streusel, stir together walnuts, flour, brown sugar, oil, and cinnamon in small bowl until blended.

3. To make cake, stir together flour, granulated sugar, baking powder, baking soda, cinnamon, and salt in large bowl. Whisk together yogurt, applesauce, butter, oil, and egg in medium bowl. Add yogurt mixture and pear to flour mixture; stir just until flour is moistened.

4. Spoon batter into pan and spread evenly. Sprinkle with streusel. Bake until toothpick inserted in center comes out clean, about 30 minutes. Let cool in pan on wire rack. To serve, cut into 12 pieces.

PER SERVING (¹⁄₁₂ of coffeecake): 215 Cal, 8 g Total Fat, 2 g Sat Fat, 0 g Trans Fat, 23 mg Chol, 215 mg Sod, 33 g Carb, 3 g Fib, 5 g Prot, 92 mg Calc.

***PointsPlus* value: 6.**

cook's note

Walnuts truly are health nuts! One study found that they are second only to blueberries in the amount of antioxidants they contain. But, eat them in moderation—walnuts are high in *PointsPlus* value (1 tablespoon has *1 PointsPlus* value).

maple–raisin bran muffins

Serves 12 • Vegetarian

1½ cups shredded bran cereal
½ cup raisins
½ cup boiling water
¼ cup canola oil
1 cup low-fat buttermilk
¼ cup pure maple syrup

1 large egg
1⅓ cups whole wheat pastry flour
1¼ teaspoons baking soda
¼ teaspoon ground cinnamon
¼ teaspoon salt
½ cup pecans, chopped

1 Stir together cereal, raisins, water, and oil in a large bowl until moistened; let cool slightly.

2 Add buttermilk, maple syrup, and egg; stir until mixed well. Whisk together flour, baking soda, cinnamon, and salt in small bowl. Add flour mixture and pecans to cereal mixture and stir just until flour mixture is moistened. Cover bowl with plastic wrap; let stand 15 minutes.

3 Meanwhile, preheat oven to 400°F. Line 12-cup muffin pan with paper liners.

4 Fill muffin cups evenly with batter. Bake until toothpick inserted into centers comes out clean, 20–25 minutes. Let cool in pan on wire rack 10 minutes. Remove muffins from pan and let cool completely on rack.

PER SERVING (1 muffin): 185 Cal, 9 g Total Fat, 1 g Sat Fat, 0 g Trans Fat, 18 mg Chol, 228 mg Sod, 26 g Carb, 5 g Fib, 5 g Prot, 73 mg Calc.

PointsPlus value: **5.**

cook's note

Using bran cereal boosts the fiber in these sweet, moist muffins. Freeze them in a resealable plastic bag up to 3 months, and pop one in the microwave for a healthy on-the-go breakfast.

Maple-Raisin Bran Muffins and Raspberry-Orange Corn Muffins, page 23

blueberry-lime loaf cake

Serves 12　•　Vegetarian

2 cups all-purpose flour
1 tablespoon grated lime zest
1 teaspoon baking powder
½ teaspoon baking soda
½ teaspoon salt
6 tablespoons unsalted butter, softened

1¼ cups sugar
⅔ cup fat-free egg substitute
1 teaspoon vanilla extract
½ cup plain low-fat Greek yogurt, at room temperature
1 cup fresh or frozen blueberries

1 Preheat oven to 350°F. Spray 4½ × 8½-inch loaf pan with nonstick spray.

2 Whisk together flour, lime zest, baking powder, baking soda, and salt in medium bowl. With an electric mixer on medium speed, beat butter until creamy, in a large bowl, about 1 minute. Add sugar and beat until light and fluffy, about 4 minutes. Reduce speed to low. Gradually beat in egg substitute. Beat in vanilla. Alternately add flour mixture and yogurt, beginning and ending with flour mixture and beating just until blended. Gently fold in blueberries.

3 Scrape batter into pan; spread evenly. Bake until toothpick inserted into center comes out clean, about 1 hour 10 minutes. Let cool in pan on wire rack 10 minutes. Remove cake from pan and let cool completely on rack.

PER SERVING (1⁄12 of cake): 232 Cal, 7 g Total Fat, 4 g Sat Fat, 0 g Trans Fat, 19 mg Chol, 223 mg Sod, 39 g Carb, 1 g Fib, 4 g Prot, 62 mg Calc.

PointsPlus* value: *6

cook's note

When buying citrus to zest, look for fruit that is unblemished and that shows no signs of shriveling. Most citrus has a coating of wax on the outside. To remove it, scrub the fruit with a vegetable brush and rinse well.

raspberry-orange corn muffins

Serves 12 • Vegetarian

1½ cups all-purpose flour
½ cup cornmeal
6 tablespoons sugar
1½ teaspoons baking powder
½ teaspoon baking soda
¼ teaspoon salt

1 cup low-fat buttermilk
3 tablespoons canola oil
1 large egg
1 tablespoon grated orange zest
1½ cups fresh or frozen raspberries

1   Preheat oven to 400°F. Line 12-cup muffin pan with paper liners.

2   Whisk together flour, cornmeal, 5 tablespoons sugar, baking powder, baking soda, and salt in large bowl. Whisk together buttermilk, oil, egg, and orange zest in small bowl. Add buttermilk mixture to flour mixture and stir just until flour mixture is moistened. Gently stir in raspberries.

3   Fill muffin cups evenly with batter and sprinkle evenly with remaining 1 tablespoon sugar. Bake until muffins spring back when lightly pressed, 15–20 minutes. Let cool in pan on wire rack 5 minutes. Remove muffins from pan and let cool on rack about 15 minutes longer. Serve warm.

PER SERVING (1 muffin): 159 Cal, 4 g Total Fat, 1 g Sat Fat, 0 g Trans Fat, 18 mg Chol, 190 mg Sod, 27 g Carb, 2 g Fib, 3 g Prot, 67 mg Calc.

PointsPlus value: *4.*

cook's note

Keep any leftover muffins in a heavy zip-close plastic bag. Store them at room temperature up to 3 days or freeze up to 3 months.

coriander-lime roasted pineapple

Serves 4 • Vegetarian • Ready in 20 minutes or less

1 pineapple, peeled and cored
1½ teaspoons canola oil
1 teaspoon coriander

1 tablespoon lime juice
1 tablespoon chopped fresh mint

1 Preheat oven to 500°F. Spray large baking sheet with nonstick spray.

2 Cut pineapple into 16 slices. Lightly brush both sides of each slice with oil; sprinkle with coriander.

3 Place pineapple slices on baking sheet. Roast until tender, about 12 minutes. Remove slices from oven; increase oven temperature to broil. Brush slices with lime juice and broil 5 inches from heat until lightly browned on edges, 1–2 minutes. Serve warm or at room temperature. Sprinkle with mint just before serving.

PER SERVING (4 slices): 75 Cal, 2 g Total Fat, 0 g Sat Fat, 0 g Trans Fat, 0 mg Chol, 1 mg Sod, 15 g Carb, 2 g Fib, 1 g Prot, 10 mg Calc.

PointsPlus value: **2.**

cook's note

To make it a meal, enjoy the pineapple with plain fat-free Greek yogurt (½ cup plain fat-free Greek yogurt per serving will increase the **PointsPlus** value by **1**).

lemon-poppy seed flax muffins

Serves 24 • Vegetarian

1½ cups all-purpose flour
1 cup sugar
¼ cup whole wheat flour
¼ cup ground flaxseeds
1 tablespoon poppy seeds
2 teaspoons baking powder
½ teaspoon salt

¾ cup fat-free milk
¼ cup canola oil
1 large egg
1 large egg white
1 tablespoon grated lemon zest
¼ cup lemon juice

1 Preheat oven to 400°F. Spray 24-cup mini-muffin pan with nonstick spray.

2 Whisk together all-purpose flour, ¾ cup sugar, whole wheat flour, flaxseeds, poppy seeds, baking powder, and salt in large bowl. Whisk together milk, oil, egg, egg white, and lemon zest in small bowl. Add milk mixture to flour mixture, stirring just until blended.

3 Fill muffin cups evenly with batter. Bake until tops spring back when lightly pressed, 10–15 minutes. Cool muffins in pan on rack.

4 Meanwhile, combine remaining ¼ cup sugar and lemon juice in small microwavable bowl. Microwave on High until bubbling, about 1 minute; stir until sugar dissolves. With a wooden skewer, poke a few holes in each muffin. Brush lemon juice mixture over muffins, brushing each a few times to allow juice to seep in. Serve muffins warm or at room temperature.

PER SERVING (1 muffin): 102 Cal, 4 g Total Fat, 1 g Sat Fat, 0 g Trans Fat, 9 mg Chol, 90 mg Sod, 17 g Carb, 1 g Fib, 2 g Prot, 28 mg Calc.

PointsPlus value: *3.*

cook's note

Flaxseeds are an excellent source of heart-healthy omega-3 fatty acids. When you eat them, grind the whole seeds in a coffee grinder, or buy them already ground (sometimes called flax meal). If you eat them whole, they pass through the digestive tract undigested and your body can't reap the healthful benefits.

**Matzo Ball Soup with Homemade
Chicken Broth, page 37**

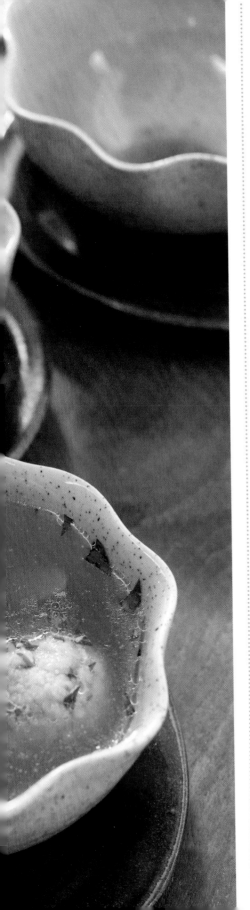

lunches

asian burgers with honey-lime slaw

Serves 4

1 pound ground lean beef (7 percent fat or less)
¼ cup plain dried bread crumbs
¼ cup finely diced onion
¼ cup plus 1 tablespoon hoisin sauce
2 tablespoons reduced-sodium soy sauce

1 tablespoon lime juice
1 tablespoon honey
4 cups thinly sliced cabbage
1 carrot, shredded
¼ red bell pepper, cut into matchstick strips
¼ cup chopped fresh cilantro

1 Combine beef, bread crumbs, onion, ¼ cup of hoisin sauce, and soy sauce in medium bowl, mixing just until combined. With damp hands, shape mixture into four (½-inch-thick) patties.

2 Spray medium nonstick skillet with nonstick spray and set over medium heat. Add patties and cook until instant-read thermometer inserted into side of each patty registers 160°F, 5–6 minutes on each side.

3 Meanwhile, whisk together remaining 1 tablespoon hoisin sauce, lime juice, and honey in large bowl. Add cabbage, carrot, bell pepper, and cilantro and toss to combine. Serve burgers with slaw.

PER SERVING (1 burger and 1 cup slaw): 252 Cal, 6 g Total Fat, 3 g Sat Fat, 0 g Trans Fat, 60 mg Chol, 745 mg Sod, 23 g Carb, 2 g Fib, 26 g Prot, 112 mg Calc.
PointsPlus value: **6.**

cook's note

To cut prep time, use 4 cups packaged coleslaw mix instead of the cabbage, carrot, and bell pepper.

lemongrass-scallion burgers

Serves 4 • Ready in 20 minutes or less

1 pound ground lean beef (7 percent fat
 or less)
2 scallions, thinly sliced
2 tablespoons reduced-sodium soy sauce
1 tablespoon minced lemongrass
1 teaspoon Asian (dark) sesame oil

1 garlic clove, minced
4 multigrain hamburger buns, toasted
½ English (seedless) cucumber, thinly sliced
4 red bell pepper rings
8 lettuce leaves

1 Combine beef, scallions, soy sauce, lemongrass, oil, and garlic in medium bowl. With damp hands, form mixture into four (½-inch-thick) patties.

2 Spray medium nonstick skillet with nonstick spray and set over medium heat. Add patties and cook until instant-read thermometer inserted into side of each patty registers 160°F, 5–6 minutes on each side.

3 Place burgers in buns with cucumber slices, pepper rings, and lettuce leaves.

PER SERVING (1 burger): 285 Cal, 8 g Total Fat, 3 g Sat Fat, 0 g Trans Fat, 60 mg Chol, 462 mg Sod, 24 g Carb, 2 g Fib, 28 g Prot, 78 mg Calc.

PointsPlus value: *7.*

cook's note

Lemongrass looks like a sturdy scallion. To use it, cut away and discard the green top and remove the toughest outer layers from the white bottom. Mince the innermost layers to release its citrusy flavor. If lemongrass is not available, substitute 1½ teaspoons each of grated lemon and lime zest in this recipe.

build a better sandwich

Sandwiches are a natural option for easy, packable, satisfying lunches—as long as you're smart about how you stack on the ingredients. Here's how to make sure your sandwich creations are good for you and low in *PointsPlus* value.

Look for lean.   When choosing sliced deli meats, select skinless turkey or chicken breast, lean roast beef, or lean ham. Making a tuna sandwich? Pick canned solid white tuna in water and use a minimal amount of reduced-fat mayonnaise—or better yet, substitute rich and creamy fat-free plain Greek yogurt for the mayo.

Just a bit of cheese, please.   Fat-free cheeses are generally lacking in flavor. For maximum taste with the least *PointsPlus* value, choose a thin slice of robust cheese such as sharp Cheddar, aged Swiss, or Provolone.

Watch the sodium.   Most deli meats are processed with generous amounts of salt. If you're watching your salt intake, choose reduced-sodium or no-salt-added deli meats and cheeses.

Avoid fatty choices.   Cold cuts such as bologna, salami, liverwurst, and pepperoni are high in fat and in *PointsPlus* values. If you love the flavor of these, treat yourself occasionally to a single thin slice on a sandwich along with a turkey breast or lean roast beef—you'll get the flavor you crave without too much fat.

Condiments count.   Have a smear of mustard, hummus, or pickle relish, or a splash of hot sauce or fat-free salad dressing on your sandwich. If you go for mayo, choose a fat-free or reduced-fat variety and have just a teaspoon or two.

Don't forget the veggies.   Think beyond lettuce and tomato and pile your sandwiches high with *0 PointsPlus* value vegetables like shredded carrots or cabbage or add cucumber, radish, or pickle slices. If you're packing your sandwich for lunch, keep the veggies in a separate container and add them just before you eat to keep the bread from getting soggy.

Choose whole grain goodness.   Whether your bread of choice is sliced bread, a roll, bun, or a wrap, choose a whole grain option for added fiber and nutrients. Choose thin-sliced whole wheat bread, a small (about 2 ounces) roll or bun, or medium (8-inch) wraps or tortillas. If you're trying to make the switch from bland white bread to robust whole wheat, sandwiches are a great start, since the fillings are so flavorful they balance the flavor of the grain.

Go for healthy sides.   Enjoy your wholesome lunch sandwich along with something equally good for you. Have a fresh veggie and low-fat dip, baked tortilla chips, a kosher dill spear, a small green salad, or veggie slaw made with light mayo—and always, a piece of fresh *0 PointsPlus* value fruit for dessert.

southwestern salsa burgers

Serves 4 • Ready in 20 minutes or less

1 pound ground lean beef (7 percent fat or less)
1 small onion, finely chopped
1 jalapeño pepper, seeded and minced
1 garlic clove, minced
2 tablespoons chopped fresh cilantro

1 teaspoon ground cumin
½ teaspoon salt
4 whole wheat hamburger buns, toasted
½ cup fat-free salsa
8 leaf lettuce leaves

1 Combine beef, onion, jalapeño, garlic, cilantro, cumin, and salt in medium bowl. With damp hands, form mixture into four (½-inch-thick) patties.

2 Spray medium nonstick skillet with nonstick spray and set over medium heat. Add patties and cook until instant-read thermometer inserted into side of each patty registers 160°F, 5–6 minutes on each side.

3 Place burgers in buns with salsa and lettuce leaves.

PER SERVING (1 burger): 268 Cal, 8 g Total Fat, 3 g Sat Fat, 0 g Trans Fat, 64 mg Chol, 717 mg Sod, 20 g Carb, 4 g Fib, 28 g Prot, 77 mg Calc.

PointsPlus value: **6.**

cook's note

Take an idea from this recipe and top your favorite burgers and sandwiches with fat-free salsa. It's a fast and flavorful *0 PointsPlus* way to add a kick of spice.

chicken sandwiches with red cabbage slaw

Serves 4 • Ready in 20 minutes or less

4 (¼-pound) skinless boneless chicken
    breasts
¼ teaspoon salt
⅛ teaspoon black pepper
3 cups thinly sliced red cabbage

¼ cup chili sauce
3 tablespoons reduced-fat mayonnaise
4 slices rye bread, toasted
4 (1-ounce) slices Swiss cheese

1 Preheat broiler.

2 Spray large nonstick skillet with nonstick spray and set over medium heat. Sprinkle chicken with salt and pepper. Place chicken in skillet and cook, turning occasionally, until well browned and cooked through, about 8 minutes.

3 Meanwhile, stir together cabbage, chili sauce, and mayonnaise in medium bowl.

4 Place bread on large baking sheet. Top each slice with 1 chicken breast. Spoon slaw evenly on chicken; top each sandwich with 1 cheese slice. Broil 5 inches from heat until cheese melts, about 1 minute.

PER SERVING (1 open-face sandwich): 394 Cal, 15 g Total Fat, 7 g Sat Fat, 0 g Trans Fat, 100 mg Chol, 816 mg Sod, 25 g Carb, 4 g Fib, 37 g Prot, 288 mg Calc.
PointsPlus value: **10.**

cook's note

Red cabbage makes a colorful slaw, but if you have green cabbage on hand, that will work fine, too. If you want to add a little sweetness to the slaw, mix in a shredded peeled apple with the cabbage.

southwestern tuna wraps

Serves 4 • Ready in 20 minutes or less

⅓ cup light mayonnaise
1 tablespoon lime juice
½ teaspoon chili powder
1 (6-ounce) can solid white tuna in water,
    drained and flaked
2 scallions, thinly sliced

1 small red bell pepper, chopped
1 jalapeño, seeded and minced
2 tablespoons chopped fresh cilantro
4 (8-inch) whole wheat tortillas
1 cup thinly sliced romaine
2 plum tomatoes, chopped

1 Stir together mayonnaise, lime juice, and chili powder in medium bowl. Add tuna, scallions, bell pepper, jalapeño, and cilantro; stir to combine.

2 Layer tortillas evenly with tuna mixture, romaine, and tomatoes. Roll up wraps tightly.

PER SERVING (1 wrap): 204 Cal, 7 g Total Fat, 1 g Sat Fat, 0 g Trans Fat, 22 mg Chol, 515 mg Sod, 23 g Carb, 4 g Fib, 13 g Prot, 31 mg Calc.

PointsPlus value: *5.*

**Meatball Sandwiches with
Sun-Dried Tomato Sauce**

meatball sandwiches with sun-dried tomato sauce

Serves 4

1 cup sun-dried tomatoes (not oil-packed)
1 cup fat-free marinara sauce
⅔ cup low-sodium chicken broth
1 pound ground skinless turkey breast
⅓ cup plain dried bread crumbs
⅓ cup grated Parmesan cheese

1 large egg white
¼ teaspoon black pepper
½ cup chopped fresh basil
4 (2-ounce) whole wheat hero rolls, toasted
½ cup shredded part-skim mozzarella cheese

1 Combine sun-dried tomatoes and enough boiling water to cover in medium bowl. Let stand until softened, about 10 minutes; drain.

2 Put sun-dried tomatoes, marinara sauce, and broth in blender and puree.

3 Stir together turkey, bread crumbs, Parmesan, egg white, and pepper in large bowl; shape into 20 meatballs.

4 Spray large nonstick skillet with nonstick spray and set over medium heat. Add meatballs and cook, turning occasionally, until browned, about 4 minutes. Add sun-dried tomato mixture and bring to boil. Reduce heat and simmer, covered, until meatballs are cooked through, 8–10 minutes. Stir in basil.

5 Fill rolls evenly with meatballs and sauce; sprinkle evenly with mozzarella.

PER SERVING (1 sandwich): 467 Cal, 13 g Total Fat, 5 g Sat Fat, 0 g Trans Fat, 90 mg Chol, 925 mg Sod, 42 g Carb, 7 g Fib, 46 g Prot, 340 mg Calc.

PointsPlus value: *12.*

cook's note

For less fat and calories—and a lower *PointsPlus* value—be sure to use ground turkey breast that is labeled "skinless."

To cook food on a rack beneath a heat source.

what you need

A broiler pan: A large, shallow drip pan topped with a slotted rack to allow fats to drain away as the food cooks. If you don't have a broiler pan, you can improvise with a flat roasting rack, a heavy-gauge cooling rack set inside a baking pan, or simply place the food in a shallow baking pan.

how it's done

Adjust the oven rack so that the food in the pan under the broiler is about 5 inches away from the heat source. Preheat the broiler for at least 5 minutes. Spray the broiler rack with nonstick spray. Season the food and place it on the rack.

Broil the food to the desired degree of doneness, taking into consideration that thicker pieces of meats and poultry will take longer to cook. Delicate fish fillets do not need to be turned while broiling, but all other foods should be turned once for even cooking.

tuna and cheddar–stuffed portobellos

Serves 4 • Ready in 20 minutes or less

4 portobello
  mushroom caps,
  stems removed
¼ teaspoon salt
¼ teaspoon black
  pepper
2 teaspoons olive oil
1 small onion, chopped
1 small carrot,
  shredded
1 (6-ounce) can solid
  white tuna in water,
  drained and flaked
1 cup fresh bread
  crumbs
2 tablespoons
  chopped fresh flat-
  leaf parsley
½ cup shredded
  reduced-fat sharp
  Cheddar cheese

① Preheat broiler. Spray large baking pan with nonstick spray.

② Scrape away black "gills" from underside of mushrooms with tip of small spoon; discard. Spray mushrooms with nonstick spray; sprinkle with 1/8 teaspoon salt and 1/8 teaspoon pepper. Place mushrooms in baking pan and broil 5 inches from heat until tender, about 3 minutes on each side.

③ Meanwhile, heat oil in large nonstick skillet over medium heat. Add onion and carrot and cook, stirring occasionally, until softened, 5 minutes. Stir in tuna, bread crumbs, parsley, and remaining 1/8 teaspoon salt and 1/8 teaspoon pepper.

④ Fill mushroom caps with tuna mixture; sprinkle evenly with cheese. Broil until cheese melts, about 1 minute.

PER SERVING (1 stuffed mushroom): 169 Cal, 7 g Total Fat, 2 g Sat Fat, 0 g Trans Fat, 22 mg Chol, 444 mg Sod, 12 g Carb, 2 g Fib, 16 g Prot, 133 mg Calc.

PointsPlus value: **4.**

matzo ball soup with homemade chicken broth

Serves 12

12 cups reduced-sodium fat-free chicken broth
1 (3-pound) chicken, cut into 8 pieces, skin and wings removed and discarded
4 carrots, sliced
2 turnips, peeled and cut into ½-inch pieces
5 sprigs fresh flat-leaf parsley
4 sprigs fresh dill

1¼ cups matzo meal
3 large eggs, lightly beaten
2 large egg whites
1 tablespoon olive oil
¾ teaspoon salt
¼ teaspoon black pepper
⅓ cup plus 1 tablespoon chopped fresh flat-leaf parsley

1 To make soup, combine broth, chicken pieces, carrots, turnips, parsley sprigs, and dill in large pot over medium-high heat; bring to boil. Reduce heat, cover, and simmer until chicken is tender, about 1 hour.

2 Meanwhile, to make matzo balls, combine matzo meal, eggs, egg whites, oil, salt, pepper, and 1/3 cup chopped parsley in medium bowl. Refrigerate 30 minutes. Form into 24 balls.

3 Using slotted spoon, remove chicken pieces from broth; reserve chicken for another use. Remove and discard parsley sprigs and dill sprigs. Return broth to simmer and add matzo balls; simmer, covered, until matzo balls are cooked through, 20–25 minutes. Sprinkle with remaining 1 tablespoon chopped parsley.

PER SERVING (1 cup soup and 2 matzo balls): 206 Cal, 7 g Total Fat, 2 g Sat Fat, 0 g Trans Fat, 94 mg Chol, 326 mg Sod, 17 g Carb, 2 g Fib, 19 g Prot, 49 mg Calc.

PointsPlus value: *5.*

cook's note

To store any leftovers, transfer to an airtight container and let cool. Cover and refrigerate up to 4 days or freeze up to 4 months. To reheat, if frozen, thaw the soup in the refrigerator overnight. Transfer to a saucepan. Cover and cook over medium heat, stirring occasionally, until heated through.

how to make homemade broths

Making your own beef, chicken, or vegetable broth is an easy way to make more flavorful and inexpensive versions than you'll find on the supermarket shelf. Substitute these homemade broths in any recipe that calls for canned broth and taste the difference.

chicken broth

Makes 8 cups

Heat 2 teaspoons canola oil in stockpot over medium-high heat. Add 1 chopped onion, 1 chopped carrot, 1 chopped celery stalk (including leaves); cook, stirring frequently, until softened, about 5 minutes. Add 12 cups water, 3 pounds chicken wings or backs, 6 sprigs parsley, 1 teaspoon salt, 1 bay leaf, and 1 sprig fresh thyme or ½ teaspoon dried thyme; bring to boil. Reduce heat and skim off any foam that rises to top. Simmer, partially covered, about 2 hours. Line colander with paper towel or double layer of cheesecloth; place over large bowl. Strain broth through colander, pressing solids with wooden spoon to extract juices; discard solids. Refrigerate broth until fat rises to surface; scrape off and discard fat. Use immediately or transfer to 1-cup containers and let cool. Cover and refrigerate up to 3 days or freeze up to 3 months.

PER SERVING (1 cup): 38 Cal, 1 g Total Fat, 0 g Sat Fat, 0 g Trans Fat, 0 mg Chol, 367 mg Sod, 3 g Carb, 0 g Fib, 5 g Prot, 10 mg Calc. *PointsPlus* value: *1.*

beef broth

Makes 8 cups

Heat 2 teaspoons canola oil in stockpot over medium-high heat. Add 4 pounds meaty beef soup bones in batches; cook, turning often, until browned on all sides, about 5 minutes. Transfer to plate. Return browned bones to stockpot. Add 12 cups water, 1 chopped onion, 1 chopped carrot, 1 chopped celery stalk (including leaves), 6 sprigs parsley, 1 bay leaf, 1 teaspoon salt, and ¼ teaspoon whole black peppercorns and bring to boil. Reduce heat and skim off any foam that rises to top. Simmer, partially covered, about 2 hours. Line colander with paper towel or double layer of cheesecloth; place over large bowl. Strain broth through colander, pressing solids with wooden spoon to extract juices; discard solids. Refrigerate until fat rises to surface; scrape off and discard fat. Use immediately or transfer to 1-cup containers, let cool, cover, and refrigerate up to 3 days or freeze up to 3 months.

PER SERVING (1 cup): 33 Cal, 1 g Total Fat, 0 g Sat Fat, 0 g Trans Fat, 0 mg Chol, 368 mg Sod, 3 g Carb, 0 g Fib, 5 g Prot, 10 mg Calc. *PointsPlus* value: *1*.

vegetable broth

Makes 6 cups

Combine 2 chopped celery stalks (including leaves), 2 sliced carrots, 1 chopped onion, 1 chopped leek, 1 peeled and chopped parsnip, 6 sliced garlic cloves, 1 bay leaf, 1 teaspoon salt, ¼ teaspoon whole black peppercorns, and 8 cups water in stockpot and bring to a boil over high heat. Reduce heat; skim off any foam that rises to top. Simmer, with pot partially covered, about 40 minutes. Line colander with paper towel or double layer of cheesecloth; place over large bowl. Strain broth through colander, pressing solids with wooden spoon to extract juices; discard solids. Use immediately or transfer to 1-cup containers and let cool. Cover and refrigerate up to 3 days or freeze up to 3 months.

PER SERVING (1 cup): 12 Cal, 0 g Total Fat, 0 g Sat Fat, 0 g Trans Fat, 0 mg Chol, 418 mg Sod, 3 g Carb, 0 g Fib, 0 g Prot, 6 mg Calc. *PointsPlus* value: *0*.

turkey noodle soup with butternut squash

Serves 6

1 pound turkey breast cutlets, cut into
   1-inch strips
6 cups reduced-sodium chicken broth
3 cups wide, yolk-free whole wheat noodles
½ small butternut squash, peeled, halved,
   seeded, and cut into ½-inch pieces
   (about 3 cups)

1 large onion, diced
1 jalapeño pepper, seeded and minced
2 yellow squash, quartered lengthwise and
   cut into 1-inch chunks
½ cup chopped fresh dill
Lime wedges

1 Spray large pot with nonstick spray and set over medium-high heat. Add turkey and cook, stirring frequently, until well browned, about 3 minutes. Transfer to plate.

2 Add broth and bring to boil. Add noodles, butternut squash, onion, and jalapeño. Reduce heat and simmer, covered, until butternut squash is almost tender, about 7 minutes. Add yellow squash and dill; cook until noodles and vegetables are just tender, about 3 minutes longer. Serve with lime wedges.

PER SERVING (about 2 cups): 225 Cal, 1 g Total Fat, 0 g Sat Fat, 0 g Trans Fat, 51 mg Chol, 602 mg Sod, 28 g Carb, 5 g Fib, 26 g Prot, 82 mg Calc.

***PointsPlus* value: 5.**

cook's note

To make it a meal, serve the soup with fresh sliced mango sprinkled with grated lime zest for dessert.

shrimp and edamame soup

Serves 4 • Ready in 20 minutes or less

2 tablespoons white or red miso
5 cups water
1½ cups frozen shelled edamame

¾ pound peeled and deveined shrimp
1 (5-ounce) bag baby spinach
2 scallions, thinly sliced

1. Whisk together miso and 1 cup of the water in small bowl until smooth; set aside.

2. Bring remaining 4 cups water to boil in large saucepan. Add edamame and cook, covered, until tender, about 5 minutes.

3. Add shrimp and cook until shrimp are just opaque in center, about 1 minute. Stir in miso mixture, spinach, and scallions and cook until spinach is wilted, 1 minute longer.

PER SERVING (about 1½ cups): 172 Cal, 5 g Total Fat, 1 g Sat Fat, 0 g Trans Fat, 131 mg Chol, 953 mg Sod, 11 g Carb, 4 g Fib, 23 g Prot, 147 mg Calc.

PointsPlus value: **4.**

cook's note

To make this soup more filling, you can add 1½ cups cooked brown rice when you add the spinach. The per-serving *PointsPlus* value will increase by *2*.

squash and apple soup with pear–blue cheese toasts

Serves 6

1½ cups reduced-sodium chicken broth
1 cup apple cider
1 (2-pound) butternut squash, seeded, peeled, and cut into ½-inch pieces
1 apple, peeled, cored, and chopped
1 onion, chopped
½ teaspoon salt
1 tablespoon lemon juice

½ teaspoon ground nutmeg
3 slices pumpernickel bread, crusts removed, toasted
1 small ripe pear, peeled, cored, and thinly sliced
3 tablespoons crumbled blue cheese, at room temperature
6 tablespoons plain low-fat Greek yogurt

1. Combine broth, cider, squash, apple, onion, and salt in large saucepan; set over medium heat and bring to boil. Reduce heat and simmer, covered, until squash is tender, about 20 minutes.

2. Let cool about 5 minutes. Pour soup in batches into blender and puree.

3. Return soup to pan; stir in lemon juice and nutmeg. Reheat over medium heat.

4. Meanwhile, to make toasts, preheat broiler. Cut each toast slice in half diagonally. Arrange pear slices evenly on toast; top with cheese. Place toasts on baking sheet and broil 5 inches from heat until cheese just begins to melt, about 1 minute. Ladle soup evenly into 6 bowls, top with yogurt, and serve with toasts.

PER SERVING (1 cup soup, 1 tablespoon yogurt, and 1 toast): 159 Cal, 2 g Total Fat, 1 g Sat Fat, 0 g Trans Fat, 4 mg Chol, 483 mg Sod, 32 g Carb, 6 g Fib, 6 g Prot, 110 mg Calc.

PointsPlus value: **4.**

cook's note

You can make the soup ahead. To do so, follow the recipe through step 2. Transfer the soup to an airtight container and let cool, then cover and refrigerate up to 4 days or freeze up to 4 months. To reheat, if frozen, thaw the soup in the refrigerator overnight. Transfer to a large saucepan, cover and cook over medium heat, stirring occasionally, until heated through, stirring in lemon juice and nutmeg. Prepare the toasts just before serving.

**Squash and Apple
Soup with Pear–Blue
Cheese Toasts**

white bean soup with cabbage

2 teaspoons olive oil
3 cups thinly sliced green cabbage
1 large carrot, sliced
1 small onion, chopped
2 garlic cloves, minced
½ teaspoon dried thyme

¼ teaspoon black pepper
2 (14½-ounce) cans reduced-sodium chicken broth
1 (14½-ounce) can diced tomatoes
2 (15 ½-ounce) cans cannellini (white kidney) beans, rinsed and drained

1 Heat oil in large saucepan over medium heat. Add cabbage, carrot, onion, garlic, thyme, and pepper. Cook, covered, until cabbage begins to wilt, about 2 minutes. Stir in broth and tomatoes. Cook, covered, until vegetables are softened, about 8 minutes.

2 Meanwhile, puree 1¼ cups of the beans in a blender or food processor. Add pureed beans and whole beans to saucepan and cook until heated through, about 2 minutes longer.

PER SERVING (about 1½ cups): 272 Cal, 3 g Total Fat, 0 g Sat Fat, 0 g Trans Fat, 0 mg Chol, 959 mg Sod, 46 g Carb, 13 g Fib, 18 g Prot, 137 mg Calc.

PointsPlus value: **6.**

cook's note

To make it a meal, assemble a salad of sliced tomatoes and cucumbers drizzled with red-wine vinegar and salt and pepper to taste to serve with the soup.

cream of broccoli soup with goat cheese

Serves 6

1 tablespoon unsalted butter	4 cups fresh broccoli florets
1 small onion, diced	⅓ cup crumbled goat cheese
3 tablespoons all-purpose flour	1 teaspoon grated lemon zest
3 cups reduced-sodium chicken broth	¼ teaspoon salt
1 cup fat-free milk	⅛ teaspoon black pepper

1 Melt butter in large saucepan over medium heat. Add onion and cook, stirring occasionally, until softened, about 5 minutes. Add flour and cook, stirring constantly, about 1 minute. Gradually add broth, stirring constantly. Stir in milk. Bring to boil, stirring occasionally.

2 Reduce heat and simmer, stirring occasionally, until mixture thickens slightly, about 2 minutes. Add broccoli and simmer, stirring occasionally, until tender, 7–8 minutes.

3 Remove pan from heat; let cool about 5 minutes. Stir in goat cheese. Transfer in batches to a food processor or blender and puree. Return soup to pan; stir in lemon zest, salt, and pepper. Reheat over medium heat (do not boil).

PER SERVING (generous ¾ cup): 95 Cal, 4 g Total Fat, 2 g Sat Fat, 0 g Trans Fat, 9 mg Chol, 437 mg Sod, 10 g Carb, 2 g Fib, 6 g Prot, 97 mg Calc.

PointsPlus value: **3.**

cook's note

To keep the soup a vibrant bright green, watch it carefully once you add the broccoli and cook until the broccoli is just barely tender. If the broccoli is overcooked, the soup will turn a drab olive color.

**Three-Mushroom Barley
Soup and Roasted
Beet and Fresh Plum
Salad, page 68**

three-mushroom barley soup

Serves 6

4 teaspoons olive oil
2 carrots, chopped
1 onion, chopped
½ teaspoon dried thyme
½ pound white button mushrooms, sliced
½ pound shiitake mushrooms, stems
    discarded, caps sliced

½ pound oyster mushrooms, sliced
3 garlic cloves, minced
6 cups reduced-sodium chicken broth
½ cup quick-cooking barley
¼ teaspoon salt
¼ teaspoon black pepper

1 Heat oil in Dutch oven over medium-high heat. Add carrots, onion, and thyme; cook, stirring occasionally, until vegetables begin to soften, 2–3 minutes. Stir in button, shiitake, and oyster mushrooms and garlic; cook, stirring occasionally, until mushrooms are lightly browned, about 15 minutes.

2 Add broth and bring to boil. Reduce heat to medium, cover, and simmer 15 minutes. Stir in barley, salt, and pepper; continue to cook, covered, until barley is tender, 18–20 minutes.

PER SERVING (1⅓ cups): 137 Cal, 4 g Total Fat, 1 g Sat Fat, 0 g Trans Fat, 0 mg Chol, 681 mg Sod, 21 g Carb, 5 g Fib, 8 g Prot, 41 mg Calc.

PointsPlus value: **4.**

cook's note
To make it a meal, finish your lunch with a crisp Granny Smith apple and a cup of unsweetened herbal tea.

coconut-ginger sweet potato soup

Serves 12　•　Vegetarian

2 teaspoons olive oil
1 onion, chopped
8 cups reduced-sodium vegetable broth
2½ pounds sweet potatoes, peeled and cut into chunks
¼ cup coarsely chopped peeled fresh ginger

½ teaspoon salt
¼ teaspoon cayenne
½ cup light coconut milk
Grated zest and juice of 1 lime
¼ cup chopped fresh cilantro leaves

1 Heat oil in large saucepan over medium-high heat. Add onion and cook, stirring frequently, until softened, about 5 minutes. Add broth, potatoes, ginger, salt, and cayenne; bring to boil. Reduce heat and simmer, partially covered, until potatoes are fork-tender, about 20 minutes.

2 Remove pan from heat; let soup cool 5 minutes. Transfer in batches to food processor or blender and puree. Return soup to saucepan. Stir in coconut milk and lime zest and juice; heat through. Serve sprinkled with cilantro.

PER SERVING (1 cup): 85 Cal, 1 g Total Fat, 0 g Sat Fat, 0 g Trans Fat, 0 mg Chol, 427 mg Sod, 18 g Carb, 2 g Fib, 1 g Prot, 28 mg Calc.

PointsPlus value: **2.**

cook's note

To store any leftovers, transfer to an airtight container and let cool. Cover and refrigerate up to 4 days or freeze up to 4 months. To reheat, if frozen, thaw the soup in the refrigerator overnight. Transfer to a saucepan. Cover and cook over medium heat, stirring occasionally, until heated through.

spicy peanut-ginger soup

Serves 8

2 red bell peppers, chopped
1 onion, chopped
1 tablespoon grated peeled fresh ginger
2 garlic cloves, minced
8 cups reduced-sodium chicken broth

1 (14½-ounce) can diced tomatoes
½ cup crunchy peanut butter
¼ teaspoon cayenne pepper
¼ teaspoon salt
Chopped fresh cilantro

1 Spray large saucepan with nonstick spray and set over medium heat. Add bell peppers, onion, ginger, and garlic; cook, stirring frequently, until vegetables are softened, about 6 minutes. Stir in broth, tomatoes, peanut butter, cayenne, and salt; bring to boil. Reduce heat and simmer, covered, stirring occasionally, until vegetables are very soft, about 20 minutes.

2 Remove pan from heat; let soup cool 5 minutes. Transfer in batches to food processor or blender and puree. Return soup to pan; reheat if necessary. Serve sprinkled with cilantro.

PER SERVING (1 cup): 138 Cal, 8 g Total Fat, 2 g Sat Fat, 0 g Trans Fat, 0 mg Chol, 747 mg Sod, 10 g Carb, 2 g Fib, 8 g Prot, 48 mg Calc.

PointsPlus value: **4.**

go for the green

Green salads are a delicious—and nutritious—option for lunch. They pack in lots of healthy *0 PointsPlus* value veggies, they're rich in antioxidants, and can be a great source of fiber. Make the most of the salads you toss together by following these tips for great taste and keeping *PointsPlus* value low.

Mix up the greens. Buy a couple of different kinds of salad greens every week and mix them together for more flavorful and colorful salads. You can't really go wrong in combining greens, so mix arugula with Bibb lettuce, watercress with leaf lettuce, and radicchio with romaine.

Make it easy. Make it simple to enjoy salads often by buying bagged prewashed greens. Or, make the minimal investment in a salad spinner and prepare your own greens. Once the greens are washed and dried, store them in an airtight plastic container or a zip-close plastic bag along with a couple of paper towels to absorb moisture. They will keep for about 5 days.

Toss with care. To make a little dressing go a long way, toss your salad with the dressing in a large bowl just before serving. You can coat up to 3 cups of salad with just a tablespoon of dressing using this technique.

Pump up the veggies. To make salads more filling, don't skimp on the veggies. Pile your plate high with lettuce, tomatoes, cucumbers, radishes, bell peppers, and carrots for a low *PointsPlus* value salad that will keep you going all afternoon.

Pack in some protein. When a salad is your main dish for lunch, pack in some protein by adding lean sliced ham, roast beef, chicken breast, turkey breast, canned solid white tuna in water, cubed tofu, a hard-boiled egg, shredded low-fat cheese, or canned beans.

Sweeten the deal. Don't forget about fresh fruits as an addition to salads. They add a touch of sweet flavor, bright color, and interesting texture. Try tossing in sliced apples, pears, figs, or peaches. Fresh orange segments or a handful of berries are delicious, too.

Limit the croutons. Croutons—even fat-free croutons—are a calorie-dense high *PointsPlus* value food (¼ cup of fat-free croutons has *1 PointsPlus* value). If you enjoy croutons, use them sparingly.

Stretch the bacon. If salad is not your favorite, a little bacon can add crunch and smoky flavor to a plate of greens. Use it wisely, though. At *1 PointsPlus* value per slice, it's easy to overdo. To make the flavor go further, finely chop one slice of crisp-cooked bacon and toss it into a salad to distribute the flavor.

Salad rules. Make it your house rule that there's salad on the table with dinner every night. If you've pre-prepped greens and veggies on the weekend, you and your family can enjoy a fresh, healthful salad even on a harried night when you're calling for pizza delivery for dinner.

Turn leftovers into lunch. Have leftover tuna, egg, or pasta salad? How about those leftover roasted vegetables lurking in the fridge? Toss a generous bowl of greens with a drizzle of dressing and put the leftovers on top. Garnish with cherry tomatoes and cucumber slices for a quick and healthy lunch.

spinach and endive salad with walnut vinaigrette

Serves 6 • *Ready in 20 minutes or less*

4 slices turkey bacon
1 tablespoon toasted walnut oil
1 tablespoon white-wine vinegar
1 tablespoon water
1 teaspoon Dijon mustard
1 garlic clove, minced

¼ teaspoon salt
¼ teaspoon black pepper
1 (5-ounce) package baby spinach
1 head Belgian endive, leaves separated
⅓ cup chopped toasted walnuts

1 Cook bacon in medium nonstick skillet over medium heat, turning occasionally, until browned, about 8 minutes. Transfer to paper towels to drain. Crumble when cool.

2 Meanwhile, whisk together oil, vinegar, water, mustard, garlic, salt, and pepper in large salad bowl; add spinach, endive, walnuts, and bacon. Toss to coat.

PER SERVING (1 cup): 97 Cal, 9 g Total Fat, 1 g Sat Fat, 0 g Trans Fat, 8 mg Chol, 239 mg Sod, 3 g Carb, 1 g Fib, 3 g Prot, 53 mg Calc.
PointsPlus value: **3.**

cook's note

Toasted walnut oil adds a rich walnut flavor to salad dressings. If it's not available, you can use olive oil in this recipe. The flavor will not be the same, but the salad will still be delicious.

wheat berry–vegetable salad with canadian bacon

Serves 6

¾ cup wheat berries, rinsed
2 cups water
3 slices Canadian bacon, chopped
2 tablespoons white-wine vinegar
1 tablespoon olive oil
¼ teaspoon salt

⅛ teaspoon black pepper
2 plum tomatoes, chopped
1 sweet onion, diced
1 cup frozen peas, thawed
¼ cup chopped fresh basil

1 Combine wheat berries and water in medium saucepan over medium-high heat; bring to boil. Reduce heat to medium-low, cover, and simmer until berries are tender, about 1 hour. Drain and transfer to large shallow dish to cool.

2 Meanwhile, spray large nonstick skillet with nonstick spray and set over medium heat. Add bacon and cook, stirring ocassionally, until browned, 2–3 minutes. Transfer to paper towels to drain.

3 Whisk together vinegar, oil, salt, and pepper in large bowl. Add wheat berries, bacon, tomatoes, onion, peas, and basil and toss well.

PER SERVING (½ cup): 145 Cal, 4 g Total Fat, 1 g Sat Fat, 0 g Trans Fat, 6 mg Chol, 286 mg Sod, 23 g Carb, 3 g Fib, 7 g Prot, 30 mg Calc.

PointsPlus value: **4.**

hoppin' john salad

Serves 6

2 tablespoons apple cider vinegar
1 tablespoon olive oil
½ teaspoon salt
¼ teaspoon black pepper
2 red bell peppers, chopped
1 yellow bell pepper, chopped
4 scallions, chopped

2 (15½-ounce) cans black-eyed peas, rinsed
   and drained
1 cup grape tomatoes, halved
1 jalapeño pepper, seeded and minced
¼ pound lean ham, diced
¼ cup chopped fresh cilantro leaves

1 Whisk together vinegar, oil, salt, and black pepper in large bowl.

2 Add bell peppers, scallions, black-eyed peas, tomatoes, jalapeño, ham, and cilantro and toss to coat. Cover and refrigerate until chilled, at least 2 hours.

PER SERVING (generous 1 cup): 191 Cal, 4 g Total Fat, 1 g Sat Fat, 0 g Trans Fat, 10 mg Chol, 657 mg Sod, 27 g Carb, 6 g Fib, 13 g Prot, 42 mg Calc.

PointsPlus value: **5.**

cook's note
To make it a meal, keep the Southern theme going and enjoy a fresh sliced peach for dessert.

salmon and white bean salad

Serves 4 • Ready in 20 minutes or less

1 teaspoon grated lemon zest
2 tablespoons lemon juice
1 tablespoon olive oil
⅛ teaspoon black pepper
1 (15½-ounce) can cannellini (white kidney) beans, rinsed and drained
1 (7½-ounce) can skinless boneless salmon, drained and flaked

1 tomato, diced
1 yellow bell pepper, diced
½ small red onion, diced
6 Kalamata olives, pitted and chopped
2 teaspoons chopped fresh basil
1 head Bibb lettuce, leaves separated

1 Whisk together lemon zest, lemon juice, olive oil, and black pepper in medium bowl. Add beans, salmon, tomato, bell pepper, onion, olives, and basil and toss to coat.

2 Divide lettuce among 4 serving plates; top with salad.

PER SERVING (about ¾ cup): 225 Cal, 7 g Total Fat, 1 g Sat Fat, 0 g Trans Fat, 44 mg Chol, 416 mg Sod, 22 g Carb, 6 g Fib, 20 g Prot, 203 mg Calc.

PointsPlus value: **6.**

cook's note

Canned salmon is a convenient staple to keep on hand. Choose skinless boneless canned salmon when you shop. It does cost a little more, but it's recipe-ready when you're in a hurry.

barley, tuna, and feta salad

Serves 6

½ cup pearl barley
1½ teaspoons grated lemon zest
¼ cup lemon juice
1 tablespoon olive oil
½ teaspoon salt
¼ teaspoon black pepper
1 large tomato, chopped
1 small green bell pepper, diced

1 (14-ounce) can quartered artichokes, drained
½ cup fresh flat-leaf parsley, chopped
2 tablespoons capers, rinsed
1 (12-ounce) can solid white tuna in water, drained and flaked
6 cups mixed baby greens
⅓ cup crumbled feta cheese

1 Bring medium pot of water to boil over medium-high heat; stir in barley. Reduce heat and simmer, covered, until barley is tender, 25 minutes. Drain in colander; rinse with cold running water to cool and drain again.

2 Whisk together lemon zest, lemon juice, oil, salt, and black pepper in large bowl. Add barley, tomato, bell pepper, artichokes, parsley, and capers, tossing to combine. Gently stir in tuna. Let stand about 30 minutes to allow flavors to blend.

3 Divide greens evenly among 6 plates and top evenly with salad; sprinkle evenly with feta. The salad can be refrigerated up to 4 hours. Let stand at room temperature about 30 minutes before serving.

PER SERVING (1⅓ cups): 215 Cal, 6 g Total Fat, 2 g Sat Fat, 0 g Trans Fat, 29 mg Chol, 719 mg Sod, 24 g Carb, 9 g Fib, 18 g Prot, 104 mg Calc.

PointsPlus value: *5.*

shrimp salad with lime and cilantro

Serves 6 • Ready in 20 minutes or less

1½ pounds cooked, peeled medium shrimp
1 cup cherry tomatoes, halved
4 scallions, thinly sliced
1 small jicama, peeled and diced
1 jalapeño pepper, seeded and diced
¼ cup chopped fresh cilantro

2 tablespoons lime juice
1 tablespoon olive oil
½ teaspoon ground cumin
¼ teaspoon salt
8 large romaine lettuce leaves
Lime wedges

1 Combine shrimp, tomatoes, scallions, jicama, jalapeño, cilantro, lime juice, oil, cumin, and salt in large bowl. Cover and refrigerate at least 2 hours or up to 6 hours.

2 Line platter with lettuce leaves. Top with shrimp salad and surround with lime wedges.

PER SERVING (1 cup): 110 Cal, 3 g Total Fat, 1 g Sat Fat, 0 g Trans Fat, 142 mg Chol, 267 mg Sod, 4 g Carb, 1 g Fib, 16 g Prot, 45 mg Calc.

PointsPlus value: **3.**

cook's note

To make it a meal, begin your lunch with a cup of gazpacho (1 cup gazpacho per serving will increase the **PointsPlus** value by **4**).

shrimp, pineapple, and avocado salad

Serves 4 • Ready in 20 minutes or less

3 tablespoons lime juice
1 tablespoon olive oil
¼ teaspoon salt
¼ teaspoon black pepper
¾ pound cooked, peeled medium shrimp

2 cups chopped fresh pineapple
2 scallions, sliced
1 avocado, pitted, peeled, and chopped
2 tablespoons chopped fresh mint

Whisk together lime juice, oil, salt, and pepper in large bowl. Add shrimp, pineapple, scallions, avocado, and mint and toss gently to combine.

PER SERVING (about 1½ cups): 235 Cal, 10 g Total Fat, 1 g Sat Fat, 0 g Trans Fat, 179 mg Chol, 958 mg Sod, 17 g Carb, 4 g Fib, 21 g Prot, 102 mg Calc.

PointsPlus value: **6.**

warm shrimp and arugula salad

Serves 4 • Ready in 20 minutes or less

¼ cup chopped fresh flat-leaf parsley
2 tablespoons grated lemon zest
1 garlic clove, minced
3 teaspoons olive oil
1 pound large peeled and deveined shrimp

2 tablespoons lemon juice
1 (6-ounce) container arugula
4 plum tomatoes, quartered
½ cucumber, peeled, seeded, and sliced
¼ cup grated Parmesan cheese

1. Spray broiler rack with nonstick spray and preheat broiler.

2. Stir together parsley, lemon zest, garlic, and 1 teaspoon oil in medium bowl; add shrimp and toss to coat.

3. Place shrimp on broiler rack and broil 5 inches from heat, turning once, until just opaque throughout, about 5 minutes.

4. Meanwhile, to make dressing, whisk together lemon juice and remaining 2 teaspoons oil in large bowl. Add arugula, tomatoes, and cucumber to dressing; toss to coat. Add Parmesan and toss gently to combine. Divide salad evenly among 4 plates. Top evenly with shrimp.

PER SERVING (about 4 shrimp and 1½ cups salad): 185 Cal, 7 g Total Fat, 2 g Sat Fat, 0 g Trans Fat, 179 mg Chol, 922 mg Sod, 7 g Carb, 2 g Fib, 23 g Prot, 247 mg Calc.

PointsPlus value: **5.**

cook's note

To change the flavor of this dish, you can use fresh basil or dill instead of parsley.

chopped salad with feta cheese

Serves 6 • Vegetarian • Ready in 20 minutes or less

1 tablespoon red-wine vinegar
1 tablespoon olive oil
⅛ teaspoon salt
⅛ teaspoon black pepper
3 cups cherry tomatoes, halved
1 English (seedless) cucumber, peeled and chopped
1 large green bell pepper, chopped

¼ cup thinly sliced red onion
¼ cup Kalamata olives, pitted and coarsely chopped
¼ cup chopped fresh flat-leaf parsley
2 tablespoons chopped fresh mint
1 tablespoon capers, drained
½ cup crumbled fat-free feta cheese

Whisk together vinegar, oil, salt, and black pepper in large bowl. Add tomatoes, cucumber, bell pepper, onion, olives, parsley, mint, and capers and toss. Add feta and toss again.

PER SERVING (1 cup): 75 Cal, 3 g Total Fat, 0 g Sat Fat, 0 g Trans Fat, 0 mg Chol, 258 mg Sod, 8 g Carb, 2 g Fib, 4 g Prot, 75 mg Calc.

PointsPlus value: **2.**

arugula and apple salad with shaved parmesan

Serves 6 • Vegetarian • Ready in 20 minutes or less

1 small shallot, minced
2 tablespoons apple cider vinegar
1 tablespoon olive oil
1 teaspoon Dijon mustard
¼ teaspoon salt
⅛ teaspoon black pepper

1 (6-ounce) bag baby arugula
2 small apples, cored and thinly sliced
⅓ cup golden raisins
¼ cup shaved Parmesan cheese
2 tablespoons toasted pine nuts

1 Whisk together shallot, vinegar, oil, mustard, salt, and pepper in large bowl.

2 Add arugula, apples, and raisins and toss to coat. Divide evenly among 6 salad plates and sprinkle evenly with Parmesan and pine nuts.

PER SERVING (1¼ cups): 118 Cal, 6 g Total Fat, 1 g Sat Fat, 0 g Trans Fat, 3 mg Chol, 203 mg Sod, 15 g Carb, 2 g Fib, 3 g Prot, 111 mg Calc.

PointsPlus value: **3.**

tuna and tomato caesar salad

Serves 4 • Ready in 20 minutes or less

2 tablespoons lemon juice
1 tablespoon olive oil
1½ teaspoons Dijon mustard
1 garlic clove, minced
1 canned anchovy fillet, minced
⅛ teaspoon salt
⅛ teaspoon black pepper

2 cups cherry tomatoes, halved
1 large head romaine lettuce, torn
2 (3-ounce) cans solid white tuna in water,
   drained and flaked
¾ cup fat-free croutons
2 tablespoons grated Parmesan cheese

1 Whisk together lemon juice, oil, mustard, garlic, anchovy, salt, and pepper in large bowl. Add tomatoes, romaine, tuna, and croutons and toss to coat.

2 Divide salad evenly among four plates; sprinkle with cheese.

PER SERVING (about 2 cups): 184 Cal, 7 g Total Fat, 2 g Sat Fat, 0 g Trans Fat, 20 mg Chol, 518 mg Sod, 17 g Carb, 6 g Fib, 15 g Prot, 139 mg Calc.

PointsPlus value: **5.**

cook's note

To make your own fat-free croutons, cut bread into ¾-inch cubes, place them on a baking sheet, and bake at 425°F until lightly browned and crisp, 6 to 8 minutes. For an even healthier option, make the croutons using whole wheat bread.

chickpea, watercress, and pear salad

Serves 4 • Ready in 20 minutes or less • Vegetarian

2 tablespoons orange juice
1 tablespoon olive oil
½ teaspoon ground cumin
¼ teaspoon salt
⅛ teaspoon black pepper
1 (15½-ounce) can chickpeas, rinsed and drained

2 large bunches watercress, tough stems discarded
1 fennel bulb, halved lengthwise and sliced
1 pear, cored and thinly sliced
2 tablespoons golden raisins
2 tablespoons slivered almonds, toasted

Whisk together orange juice, oil, cumin, salt, and pepper in large bowl. Add chickpeas, watercress, fennel, pear, raisins, and almonds and toss to coat.

PER SERVING (about 1½ cups): 244 Cal, 8 g Total Fat, 1 g Sat Fat, 0 g Trans Fat, 0 mg Chol, 362 mg Sod, 38 g Carb, 9 g Fib, 10 g Prot, 152 mg Calc.

PointsPlus value: **6.**

cook's note

Fresh fennel adds a mild anise flavor to this salad. If it's not to your liking, use a small, thinly sliced red bell pepper in this recipe instead.

asparagus and avocado salad

Serves 6 • Vegetarian

1 bunch asparagus, trimmed and cut into
  1-inch pieces
2 teaspoons grated lemon zest
3 tablespoons lemon juice
1 tablespoon olive oil
1 teaspoon Dijon mustard
½ teaspoon salt

¼ teaspoon black pepper
1 cucumber, peeled, seeded, and diced
1 avocado, halved, peeled, pitted, and diced
1 pint grape tomatoes, halved
6 radishes, halved and sliced
⅓ cup thinly sliced red onion
¼ cup chopped fresh dill

1 Bring medium pot two thirds full of water to boil. Add asparagus and cook 1 minute; drain, cool under cold running water, and drain again. Pat dry with paper towels.

2 Whisk together lemon zest, lemon juice, oil, mustard, salt, and pepper in large bowl. Add asparagus, cucumber, avocado, tomatoes, radishes, onion, and dill and toss to coat.

PER SERVING (1¼ cups): 94 Cal, 6 g Total Fat, 1 g Sat Fat, 0 g Trans Fat, 0 mg Chol, 226 mg Sod, 9 g Carb, 4 g Fib, 3 g Prot, 38 mg Calc.

PointsPlus value: *2.*

cook's note

To add more good-for-you greens to this salad, serve it on a bed of baby spinach, arugula, or watercress.

green salad with roasted corn and cumin vinaigrette

Serves 4 • Vegetarian

1 cup fresh or thawed frozen corn kernels
3 tablespoons white wine vinegar
1 teaspoon olive oil
½ teaspoon ground cumin
½ teaspoon salt
½ teaspoon black pepper
1 small head Bibb lettuce, torn into bite-size pieces

½ small head romaine, torn into bite-size pieces
½ avocado, pitted, peeled, and chopped
1 small red onion, thinly sliced
1 cup cherry tomatoes, halved

1 Preheat oven to 425°F. Spray large rimmed baking sheet with nonstick spray.

2 Spread corn on baking sheet and roast, stirring twice, until lightly browned, 25 minutes. Let cool slightly.

3 Whisk together vinegar, oil, cumin, salt, and pepper in large bowl. Add Bibb, romaine, avocado, onion, tomatoes, and corn and toss to coat.

PER SERVING (1½ cups): 103 Cal, 4 g Total Fat, 1 g Sat Fat, 0 g Trans Fat, 0 mg Chol, 310 mg Sod, 16 g Carb, 5 g Fib, 3 g Prot, 50 mg Calc.
***PointsPlus* value: 3.**

cook's note

To add more protein and fiber to this salad, toss in 1 cup rinsed and drained canned black beans or red kidney beans (the per-serving *PointsPlus* value will increase by *1*).

Green Salad with Roasted Corn and Cumin Vinaigrette

romaine and radicchio salad with stilton dressing

Serves 6 • Vegetarian • Ready in 20 minutes or less

4 ounces French baguette, cut into ¾-inch cubes
½ cup crumbled Stilton cheese
⅓ cup plain low-fat Greek yogurt
3 tablespoons reduced-fat mayonnaise
2 tablespoons white-wine vinegar

¾ teaspoon Worcestershire sauce
⅛ teaspoon black pepper
2 small heads romaine lettuce, chopped
1 head radicchio, chopped
3 plum tomatoes, cut into thin wedges
½ small red onion, chopped

1 Preheat oven to 425°F.

2 Spread bread cubes on baking sheet. Bake until lightly browned and crisp, 6–8 minutes. Cool on baking sheet.

3 To make dressing, whisk together cheese, yogurt, mayonnaise, vinegar, Worcestershire sauce, and pepper in small bowl. Combine lettuce, radicchio, tomatoes, onion, and cooled bread cubes in large bowl. Drizzle dressing over lettuce mixture and toss to coat.

PER SERVING (2 cups): 154 Cal, 5 g Total Fat, 3 g Sat Fat, 0 g Trans Fat, 10 mg Chol, 351 mg Sod, 21 g Carb, 5 g Fib, 9 g Prot, 148 mg Calc.

PointsPlus value: *4.*

tangy tomatillo salad

Serves 6 • Vegetarian • Ready in 20 minutes or less

⅓ cup plain fat-free yogurt
2 tablespoons lime juice
1 garlic clove, minced
1 teaspoon ground cumin
½ teaspoon salt
1 (12-ounce) can tomatillos, rinsed, drained,
  and chopped

1 large yellow bell pepper, chopped
1 large cucumber, peeled and chopped
1 small red onion, chopped
¼ cup chopped fresh cilantro

1 Whisk together yogurt, lime juice, garlic, cumin, and salt in large bowl.

2 Add tomatillos, bell pepper, cucumber, onion, and cilantro and toss to coat.

PER SERVING (¾ cup): 43 Cal, 1 g Total Fat, 0 g Sat Fat, 0 g Trans Fat, 0 mg Chol, 270 mg Sod, 8 g Carb, 2 g Fib, 2 g Prot, 48 mg Calc.

PointsPlus value: *1.*

hearts of romaine with creamy lime dressing

Serves 6 • Vegetarian • Ready in 20 minutes or less

1 garlic clove
¼ cup reduced-fat mayonnaise
1 teaspoon grated lime zest
3 tablespoons lime juice
1 teaspoon Dijon mustard
¼ teaspoon salt

¼ cup grated Parmesan cheese
2 hearts of romaine lettuce, chopped
1 small carrot, shredded
1 cup shredded red cabbage
1 cup fat-free croutons

1 Put garlic in food processor and pulse until minced. Add mayonnaise, lime zest and juice, mustard, and salt. Pulse until blended. Add Parmesan and pulse to combine.

2 Combine lettuce, carrot, cabbage, and croutons in large bowl. Add dressing and toss to coat.

PER SERVING (2 cups): 93 Cal, 4 g Total Fat, 1 g Sat Fat, 0 g Trans Fat, 6 mg Chol, 420 mg Sod, 11 g Carb, 2 g Fib, 4 g Prot, 100 mg Calc.

PointsPlus value: *2.*

green salad with apple and fennel

Serves 6 • Vegetarian • Ready in 20 minutes or less

2 tablespoons white-wine vinegar
1 tablespoon olive oil
1 teaspoon honey
¾ teaspoon salt
¼ teaspoon black pepper
1 head Bibb or Boston lettuce, cut into bite-size pieces

1 bunch watercress, trimmed
1 red apple, cored and thinly sliced
½ fennel bulb, halved and thinly sliced, feathery fronds chopped
¼ cup thinly sliced red onion
¼ cup chopped toasted walnuts

1 Whisk together vinegar, oil, honey, salt, and pepper in large bowl.

2 Add lettuce, watercress, apple, fennel, and onion to bowl and toss to coat. Sprinkle with walnuts.

PER SERVING (1¼ cups): 86 Cal, 6 g Total Fat, 1 g Sat Fat, 0 g Trans Fat, 0 mg Chol, 313 mg Sod, 9 g Carb, 2 g Fib, 2 g Prot, 45 mg Calc.

PointsPlus value: 3.

spinach and orange salad with almonds

Serves 6 • Vegetarian • Ready in 20 minutes or less

2 tablespoons orange juice
1 tablespoon apple cider vinegar
1 tablespoon olive oil
1 teaspoon honey
1 teaspoon Dijon mustard

¼ teaspoon salt
⅛ teaspoon black pepper
1 (8-ounce) package baby spinach
1 navel orange, peeled and cut into sections
¼ cup sliced almonds, toasted

1 Whisk together orange juice, vinegar, oil, honey, mustard, salt, and pepper in large bowl.

2 Add spinach, orange, and almonds and toss to coat.

PER SERVING (1 cup): 68 Cal, 4 g Total Fat, 0 g Sat Fat, 0 g Trans Fat, 0 mg Chol, 148 mg Sod, 6 g Carb, 2 g Fib, 2 g Prot, 58 mg Calc.

PointsPlus value: **2.**

apple, celery, and walnut salad with dijon dressing

Serves 6 • Vegetarian • Ready in 20 minutes or less

½ bunch celery
2 tablespoons white-wine vinegar
1 tablespoon olive oil
2 teaspoons Dijon mustard
½ teaspoon maple syrup
¼ teaspoon salt

⅛ teaspoon black pepper
1 red apple, cored and cut into matchstick strips
2 tablespoons chopped fresh flat-leaf parsley
¼ cup chopped toasted walnuts

1 Reserve leaves of celery; cut stalks into matchstick strips.

2 Whisk together vinegar, oil, mustard, maple syrup, salt, and pepper in large bowl. Add celery strips, celery leaves, apple, and parsley and toss to coat. Sprinkle with walnuts.

PER SERVING (¾ cup): 79 Cal, 6 g Total Fat, 1 g Sat Fat, 0 g Trans Fat, 0 mg Chol, 270 mg Sod, 7 g Carb, 2 g Fib, 1 g Prot, 27 mg Calc.

PointsPlus value: **2.**

roasted beet and fresh plum salad

Serves 6 • Vegetarian

1 pound beets, trimmed
3 tablespoons orange juice
1 tablespoon olive oil
1 tablespoon white-wine vinegar
1 teaspoon Dijon mustard
½ teaspoon salt

⅛ teaspoon black pepper
4 large black plums, halved, pitted, and cut
  into thin wedges
1 small shallot, finely chopped
8 cups mixed baby greens
3 tablespoons chopped toasted walnuts

1. Preheat oven to 425°F.

2. Wrap beets in large sheet of foil and place on baking sheet. Roast until easily pierced with paring knife, about 1 hour 5 minutes. Let cool in foil 1 hour. Peel beets and cut into wedges.

3. To make dressing, whisk together the orange juice, oil, vinegar, mustard, salt, and pepper in large serving bowl.

4. Combine beets, plums, and shallot in medium bowl. Add 4 tablespoons of the dressing and toss to combine.

5. Add greens to dressing in serving bowl and toss to coat. Spoon beet mixture on top of greens; sprinkle with walnuts.

PER SERVING (1⅔ cups): 118 Cal, 5 g Total Fat, 1 g Sat Fat, 0 g Trans Fat, 0 mg Chol, 278 mg Sod, 17 g Carb, 4 g Fib, 3 g Prot, 54 mg Calc.

PointsPlus value: **3.**

cook's note

Goat cheese and roasted beets are a classic pairing. If you add 6 ounces of crumbled goat cheese to this salad, the per-serving *PointsPlus* value will increase by *3*.

heirloom tomato salad with feta and capers

Serves 4 • Vegetarian

2 large heirloom tomatoes, thickly sliced
2 tablespoons minced shallots
2 tablespoons red-wine vinegar
1 tablespoon reduced-sodium vegetable broth
1 tablespoon olive oil

1 teaspoon Dijon mustard
⅛ teaspoon salt
⅛ teaspoon black pepper
¼ cup crumbled feta cheese
¼ cup thinly sliced fresh basil leaves
1 tablespoon capers, drained

1 Arrange tomatoes on large serving platter.

2 Whisk together shallots, vinegar, broth, oil, mustard, salt, and pepper in small bowl; drizzle over tomatoes. Sprinkle with feta, basil, and capers.

PER SERVING (¼ of salad): 79 Cal, 6 g Total Fat, 2 g Sat Fat, 0 g Trans Fat, 8 mg Chol, 282 mg Sod, 5 g Carb, 1 g Fib, 2 g Prot, 64 mg Calc.

PointsPlus value: *2.*

cook's note

If heirloom tomatoes are not available, you can use regular large tomatoes. Scatter a few yellow cherry tomatoes on the salad to make it even more colorful.

Artichoke–White Bean
Dip with Veggies and
Pita Chips, page 93

appetizers
and snacks

honeydew and prosciutto skewers

Serves 2 • Ready in 20 minutes or less

2 cups honeydew melon cubes
3 thin slices prosciutto, halved
2 teaspoons grated lime zest

1 tablespoon lime juice
¼ teaspoon cracked black pepper

Thread honeydew and prosciutto alternately on four (6-inch) bamboo skewers. Sprinkle with lime zest and juice and pepper.

PER SERVING (2 skewers): 111 Cal, 3 g Total Fat, 1 g Sat Fat, 0 g Trans Fat, 19 mg Chol, 426 mg Sod, 17 g Carb, 2 g Fib, 7 g Prot, 20 mg Calc.

PointsPlus value: *3.*

cook's note

Sweet fresh fruit and salty cured prosciutto is a sophisticated and elegant pairing. Almost any kind of fruit is delicious in this recipe. Try cantaloupe or watermelon cubes or peach, nectarine, or plum slices instead of the honeydew.

bacon-cheddar cheese tarts

Serves 12

1 teaspoon olive oil
1 sweet onion, quartered and thinly sliced
¼ teaspoon salt
3 slices Canadian bacon, finely chopped
¼ cup fat-free egg substitute
2 tablespoons fat-free half-and-half

½ teaspoon Dijon mustard
⅛ teaspoon black pepper
24 frozen mini–phyllo tart shells
⅓ cup finely shredded reduced-fat sharp
   Cheddar cheese

1 Heat oil in medium nonstick skillet over medium heat. Add onion and salt; cover and cook until onion is softened, about 5 minutes. Uncover and cook, stirring frequently, until onion is golden brown, about 12 minutes. Transfer to plate. Add bacon to skillet and cook until lightly browned, about 2 minutes.

2 Preheat oven to 350°F. In small bowl, whisk together egg substitute, half-and-half, mustard, and pepper. Arrange tart shells on baking sheet. Spoon onions evenly into shells. Sprinkle bacon evenly over onions. Pour about 1 teaspoon egg mixture into each tart. Sprinkle tops evenly with cheese and bake until egg mixture is set, about 15 minutes. Serve warm.

PER SERVING (2 tarts): 66 Cal, 4 g Total Fat, 0 g Sat Fat, 0 g Trans Fat, 6 mg Chol, 188 mg Sod, 6 g Carb, 0 g Fib, 4 g Prot, 40 mg Calc.

PointsPlus value: **2.**

grilled beef bruschetta with goat cheese and fig jam

Serves 6

1 (½-pound) beef tenderloin, trimmed
¼ teaspoon salt
⅛ teaspoon black pepper
1 (10-inch) whole wheat baguette

¼ cup fig jam
1 cup lightly packed baby spinach
¼ cup crumbled goat cheese
1 tablespoon minced scallions

1 Spray grill rack with nonstick spray. Preheat grill to medium-high heat or prepare medium-high fire.

2 Sprinkle tenderloin with salt and pepper. Place on grill rack and grill, turning once, until instant-read thermometer inserted into center registers 145°F, about 10 minutes. Transfer to cutting board and let stand 5 minutes. Slice tenderloin across grain into 12 thin slices.

3 Cut baguette on diagonal into 12 (½-inch) slices; lightly spray with nonstick spray. Place baguette slices on grill rack and grill until well marked, about 1 minute per side. Spread baguette slices evenly with fig jam and top with spinach, beef, and goat cheese. Sprinkle evenly with scallions and arrange on platter.

PER SERVING (2 bruschetta): 171 Cal, 4 g Total Fat, 2 g Sat Fat, 0 g Trans Fat, 25 mg Chol, 272 mg Sod, 21 g Carb, 2 g Fib, 12 g Prot, 49 mg Calc.

PointsPlus value: **4.**

cook's note
You can make the bruschetta with a ½-pound pork tenderloin instead of the beef. To prepare the pork, grill it until an instant-read thermometer inserted in the center registers 145°F, about 15 minutes.

Grilled Beef Bruschetta with Goat Cheese and Fig Jam and Shrimp with Tomato-Chipotle Relish, page 84

ginger-lime chicken skewers

Serves 6

3 tablespoons reduced-sodium soy sauce
2 tablespoons rice vinegar
2 tablespoons lime juice
2 tablespoons grated peeled fresh ginger

1 tablespoon sugar
1 pound skinless boneless chicken breast,
  cut into 2-inch chunks
Chopped fresh cilantro

1 Spray broiler rack with nonstick spray. Preheat broiler.

2 To make basting sauce, combine soy sauce, vinegar, lime juice, ginger, and sugar in small saucepan; bring to boil over medium-high heat. Cook, stirring often, until sauce is reduced to 1/3 cup, about 6 minutes.

3 Meanwhile, thread chicken onto six (8-inch) metal skewers. Arrange skewers on broiler rack; brush with half of sauce. Broil 4 inches from heat, turning once and basting with remaining sauce, until chicken is cooked through, 8–10 minutes. Sprinkle chicken with cilantro. Serve hot or warm.

PER SERVING (1 skewer): 95 Cal, 2 g Total Fat, 1 g Sat Fat, 0 g Trans Fat, 42 mg Chol, 304 mg Sod, 3 g Carb, 0 g Fib, 16 g Prot, 11 mg Calc.
PointsPlus value: **2.**

cook's note
Use this sweet and tangy sauce for basting broiled shrimp or scallops, too.

italian sausage and spinach–stuffed mushrooms

Serves 12

24 large button mushrooms
¼ pound spicy Italian turkey sausage, casings removed
½ red onion, finely chopped
1 large garlic clove, minced
2 cups packed baby spinach

¾ cup cooked brown rice
¼ cup spreadable light garlic-and-herb cheese
3 tablespoons seasoned dried bread crumbs
⅓ cup grated Parmesan cheese

1 Remove stems from mushrooms; set caps aside and finely chop stems. Spray large nonstick skillet with nonstick spray and set over medium heat. Add mushroom stems, turkey sausage, onion, and garlic. Cook, breaking up sausage with side of spoon, until sausage is cooked and mixture is dry, about 8 minutes. Stir in spinach and cook until wilted, about 2 minutes. Remove skillet from heat; let cool 10 minutes. Stir rice, garlic-and-herb cheese, bread crumbs, and 3 tablespoons Parmesan into sausage mixture.

2 Preheat oven to 375°F. Spray rimmed baking sheet with nonstick spray. Spoon filling by rounded tablespoonfuls into mushroom caps, pressing firmly. Arrange mushrooms on prepared baking sheet. Sprinkle evenly with remaining Parmesan. Bake until mushrooms are tender, 18–20 minutes. Serve warm.

PER SERVING (2 stuffed mushrooms): 66 Cal, 2 g Total Fat, 1 g Sat Fat, 0 g Trans Fat, 8 mg Chol, 181 mg Sod, 7 g Carb, 1 g Fib, 5 g Prot, 47 mg Calc.
***PointsPlus* value: 2.**

cook's note

For this recipe, buy the mushrooms at a market where you can select them yourself, rather than purchasing them in a sealed plastic container. That way, you can pick out the largest button mushrooms that are the perfect size for stuffing.

roasted potato slices with smoked salmon spread

Serves 12

4 small red potatoes
1½ teaspoons olive oil
⅛ teaspoon salt
⅓ cup plain fat-free Greek yogurt
2 ounces smoked salmon, finely chopped

1 tablespoon chopped fresh dill
½ teaspoon finely grated lemon zest
Pinch black pepper
1 tablespoon snipped fresh chives

1 Preheat oven to 425°F. Spray large baking sheet with nonstick spray.

2 Trim off and discard thin slice from opposite ends of each potato. Cut each potato into six (¼-inch) slices. Put slices in medium bowl and toss with oil and salt. Arrange on baking sheet in single layer. Bake until browned on bottom, about 12 minutes. Turn with spatula and continue to bake until browned and crisp, about 12 minutes longer.

3 Meanwhile, mix yogurt, salmon, dill, lemon zest, and pepper in small bowl.

4 Top each potato slice with about 1 teaspoon salmon mixture and sprinkle evenly with chives. Serve warm or at room temperature.

PER SERVING (2 potato slices): 56 Cal, 1 g Total Fat, 0 g Sat Fat, 0 g Trans Fat, 1 mg Chol, 131 mg Sod, 10 g Carb, 1 g Fib, 2 g Prot, 14 mg Calc.

PointsPlus value: *1.*

cook's note

No time to make the roasted potatoes? Serve the salmon spread on store-bought baked potato chips instead.

tuna crostini with lemony white bean spread

Serves 8

1 (15½-ounce) can cannellini (white kidney) beans, rinsed and drained
1 tablespoon chopped fresh flat-leaf parsley
1 teaspoon grated lemon zest
1 tablespoon lemon juice
3 teaspoons olive oil
1 garlic clove, minced
1 (½-pound) tuna steak, about 1 inch thick
¼ teaspoon salt
⅛ teaspoon black pepper
1 (8-ounce) whole wheat baguette, cut on the diagonal into 16 slices, toasted
2 scallions, thinly sliced
16 thin slices English (seedless) cucumber

1 Combine beans, parsley, lemon zest, lemon juice, 2 teaspoons of oil, and garlic in medium bowl; coarsely mash with fork.

2 Heat remaining 1 teaspoon oil in medium skillet over medium-high heat. Sprinkle tuna with salt and pepper. Add tuna; cook 2–3 minutes per side for medium-rare or until desired doneness. Transfer tuna to cutting board; let stand about 5 minutes.

3 Cut tuna into 16 slices. Spread each baguette slice with about 1 tablespoon of bean mixture; sprinkle with scallions. Top each with 1 slice cucumber, then with 1 slice tuna.

PER SERVING (2 crostini): 176 Cal, 4 g Total Fat, 1 g Sat Fat, 0 g Trans Fat, 17 mg Chol, 338 mg Sod, 22 g Carb, 4 g Fib, 13 g Prot, 70 mg Calc.

PointsPlus value: **4.**

how to

pan sear

To cook food in a skillet over medium-high heat using very little oil for a short amount of time.

what you need

A heavy-bottomed skillet big enough to hold the food you are cooking in a single layer with at least 1 inch between the pieces. A cast iron or stainless steel skillet is an excellent choice.

how it's done

Heat the skillet over medium-high heat until a drop of water sizzles when dropped onto the surface, about 5 minutes. Add just enough oil to lightly coat the bottom (1 teaspoon of oil will coat a 12-inch skillet). Season the food and add it to the skillet. Wait 2 to 3 minutes for the color of the food to begin to change from the bottom up: Seafood will turn opaque; beef and pork will turn brown. Turn the food over and continue cooking to the desired doneness.

Chicken, Mushroom, and Spinach
Quesadillas and Sweet Onion
Pico de Gallo, page 96

chicken, mushroom, and spinach quesadillas

Serves 8 • Ready in 20 minutes or less

2 teaspoons canola oil
1 (10-ounce) package white mushrooms, thinly sliced
¼ teaspoon salt
3 cups baby spinach

1½ cups shredded cooked chicken breast
3 ounces reduced-fat goat cheese, crumbled
4 (8-inch) whole wheat tortillas
½ cup Sweet Onion Pico de Gallo (page 96)

1 Heat oil in large nonstick skillet over medium heat. Add mushrooms and salt and cook, stirring occasionally, until tender, about 8 minutes. Add spinach and cook, stirring, until spinach has wilted, 1 minute.

2 Sprinkle one quarter of mushroom mixture, chicken, and goat cheese on half of each tortilla. Fold unfilled half of each tortilla over filling, pressing down lightly.

3 Wipe out skillet and spray with nonstick spray; set over medium heat. Cook quesadillas, one at a time, until crisp and heated through, about 3 minutes per side. Cut each quesadilla into 4 wedges; arrange on platter. Serve with pico de gallo.

PER SERVING (2 quesadilla wedges and 1 tablespoon pico de gallo): 140 Cal, 5 g Total Fat, 2 g Sat Fat, 0 g Trans Fat, 26 mg Chol, 309 mg Sod, 12 g Carb, 2 g Fib, 13 g Prot, 27 mg Calc.

PointsPlus value: *4.*

cook's note

If you don't have time to make the Sweet Onion Pico de Gallo, serve the quesadillas with store-bought pico de gallo or fat-free salsa.

gefilte fish

Serves 12

3 carrots, sliced
2 small onions, sliced
2 pounds skinless cod fillet, cut into chunks
2 large eggs
¼ cup matzo meal
¾ teaspoon salt

¼ teaspoon black pepper
8 cups low-sodium fish broth
4 cups water
1 parsnip, peeled and sliced
¼ cup prepared horseradish in vinegar, drained

1. Combine 1 carrot and 1 onion in food processor and pulse until chopped. Add cod, eggs, matzo meal, salt, and pepper; pulse until mixture is fairly smooth. Transfer to medium bowl, cover, and refrigerate.

2. Combine broth, water, parsnip, remaining 2 carrots, and remaining onion in large pot. Bring to boil over high heat. Reduce heat, cover, and simmer 20 minutes.

3. Meanwhile, with damp hands, form fish mixture into 12 ovals, using about 1/3 cup for each. Increase heat to medium-high and drop ovals into broth mixture; return to simmer. Cover, reduce heat to medium-low, and simmer until gefilte fish is cooked through, 50–55 minutes. Remove from heat and cool in pot.

4. Transfer gefilte fish and vegetables to large plastic container and spoon in enough broth to cover; reserve remaining broth for another use. Chill gefilte fish and vegetables at least 2 hours or up to 2 days. With slotted spoon, transfer to platter; serve with horseradish.

PER SERVING (1 piece gefilte fish, ¼ cup vegetables, and 1 teaspoon horseradish): 131 Cal, 3 g Total Fat, 1 g Sat Fat, 0 g Trans Fat, 71 mg Chol, 309 mg Sod, 9 g Carb, 2 g Fib, 18 g Prot, 38 mg Calc.

PointsPlus value: **3.**

cook's note

The flavor of this delicate dish deepens and improves as the gefilte fish sit in the poaching liquid, so make it a day or two ahead if you can.

smoked trout spread with dill

Serves 12

3 ounces light cream cheese (Neufchâtel)
½ cup plain fat-free Greek yogurt
1 tablespoon lemon juice
3 ounces skinless smoked trout fillet,
    broken into pieces

2 tablespoons chopped fresh dill
1 tablespoon minced red onion
⅛ teaspoon black pepper
Small dill sprigs
36 thin whole grain crackers

1 Combine cream cheese, yogurt, and lemon juice in food processor and pulse until blended. Add trout, chopped dill, onion, and pepper and pulse until blended. Scrape spread into small bowl, cover, and refrigerate until chilled, at least 2 hours.

2 Just before serving, transfer spread to serving bowl; garnish with dill sprigs. Serve with crackers.

PER SERVING (3 tablespoons trout spread and 3 crackers): 71 Cal, 4 g Total Fat, 1 g Sat Fat, 0 g Trans Fat, 13 mg Chol, 104 mg Sod, 5 g Carb, 0 g Fib, 5 g Prot, 27 mg Calc.
PointsPlus value: *2.*

cook's note

To store any leftovers, transfer spread to an airtight container, cover, and refrigerate for up to 4 days.

shrimp with tomato-chipotle relish

Serves 6 • Ready in 20 minutes or less

1 pound tomatoes, seeded and chopped
¼ cup diced red onion
2 tablespoons chopped fresh cilantro
2 teaspoons lime juice
½ teaspoon ground chipotle chile

1½ teaspoons canola oil
1 small garlic clove, minced
⅛ teaspoon salt
1¼ pounds large cooked shrimp
6 lime wedges

1 To make relish, stir together tomatoes, onion, cilantro, lime juice, chipotle, oil, garlic, and salt in medium bowl.

2 Spoon about ¼ cup of relish into each of 6 small bowls; top evenly with shrimp. Serve with lime wedges.

PER SERVING (about 4 shrimp and ¼ cup relish): 83 Cal, 2 g Total Fat, 0 g Sat Fat, 0 g Trans Fat, 107 mg Chol, 186 mg Sod, 5 g Carb, 1 g Fib, 12 g Prot, 34 mg Calc.
PointsPlus value: **2.**

cook's note
This smoky tomato relish is also delicious to serve with baked tortilla chips, tacos, or tostadas.

grilled shrimp with mango-ginger dipping sauce

Serves 6

2 teaspoons olive oil
1 teaspoon grated lime zest
5 tablespoons lime juice
1 jalapeño pepper, seeded and minced
1 teaspoon grated peeled fresh ginger
¼ teaspoon plus ⅛ teaspoon salt

1¼ pounds large peeled and deveined
　shrimp (about 18 shrimp)
1½ large ripe mangoes, peeled and pitted
3 tablespoons minced red onion
1 tablespoon chopped fresh cilantro

1 Spray grill rack with nonstick spray; preheat grill to high or prepare high fire.

2 Combine oil, lime zest, 2 tablespoons of lime juice, half of jalapeño, ½ teaspoon of ginger, and ¼ teaspoon salt in zip-close plastic bag; add shrimp. Squeeze out air and seal bag; turn to coat shrimp. Refrigerate 30 minutes.

3 Meanwhile, to make sauce, combine mangoes, remaining 3 tablespoons lime juice, and remaining ½ teaspoon ginger in food processor or blender and puree. Transfer to small bowl and stir in onion, cilantro, and remaining half of jalapeño and 1/8 teaspoon salt.

4 Remove shrimp from bag and discard marinade; place shrimp on grill rack and grill until just opaque in center, 2–3 minutes on each side. Serve shrimp hot or at room temperature with dipping sauce.

PER SERVING (3 shrimp and ¼ cup sauce): 141 Cal, 2 g Total Fat, 0 g Sat Fat, 0 g Trans Fat, 146 mg Chol, 802 mg Sod, 15 g Carb, 2 g Fib, 17 g Prot, 75 mg Calc.
PointsPlus value: **4.**

cook's note
To make it a meal, serve this appetizer with Chicken, Black Bean, and Corn Chili on page 151.

crispy coconut shrimp with pineapple salsa

Serves 4

6 tablespoons flaked unsweetened coconut
¼ cup panko bread crumbs
2 tablespoons all-purpose flour
½ teaspoon salt
4 large egg whites
24 medium shrimp (about ½ pound), peeled
   with tails left on, deveined, butterflied,
   and patted dry

2 cups diced fresh pineapple
1 jalapeño pepper, seeded and minced
¼ cup chopped fresh cilantro
2 tablespoons lime juice

1 Preheat oven to 450°F. Spray baking sheet with nonstick spray.

2 Combine coconut, panko, flour, and salt in large shallow dish. Beat egg whites in large bowl until frothy; add shrimp to egg whites and toss to coat. Lift shrimp from egg whites one at a time, letting excess drip back into bowl; coat shrimp with coconut mixture, pressing gently to help it adhere. Place shrimp in single layer on baking sheet. Spray shrimp lightly with nonstick spray. Bake until golden outside and opaque inside, 8–10 minutes.

3 Meanwhile, to make salsa, stir together pineapple, jalapeño, cilantro, and lime juice in medium bowl. Serve shrimp with salsa.

PER SERVING (6 shrimp and ½ cup salsa): 180 Cal, 6 g Total Fat, 4 g Sat Fat, 0 g Trans Fat, 63 mg Chol, 664 mg Sod, 20 g Carb, 3 g Fib, 12 g Prot, 52 mg Calc.
PointsPlus value: **5.**

cook's note

If you have canned pineapple rings packed in juice on hand, you can dice them and use them instead of fresh pineapple.

**Crispy Coconut Shrimp
with Pineapple Salsa**

steamed shrimp dumplings with soy dipping sauce

Serves 6

2 cups coleslaw mix
2 scallions, cut into 1-inch pieces
¾ cup lightly packed fresh cilantro leaves
24 medium shrimp (about ½ pound), peeled and deveined
1 large egg white
1 teaspoon sesame oil

24 (3-inch) round wonton wrappers
3 tablespoons reduced-sodium soy sauce
2 tablespoons unseasoned rice vinegar
1 tablespoon water
½ teaspoon chili-garlic paste
2 tablespoons thinly sliced scallions

1 Bring medium saucepan two thirds full of water to boil over high heat. Add coleslaw mix and cook until wilted, about 30 seconds. Drain, rinse under cold running water, and drain again. Pat dry with paper towels.

2 Put scallions and cilantro in food processor; pulse until finely chopped. Add shrimp and coleslaw mix and continue to pulse until finely chopped. Add egg white and sesame oil and pulse until blended.

3 Lay wonton wrappers on work surface and spoon 1 level tablespoon of shrimp mixture into center of each. Gather up edges, pleating wonton wrappers around filling, but leaving filling uncovered at top. Press down lightly on filling with moistened finger so that dumplings resemble small flowers.

4 Fill large, deep skillet with 1 inch water. Set steamer basket in skillet and spray basket with nonstick spray. Arrange half of dumplings in basket. Set skillet over high heat and bring to boil; reduce heat to medium, cover skillet tightly, and steam dumplings until filling is firm and cooked through, about 10 minutes. Transfer dumplings to platter and cover to keep warm. Repeat with remaining dumplings.

5 Meanwhile, to make sauce, stir together soy sauce, rice vinegar, water, and chili-garlic paste in small bowl; sprinkle with scallions. Serve dumplings with sauce.

PER SERVING (4 dumplings and 1 tablespoon sauce): 136 Cal, 1 g Total Fat, 0 g Sat Fat, 0 g Trans Fat, 41 mg Chol, 479 mg Sod, 22 g Carb, 2 g Fib, 8 g Prot, 39 mg Calc.
PointsPlus value: **3.**

cook's note

Wonton wrappers come in round and square varieties. If you can't find round ones, you can use a 3-inch biscuit cutter to cut rounds from square wonton wrappers.

crabmeat and avocado salad in endive

Serves 6 • Ready in 20 minutes or less

3 ounces crabmeat, picked over
1 plum tomato, diced
¼ avocado, halved, peeled, pitted, and
   diced
1 tablespoon minced red onion
1 tablespoon chopped fresh flat-leaf parsley

¼ teaspoon grated lemon zest
1 tablespoon lemon juice
⅛ teaspoon seafood seasoning
12 large Belgian endive leaves (from about
   2 heads endive)

Toss together crabmeat, tomato, avocado, onion, parsley, lemon zest and juice, and seafood seasoning in medium bowl. Spoon 1 heaping tablespoon of crabmeat mixture into each endive leaf and arrange on serving platter. Serve at once, or cover and refrigerate up to 1 hour.

PER SERVING (2 stuffed endive leaves): 27 Cal, 1 g Total Fat, 0 g Sat Fat, 0 g Trans Fat, 14 mg Chol, 74 mg Sod, 2 g Carb, 1 g Fib, 3 g Prot, 23 mg Calc.

PointsPlus value: *1.*

cook's note

To make this appetizer for serving with the Christmas Dinner menu (page 380), double all the ingredients and prepare as directed.

10 simple snacks

Try these quick and tasty ways to stave off afternoon hunger—each with a **PointsPlus** value of only **2**.

HAM SANDWICH

Spread 1 slice reduced-calorie whole wheat bread with 1 teaspoon Dijon mustard. Top with 1 ounce lean ham and 2 tomato slices.

TURKEY ON RYE

Top 2 crispy light rye crackers with 1 ounce of lean skinless turkey breast and 2 or 3 radish slices.

CHICKEN SOUP

Prepare a packet of instant chicken-noodle soup mix, stirring in 1 cup of baby spinach when the soup comes to a boil.

CHEESE TORTILLA

Sprinkle a 4-ounce fat-free tortilla with 1 tablespoon shredded reduced-fat Monterey Jack cheese and bake at 425°F until the cheese melts, 2 to 3 minutes. Top with 2 tablespoons fat-free salsa.

RICE CAKE WITH PEANUT BUTTER

Spread 1 multigrain rice cake with 1 teaspoon creamy peanut butter and top with 2 or 3 thin slices of apple.

CARROTS AND SALSA

Dip 6 baby carrots into ½ cup fat-free salsa.

CHERRY TOMATOES AND RANCH DRESSING

Dip 1½ cups cherry tomatoes into 2 tablespoons fat-free ranch dressing.

CHILI POPCORN

Toss 2 cups of air-popped popcorn with ¼ teaspoon chili powder.

FRESH BERRY YOGURT

Mash ¼ cup sliced fresh strawberries in a small bowl; stir in ½ cup plain fat-free yogurt.

RASPBERRY REFRESHER

Puree 1 cup frozen unsweetened raspberries, ½ cup ice cubes, ½ cup seltzer water, and 1 teaspoon honey in a blender.

baked parmesan oysters

Serves 6

Kosher salt
¼ cup plain dried whole wheat bread
   crumbs
1 shallot, minced
2 tablespoons chopped fresh flat-leaf
   parsley

1 garlic clove, minced
2 teaspoons olive oil
1 dozen oysters, shucked, on the half shell
3 tablespoons grated Parmesan cheese

1 Preheat oven to 425°F. Spread kosher salt to a depth of ½ inch in large baking pan.

2 Stir together bread crumbs, shallot, parsley, garlic, and oil in small bowl. Nestle oysters in their shells in salt to keep them level. Spoon about 2 teaspoons bread crumb mixture over each oyster; sprinkle evenly with Parmesan.

3 Bake until oysters are cooked through and topping is golden, about 10 minutes. Place oysters on serving platter; discard salt.

PER SERVING (2 stuffed oysters): 58 Cal, 3 g Total Fat, 1 g Sat Fat, 0 g Trans Fat, 14 mg Chol, 86 mg Sod, 4 g Carb, 0 g Fib, 4 g Prot, 64 mg Calc.

PointsPlus value: *2.*

creamy salsa dip with vegetables

Serves 6 • Vegetarian

8 ounces fat-free cream cheese
4 ounces light cream cheese (Neufchâtel)
¼ cup mild fat-free salsa
2 ounces shredded low-fat sharp Cheddar
   cheese

2 scallions, thinly sliced
2 tablespoons chopped fresh cilantro
   (optional)
3 cups assorted cut-up vegetables

1 Combine fat-free cream cheese, light cream cheese, and salsa in large bowl and beat with electric mixer on medium speed until well combined. Stir in Cheddar, scallions, and cilantro, if using.

2 Spoon into serving bowl, cover, and refrigerate 2 hours or up to 2 days. Serve with vegetables.

PER SERVING (¼ cup dip and ½ cup vegetables): 133 Cal, 6 g Total Fat, 4 g Sat Fat, 0 g Trans Fat, 23 mg Chol, 479 mg Sod, 8 g Carb, 1 g Fib, 11 g Prot, 246 mg Calc.

PointsPlus value: *3.*

spiced ginger-carrot dip

Serves 6 • Vegetarian

1 pound carrots, cut into 1-inch pieces
1 tablespoon olive oil
1 small garlic clove, minced
1½ teaspoons lemon juice
1 teaspoon grated peeled fresh ginger
1 teaspoon paprika

½ teaspoon ground cumin
½ teaspoon salt
¼ teaspoon cinnamon
¼ teaspoon ground coriander
Pinch cayenne
1 tablespoon chopped fresh cilantro

1 Combine carrots and enough water to cover in large saucepan and bring to boil. Cook until fork-tender, about 20 minutes. Drain in colander and let cool 5 minutes.

2 Put carrots, oil, garlic, lemon juice, ginger, paprika, cumin, salt, cinnamon, coriander, and cayenne in food processor and process until smooth. Transfer to serving bowl; sprinkle with cilantro. Serve warm or at room temperature.

PER SERVING (¼ cup dip): 55 Cal, 3 g Total Fat, 0 g Sat Fat, 0 g Trans Fat, 0 mg Chol, 250 mg Sod, 8 g Carb, 2 g Fib, 1 g Prot, 31 mg Calc.
PointsPlus value: **2.**

cook's note

To make it a meal, serve this dip as a sandwich for lunch. Spread the dip in a whole-wheat sandwich thin topped with shredded lettuce and tomato and cucumber slices (1 whole-wheat sandwich thin per serving will increase the *PointsPlus* value by **3**).

artichoke–white bean dip with veggies and pita chips

Serves 4 • Vegetarian

½ (14-ounce) can artichoke hearts, drained
⅓ cup canned cannellini (white kidney) beans, rinsed and drained
2 tablespoons grated Parmesan cheese
1½ teaspoons olive oil
½ garlic clove, finely chopped
½ teaspoon grated lemon zest
1½ teaspoons lemon juice

Pinch cayenne pepper
1 tablespoon chopped fresh flat-leaf parsley
2 large multigrain or whole wheat pita breads
¾ teaspoon paprika
2 cups assorted vegetables, such as cucumber spears, bell pepper strips, and steamed and cooled green beans

1 Combine artichoke hearts, beans, Parmesan, oil, garlic, lemon zest and juice, and cayenne in food processor; pulse until smooth. Transfer dip to serving bowl and stir in parsley. Cover and refrigerate.

2 Preheat oven to 375°F. Split each pita in half horizontally to make 2 rounds. Place halves, rough sides up, on ungreased baking sheet. Spray lightly with olive oil nonstick spray, sprinkle evenly with paprika, and cut each round into 8 wedges. Bake until wedges are browned and crisp, 7–8 minutes.

3 Place dip in center of serving platter; arrange vegetables and chips around dip.

PER SERVING (3 tablespoons dip, ½ cup vegetables, and 8 chips): 173 Cal, 4 g Total Fat, 1 g Sat Fat, 0 g Trans Fat, 2 mg Chol, 352 mg Sod, 29 g Carb, 8 g Fib, 7 g Prot, 79 mg Calc.

PointsPlus value: *4.*

red pepper–basil dip with spring vegetables

Serves 6 • Vegetarian

2 garlic cloves, unpeeled
¾ cup canned cannellini (white kidney) beans, rinsed and drained
1 (7-ounce) jar roasted red bell peppers (not packed in oil), rinsed and drained
2½ tablespoons plain fat-free Greek yogurt
½ tablespoon lemon juice

¼ teaspoon salt
Pinch cayenne pepper
¼ cup lightly packed fresh basil
1 cup baby carrots
1 cup sugar snap peas, trimmed
1 cup small radishes, trimmed

1 To make dip, put garlic in small saucepan and cover with water; bring to boil. Reduce heat and simmer 5 minutes. Drain, cool garlic under cold running water, and remove and discard papery peel. Put garlic in food processor and pulse until minced. Add beans and bell peppers; pulse until smooth. Add yogurt, lemon juice, salt, and cayenne; pulse until blended. Add basil and pulse until chopped. Transfer to serving bowl, cover, and refrigerate at least 2 hours and up to 2 days.

2 Place dip in center of large serving platter; arrange vegetables around dip.

PER SERVING (½ cup vegetables and 3 tablespoons dip): 57 Cal, 0 g Total Fat, 0 g Sat Fat, 0 g Trans Fat, 0 mg Chol, 246 mg Sod, 11 g Carb, 3 g Fib, 4 g Prot, 39 mg Calc.
PointsPlus value: *1*.

cook's note

To make this dip for serving with the spring Easter Dinner menu (page 379), double all the ingredients and prepare as directed.

mango-poblano salsa

Serves 8 • Vegetarian • Ready in 20 minutes or less

1 poblano pepper
2 cups diced, peeled, and pitted mango
¼ cup diced red onion
2 tablespoons chopped fresh cilantro

1 garlic clove, minced
1 tablespoon lime juice
¼ teaspoon salt

1. Preheat broiler. Place poblano on baking sheet and broil 5 inches from heat, turning occasionally, until blackened on all sides, about 4 minutes. Place poblano in paper bag and fold closed. Let steam 10 minutes.

2. Meanwhile, combine mango, onion, cilantro, garlic, lime juice, and salt in a medium bowl. When cool enough to handle, peel poblano, discard seeds, and chop. Add poblano to mango mixture; stir gently. Serve at once or store, covered, in refrigerator up to 2 days.

PER SERVING (¼ cup): 30 Cal, 0 g Total Fat, 0 g Sat Fat, 0 g Trans Fat, 0 mg Chol, 75 mg Sod, 7 g Carb, 1 g Fib, 1 g Prot, 8 mg Calc.

***PointsPlus* value: *1*.**

cook's note

To make it a meal, serve this salsa with grilled shrimp (3 ounces of cooked shrimp per serving will increase the *PointsPlus* value by *2*).

sweet onion pico de gallo

Serves 6 • Vegetarian • Ready in 20 minutes or less

1 pound plum tomatoes (about 6), chopped
1 cup chopped sweet onion
½ cup chopped fresh cilantro
2 tablespoons lime juice

1 jalapeño pepper, seeded and minced
½ teaspoon salt
¼ teaspoon black pepper

Stir together all ingredients in large bowl. Cover and chill at least 30 minutes or up to 4 hours. Stir before serving.

PER SERVING (⅓ cup): 25 Cal, 0 g Total Fat, 0 g Sat Fat, 0 g Trans Fat, 0 mg Chol, 203 mg Sod, 6 g Carb, 1 g Fib, 1 g Prot, 15 mg Calc.

PointsPlus value: **1.**

cook's note

To make it a meal, serve a bowl of this spicy salsa alongside broiled lean boneless pork chops (a 4-ounce lean boneless pork chop per serving will increase the ***PointsPlus*** value by **4**).

italian spinach balls with marinara dip

Serves 6 • Vegetarian

1 teaspoon olive oil
1 onion, chopped
1 garlic clove, minced
1 (10-ounce) package frozen chopped
    spinach, thawed and squeezed dry
½ cup shredded Gruyère cheese

¼ cup grated Parmesan cheese
1 large egg white
½ teaspoon dried oregano
¼ teaspoon salt
⅔ cup seasoned dried bread crumbs
1¼ cups fat-free marinara sauce, warmed

1 Preheat oven to 350°F. Spray rimmed baking sheet with nonstick spray.

2 Heat oil in large nonstick skillet over medium heat. Add onion and cook, stirring occasionally, until softened, about 8 minutes. Stir in garlic and cook 1 minute. Let cool 10 minutes.

3 Combine spinach, Gruyère, Parmesan, egg white, oregano, salt, 1/3 cup bread crumbs, and cooled onion in food processor; pulse until well blended. Shape mixture into about thirty-six (1-inch) balls. Place remaining 1/3 cup bread crumbs on piece of wax paper and roll balls in crumbs to coat. Place balls 1 inch apart on baking sheet. Bake until firm, about 12 minutes. Serve warm with marinara sauce.

PER SERVING (6 balls and 3 tablespoons sauce): 152 Cal, 7 g Total Fat, 3 g Sat Fat, 0 g Trans Fat, 14 mg Chol, 605 mg Sod, 15 g Carb, 2 g Fib, 8 g Prot, 231 mg Calc.

PointsPlus value: *4.*

creamed mushroom toasts

Serves 6 • Vegetarian

2 teaspoons olive oil
1 small onion, chopped
2 garlic cloves, minced
⅛ teaspoon dried oregano
¼ pound cremini mushrooms, chopped
2 ounces shiitake mushrooms, stemmed
    and chopped
⅛ teaspoon salt

⅛ teaspoon black pepper
2 ounces light cream cheese (Neufchâtel),
    softened
2 tablespoons grated Parmesan cheese
2 tablespoons fat-free milk
1 tablespoon chopped fresh flat-leaf parsley
1 (12-ounce) whole wheat baguette, cut on
    the diagonal into 18 slices, toasted

1 Heat oil in medium nonstick skillet over medium heat. Add onion, garlic, and oregano; cook, stirring, 2 minutes. Add mushrooms, salt, and pepper; cook, stirring occasionally, until mushrooms are browned, 8–10 minutes. Remove from heat and stir in cream cheese, Parmesan, milk, and parsley.

2 Top each baguette slice with 1 tablespoon mushroom mixture.

PER SERVING (3 toasts): 202 Cal, 6 g Total Fat, 2 g Sat Fat, 0 g Trans Fat, 9 mg Chol, 389 mg Sod, 27 g Carb, 4 g Fib, 10 g Prot, 115 mg Calc.

PointsPlus value: **5.**

chickpea and tomato pita pizzas

Serves 6 • Vegetarian • Ready in 20 minutes or less

2 (6-inch) whole wheat pitas
1 cup canned chickpeas, rinsed and drained
1 garlic clove, minced
¼ teaspoon red pepper flakes
2 large plum tomatoes, thinly sliced

1 cup shredded part-skim mozzarella cheese
¼ cup freshly grated Parmesan cheese
¼ cup lightly packed fresh basil, thinly sliced

1 Preheat oven to 425°F. Spray large baking sheet with nonstick spray.

2 Split pitas in half horizontally to make 4 rounds. Place, rough sides up, on baking sheet.

3 Place chickpeas in small bowl and mash with fork. Stir in garlic and red pepper flakes. Spread pitas with chickpea mixture. Arrange tomato slices over chickpeas. Sprinkle evenly with mozzarella and Parmesan. Bake until pitas are crisp and cheese is melted, about 8 minutes.

4 Transfer pizzas to cutting board and sprinkle with basil. Cut each into 6 wedges; serve hot.

PER SERVING (4 wedges): 170 Cal, 6 g Total Fat, 3 g Sat Fat, 0 g Trans Fat, 13 mg Chol, 350 mg Sod, 19 g Carb, 3 g Fib, 11 g Prot, 214 mg Calc.

PointsPlus value: *4.*

cook's note

To make the pizzas for serving with the Come for Cocktails menu (page 379), double all the ingredients and prepare as directed, mashing the chickpeas in a large bowl and baking the pizzas on 2 large baking sheets.

curry-roasted cauliflower and broccoli with yogurt-mint sauce

Serves 6 • Vegetarian

2 tablespoons lemon juice
1 tablespoon olive oil
½ teaspoon ground cumin
½ teaspoon curry powder
¼ teaspoon chili powder
⅛ teaspoon cayenne pepper
⅛ teaspoon salt

½ small bunch broccoli, trimmed and cut into small florets
½ small head cauliflower, trimmed and cut into small florets
¾ cup plain low-fat Greek yogurt
3 tablespoons chopped fresh mint

1 Preheat oven to 400°F. Spray large rimmed baking sheet with nonstick spray.

2 Stir together 1 tablespoon of lemon juice, oil, ¼ teaspoon of cumin, curry powder, chili powder, cayenne, and salt in large bowl. Add broccoli and cauliflower and toss to coat.

3 Spread vegetables on baking sheet; roast 15 minutes. Stir and continue to roast until vegetables are tender and begin to brown, about 5 minutes longer.

4 Meanwhile, to make sauce, stir together yogurt, mint, remaining 1 tablespoon lemon juice, and remaining ¼ teaspoon cumin in serving bowl. Serve vegetables hot or at room temperature with dip.

PER SERVING (about ½ cup vegetables and 2 tablespoons dip): 71 Cal, 3 g Total Fat, 1 g Sat Fat, 0 g Trans Fat, 3 mg Chol, 90 mg Sod, 7 g Carb, 2 g Fib, 5 g Prot, 73 mg Calc.
PointsPlus value: **2.**

cook's note

To make the vegetables and dip for serving with the Come for Cocktails menu (page 379), double all the ingredients and prepare as directed, baking the vegetables on a large rimmed baking sheet.

toasted snack mix

Serves 20 • Vegetarian

3 tablespoons butter
1 tablespoon packed light-brown sugar
1 tablespoon reduced-sodium soy sauce
2 teaspoons hot pepper sauce
6 cups air-popped popcorn
4 cups corn-cereal squares

3 cups reduced-fat cheese-flavored baked snack crackers
2 cups unsalted pretzel twists
½ cup lightly salted cocktail peanuts
2 teaspoons chili powder

1 Preheat oven to 250°F. Spray large shallow roasting pan with nonstick spray.

2 Melt butter in small saucepan over low heat. Stir in brown sugar, soy sauce, and pepper sauce. Place popcorn, cereal, snack crackers, pretzels, and peanuts in roasting pan. Drizzle butter mixture over popcorn mixture and sprinkle with chili powder; stir to coat. Bake until crisp, stirring occasionally, about 45 minutes.

3 Turn mixture out onto sheet of foil to cool.

PER SERVING (½ cup): 129 Cal, 5 g Total Fat, 2 g Sat Fat, 0 g Trans Fat, 5 mg Chol, 242 mg Sod, 18 g Carb, 1 g Fib, 3 g Prot, 37 mg Calc.

PointsPlus value: **3.**

cook's note

You can store this crispy snack mix in an airtight container for up to a week. It's great to have on hand when you're craving a snack that's sweet and salty.

**Pork Chops and Rice with
Mole Sauce page 128**

beef, pork, and lamb

herb-roasted beef tenderloin and root vegetables

Serves 8

1 pound small red potatoes, halved or
    quartered if large
1 pound baby carrots
1 large onion, cut into 8 wedges
4 teaspoons olive oil
2 teaspoons plus 1 tablespoon chopped
    fresh thyme

1 teaspoon salt
¾ teaspoon black pepper
1 (2-pound) beef tenderloin, trimmed
2 garlic cloves, minced
1½ pounds green beans, trimmed

1   Preheat oven to 450°F. Place potatoes, carrots, and onion on large rimmed baking sheet. Drizzle with 2 teaspoons of oil, sprinkle with 2 teaspoons thyme, ½ teaspoon salt, and ¼ teaspoon pepper and toss to coat. Roast 30 minutes.

2   Meanwhile, rub beef with garlic, ¼ teaspoon remaining salt, and ¼ teaspoon remaining pepper. Spray large skillet with nonstick spray and set over medium-high heat. Place beef in skillet and cook, turning occasionally, until browned on all sides, 10–12 minutes. Rub remaining 1 tablespoon thyme over meat.

3   Turn vegetables and push them to sides of baking sheet. Place beef on rack in center of baking sheet and roast until vegetables are browned and tender and instant-read thermometer inserted into center of beef registers 145°F, about 25 minutes. Transfer vegetables to serving platter and cover loosely with foil. Transfer beef to cutting board, cover loosely with foil, and let stand 10 minutes.

4   Meanwhile, place green beans on large rimmed baking sheet; drizzle with remaining 2 teaspoons oil, ¼ teaspoon salt, and ¼ teaspoon pepper. Roast, stirring once, until crisp-tender, 10 minutes. Cut beef across grain into 16 slices and serve with vegetables.

PER SERVING (2 slices beef with 1 cup vegetables): 268 Cal, 9 g Total Fat, 3 g Sat Fat, 0 g Trans Fat, 66 mg Chol, 374 mg Sod, 23 g Carb, 5 g Fib, 26 g Prot, 67 mg Calc.

PointsPlus value: **7.**

cook's note

To make it a meal, start with a salad of watercress and plum tomatoes tossed with balsamic vinegar and salt and pepper to taste. Finish on an elegant note by serving small bowls of fresh rasberries.

wine-braised beef brisket

Serves 6

2 teaspoons olive oil
2 pounds center-cut brisket, trimmed
½ teaspoon ground cumin
½ teaspoon salt
⅛ teaspoon black pepper
1 small onion, chopped
1 carrot, chopped

1 celery stalk, chopped
¼ cup dry red wine or reduced-sodium beef
   broth
2 garlic cloves, minced
½ teaspoon dried oregano
1 (14-ounce) can diced tomatoes
½ cup water

1 Heat oil in Dutch oven over medium-high heat. Sprinkle brisket all over with cumin, salt, and pepper; add to Dutch oven and cook until browned, about 4 minutes on each side. Transfer to plate and set aside.

2 Return Dutch oven to stovetop and add onion, carrot, celery, wine, garlic, and oregano; bring to boil and cook until wine nearly evaporates, about 2 minutes. Stir in tomatoes and water and bring to simmer. Add brisket; cover, reduce heat to medium low, and simmer, turning occasionally, just until tender, about 3 hours.

3 Place brisket on cutting board; cut into 24 thin slices, keeping shape of brisket intact. Lay slices in sauce in Dutch oven and bring to simmer over medium heat; cover, reduce heat, and simmer until brisket is very tender, about 1 hour.

PER SERVING (4 slices brisket and ¼ cup sauce): 207 Cal, 7 g Total Fat, 2 g Sat Fat, 1 g Trans Fat, 89 mg Chol, 338 mg Sod, 5 g Carb, 2 g Fib, 30 g Prot, 24 mg Calc.
PointsPlus value: **5.**

cook's note
To make the brisket for serving with the Passover Dinner menu (page 379), double all the ingredients and prepare as directed.

merlot-braised beef roast and vegetables

Serves 8

1 (2-pound) beef bottom round roast, trimmed
1 teaspoon salt
¼ teaspoon black pepper
2 teaspoons olive oil
1½ cups reduced-sodium beef broth
1 cup merlot or other dry red wine
4 garlic cloves, minced

4 medium parsnips, peeled and cut into 1-inch pieces
3 carrots, cut into 1-inch pieces
3 medium red potatoes, scrubbed and each cut into 6 wedges
2 onions, each cut into 6 wedges
2 canned anchovy fillets, minced
2 teaspoons minced fresh rosemary

1 Preheat oven to 350°F.

2 Sprinkle beef with salt and pepper. Heat oil in Dutch oven over medium-high heat. Add beef and cook, turning occasionally, until browned on all sides, about 8 minutes. Add broth and wine, stirring to scrape any browned bits from bottom of Dutch oven. Add garlic and bring to boil. Cover, transfer pot to oven, and bake 1 hour, turning halfway through.

3 Remove pot from oven and stir in parsnips, carrots, potatoes, onions, anchovies, and rosemary. Cover and bake until beef and vegetables are fork-tender, about 2 hours. Transfer beef to cutting board and let cool 10 minutes. Cut into 16 slices and serve with vegetables and broth.

PER SERVING (2 slices beef with about ½ cup vegetables and broth): 322 Cal, 6 g Total Fat, 2 g Sat Fat, 0 g Trans Fat, 82 mg Chol, 484 mg Sod, 29 g Carb, 5 g Fib, 36 g Prot, 56 mg Calc.
***PointsPlus* value: 8.**

cook's note

You can use any sturdy root vegetables in this recipe. Try rutabagas, turnips, or celery root to replace the parsnips or carrots.

**Merlot-Braised Beef
Roast and Vegetables**

grilled flank steak with tomato-mint salsa

Serves 8

1 (2-pound) flank steak, trimmed
2 garlic cloves, minced
¼ teaspoon salt
¼ teaspoon black pepper
1 large tomato, chopped
½ cup chopped fresh flat-leaf parsley

¼ cup chopped fresh mint
2 tablespoons crumbled fat-free feta cheese
1 teaspoon grated lemon zest
2 tablespoons lemon juice
1 tablespoon olive oil

1. Spray grill rack with nonstick spray and preheat grill to medium high or prepare a medium-high fire.

2. Rub steak with garlic, salt, and pepper. Place on grill rack and grill, turning occasionally, until instant-read thermometer inserted into side of steak registers 145°F, 20–25 minutes. Transfer to cutting board and let stand 10 minutes.

3. Meanwhile, to make salsa, stir together tomato, parsley, mint, feta, lemon zest and juice, and oil in medium bowl. Cut steak across grain into 24 slices. Serve with salsa.

PER SERVING (about 3 slices beef and about 2 tablespoons salsa): 207 Cal, 6 g Total Fat, 2 g Sat Fat, 0 g Trans Fat, 82 mg Chol, 140 mg Sod, 2 g Carb, 1 g Fib, 34 g Prot, 24 mg Calc.

PointsPlus value: **5.**

cook's note

To make it a meal, grill a vegetable side dish while you grill the steak. Cut 4 zucchini lengthwise into quarters; spray lightly with nonstick spray. Grill, turning occasionally, until crisp-tender, 6–8 minutes. Season to taste with salt and pepper.

grilled t-bone steak with portuguese piri-piri sauce

Serves 6

2 red bell peppers, chopped
1 jalapeño pepper
2 tablespoons lime juice
2 teaspoons olive oil
2 teaspoons sugar

¾ teaspoon salt
2 garlic cloves, minced
1 teaspoon ground cumin
2 (1¼-pound) T-bone steaks, trimmed

1 Combine bell peppers, jalapeño, lime juice, oil, sugar, and ¼ teaspoon salt in blender; puree. Refrigerate 1 cup of sauce for serving.

2 Add garlic and cumin to remaining sauce. Divide sauce between 2 large zip-close plastic bags; add 1 steak to each bag. Squeeze out air and seal bag; turn to coat meat. Refrigerate, turning bags occasionally, at least 2 hours or up to 8 hours.

3 Spray grill rack with nonstick spray; preheat grill to medium heat or prepare a medium-high fire.

4 Remove steaks from marinade; discard marinade. Sprinkle steaks with remaining ½ teaspoon salt. Place steaks on grill rack; grill until well marked and instant-read thermometer inserted into side registers 145°F, 4–5 minutes on each side; transfer to cutting board and let stand 10 minutes. Cut each steak into thirds. Serve with sauce.

PER SERVING (⅓ of 1 steak and 2½ tablespoons sauce): 251 Cal, 11 g Total Fat, 4 g Sat Fat, 0 g Trans Fat, 95 mg Chol, 341 mg Sod, 5 g Carb, 1 g Fib, 33 g Prot, 16 mg Calc.
PointsPlus value: **6.**

cook's note

To make it a meal, serve this hearty steak with Chili-Lime Corn on the Cob on page 299.

Grilled Sirloin with Coffee-Molasses
Barbeque Sauce, Grill-Roasted
Fingerling Potatoes, page 300,
and Spinach and Endive Salad
with Walnut Vinaigrette, page 51

grilled sirloin with coffee-molasses barbecue sauce

Serves 6

½ cup strong brewed coffee
¼ cup ketchup
¼ cup bottled steak sauce
¼ cup molasses
¼ cup white-wine vinegar
1 tablespoon chili powder
1 tablespoon Dijon mustard

1 tablespoon hot pepper sauce
1 teaspoon paprika
1 large garlic clove, minced
1 (1¼-pound) top sirloin steak, 1¼ inches
    thick, trimmed
¼ teaspoon salt
¼ teaspoon black pepper

1 To prepare sauce, stir together coffee, ketchup, steak sauce, molasses, vinegar, chili powder, mustard, pepper sauce, paprika, and garlic in medium saucepan. Bring to boil over medium-high heat, stirring occasionally. Reduce heat to low and simmer, stirring frequently, until sauce thickens, about 20 minutes. Transfer half of sauce to serving bowl; set aside for serving.

2 Spray grill rack with nonstick spray; preheat grill to medium or prepare medium fire.

3 Sprinkle steak with salt and pepper and place on grill rack. Cover grill and cook steak 8 minutes on each side. Uncover grill; continue to cook steak, turning and brushing it frequently with remaining half of sauce, until instant-read thermometer inserted into center of steak registers 145°F, about 10 minutes longer. Transfer to cutting board and let stand 5 minutes; cut on diagonal into 24 very thin slices. Serve with remaining sauce.

PER SERVING (4 slices steak and 2 tablespoons sauce): 180 Cal, 5 g Total Fat, 2 g Sat Fat, 1 g Trans Fat, 53 mg Chol, 552 mg Sod, 16 g Carb, 1 g Fib, 19 g Prot, 40 mg Calc.

PointsPlus value: **5.**

the skinny on cooking lean beef

Portion size still counts—even when you're eating lean cuts of beef. A 3-ounce cooked portion of steak, roast, or burger is about the size of a deck of cards. Restaurant steaks can be 12 ounces or more, so ask for a doggie bag and enjoy several meals with the leftovers.

Consumer demand for lean beef has led beef producers and processors to breed leaner beef and to trim away more fat before selling at retail. To further reduce fat and *PointsPlus* value, always trim away any visible fat from beef and other meats before cooking. Weight Watchers recipes always call for meats to be trimmed for just this reason.

Supermarket meat counters can be so confusing that you don't know what to buy. To make it simple, choose beef labeled with the words "round" or "loin" and you'll be guaranteed a lean cut.

When you choose lean beef, you'll enjoy it more if you prepare the meat using the cooking methods best suited for the cut. Here's a guide to some of the most popular lean cuts (all at 7 grams or less fat in a 3-ounce serving), and the page where you'll find the how-to techniques for cooking them.

And don't forget everyone's favorite: A 3-ounce serving of 95% lean ground beef has just 5 grams of fat.

Lean Beef Cut	Best Way to Cook
Beef eye round roast	Roast, page 166
Beef top round roast	Roast, page 166
Beef top round steak	Marinate first, then stir-fry, page 206; broil, page 36; or grill, page 239
Top sirloin steak	Stir-fry, page 206; pan sear, page 79; broil, page 36; or grill, page 239
Brisket (flat half)	Braise, page 133
Beef bottom round roast	Braise, page 133
Top loin (strip) steak	Stir-fry, page 206; broil, page 36; or grill, page 239
Flank steak	Stir-fry, page 206; broil, page 36; or grill, page 239
Beef tenderloin steak (filet mignon)	Pan sear, page 79; broil, page 36; or grill, page 239

red curry beef, napa cabbage, and noodle salad

Serves 4

4 ounces rice stick noodles
3 tablespoons lime juice
2 tablespoons reduced-sodium soy sauce
1 tablespoon packed light brown sugar
2 teaspoons grated peeled fresh ginger
1 teaspoon Asian fish sauce
½ teaspoon Thai red curry paste
¾ pound sirloin steak, cut on the diagonal
    into ¼-inch strips

2 teaspoons canola oil
4 cups thinly sliced Napa cabbage
½ seedless (English) cucumber, cut into
    matchstick-thin strips
½ cup shredded carrots
½ cup chopped fresh cilantro

1 Place noodles in large bowl and add enough hot water to cover. Let noodles stand until softened, about 10 minutes. Drain in colander, then rinse under cold running water; drain again. Transfer noodles to large bowl.

2 To make dressing, whisk together lime juice, soy sauce, sugar, ginger, fish sauce, and curry paste in small bowl. Put beef in medium bowl. Add 2 tablespoons of dressing and toss to coat. Reserve remaining dressing.

3 Heat large skillet or wok over high heat until a drop of water sizzles on it. Pour in oil and swirl to coat pan. Add beef and stir-fry until lightly browned, about 3 minutes.

4 Add cabbage, cucumber, carrots, cilantro, and reserved dressing to noodles and toss to coat; divide evenly among 4 plates. Top noodles evenly with beef.

PER SERVING (about 2 cups): 294 Cal, 6 g Total Fat, 1 g Sat Fat, 0 g Trans Fat, 55 mg Chol, 474 mg Sod, 35 g Carb, 3 g Fib, 25 g Prot, 83 mg Calc.

PointsPlus value: *7.*

orange-basil beef and broccoli stir-fry

Serves 6

4 navel oranges
1 tablespoon cornstarch
¼ teaspoon red pepper flakes
3 tablespoons reduced-sodium soy sauce
1 (1¼-pound) flank steak, trimmed, halved lengthwise, and thinly sliced crosswise
4 cups broccoli florets

⅓ cup water
1 yellow squash, cut in half lengthwise and sliced
3 scallions, cut into 1-inch pieces
3 large garlic cloves, minced
1 tablespoon minced peeled fresh ginger
¼ cup chopped fresh basil

1. Grate 1 teaspoon orange zest from 1 orange, then squeeze ¾ cup juice (from about 2 oranges) into measuring cup. Stir in orange zest, cornstarch, pepper flakes, and 2 tablespoons soy sauce. Remove peel and white pith from remaining oranges and cut into segments.

2. Spray nonstick wok or large deep nonstick skillet with nonstick spray and set over medium heat. Toss beef with remaining 1 tablespoon soy sauce in large bowl. Add half of beef to wok; stir-fry just until beef is no longer pink, about 1 minute. Transfer to plate. Repeat with remaining beef.

3. Add broccoli and water to wok. Cover and cook 1 minute. Uncover, add squash, and stir-fry 1 minute. Stir in scallions, garlic, and ginger; stir-fry until fragrant, about 1 minute. Stir orange juice mixture and add to wok. Stir-fry until sauce thickens, about 1 minute. Stir in beef and basil; cook until heated through. Spoon mixture onto platter and top with orange segments.

PER SERVING (about 1⅔ cups): 244 Cal, 9 g Total Fat, 5 g Sat Fat, 0 g Trans Fat, 48 mg Chol, 820 mg Sod, 19 g Carb, 5 g Fib, 23 g Prot, 87 mg Calc.

PointsPlus value: **6.**

roasted red pepper beef stew

Serves 4

1 (7-ounce) jar roasted red peppers (not in oil), drained
1 pound bottom round steak, trimmed and cut into 1-inch chunks
1 teaspoon ground cumin
½ teaspoon salt
¼ teaspoon black pepper
1 large onion, chopped
1 celery stalk, chopped

3 garlic cloves, minced
1 teaspoon smoked sweet paprika
½ cup reduced-sodium beef broth
3 large carrots, halved lengthwise and cut into 2-inch pieces
1 (28-ounce) can diced tomatoes
8 ounces green beans, trimmed and cut into 1-inch pieces
¼ cup chopped fresh flat-leaf parsley

1 Preheat oven to 325°F. Put roasted peppers in food processor or blender and process until smooth.

2 Sprinkle beef with cumin, salt, and pepper. Spray Dutch oven with nonstick spray and set over medium-high heat. Add beef and cook, stirring occasionally, until browned, about 4 minutes. Transfer to plate.

3 Add onion and celery to Dutch oven and cook, stirring occasionally, until softened and browned, 5 minutes. Add garlic and paprika and cook, stirring constantly, until fragrant, 30 seconds.

4 Add broth and simmer until it has almost evaporated, about 2 minutes. Add beef, carrots, tomatoes, and roasted peppers. Bring to simmer, cover, and transfer to oven. Bake until beef is very tender, about 1½ hours. Stir in beans and bake 10 minutes longer. Remove from oven and stir in parsley.

PER SERVING (1 cup): 399 Cal, 6 g Total Fat, 2 g Sat Fat, 0 g Trans Fat, 84 mg Chol, 780 mg Sod, 25 g Carb, 6 g Fib, 38 g Prot, 136 mg Calc.

PointsPlus value: *8.*

cook's note

To make it a meal, spoon the beef stew over creamy polenta (½ cup cooked polenta per serving will increase *PointsPlus* value by *3*).

chili beef and pasta bake

Serves 8

3 cups whole wheat penne
1 pound ground lean beef (7 percent fat or less)
1 large onion, chopped
2 garlic cloves, minced
1 (28-ounce) can diced tomatoes
1 tablespoon chili powder

1 teaspoon ground cumin
¾ teaspoon salt
½ teaspoon black pepper
1 cup part-skim ricotta cheese
1 cup shredded reduced-fat Monterey Jack cheese

1. Preheat oven to 350°F. Spray 9 × 13-inch baking dish with nonstick spray.

2. Cook penne according to package directions omitting salt, if desired. Drain and transfer to large bowl.

3. Meanwhile, cook beef, onion, and garlic in large nonstick skillet over medium heat, breaking up beef with wooden spoon, until beef is browned, about 8 minutes. Stir in tomatoes, chili powder, cumin, salt, and pepper; simmer, stirring occasionally, until sauce thickens slightly, about 15 minutes.

4. Stir beef mixture, ricotta, and ½ cup Monterey Jack into penne; transfer to baking dish. Sprinkle with remaining ½ cup Monterey Jack. Bake until heated through and lightly browned, about 25 minutes.

PER SERVING (about 1¼ cups): 348 Cal, 9 g Total Fat, 5 g Sat Fat, 0 g Trans Fat, 47 mg Chol, 671 mg Sod, 44 g Carb, 5 g Fib, 26 g Prot, 253 mg Calc.

PointsPlus value: **9.**

cook's note

Serve this homey casserole with a simple tossed salad. Combine 8 cups torn romaine, 4 plum tomatoes, cut into wedges, 1 red bell pepper, cut into thin strips, and 1 small red onion, thinly sliced, and toss with a squeeze of lemon juice and salt and pepper to taste.

Chili Beef and Pasta Bake

Italian Beef and Mushroom Meat Loaf

italian beef and mushroom meat loaf

Serves 6

2 teaspoons olive oil
1 large onion, chopped
½ pound fresh cremini mushrooms, sliced
2 garlic cloves, minced
1½ pounds ground lean beef (7 percent fat or less)
1 cup tomato sauce
½ cup plain dried bread crumbs

2 large egg whites, lightly beaten
2 teaspoons Worcestershire sauce
1 teaspoon dried basil
1 teaspoon dried oregano
¾ teaspoon salt
¼ teaspoon black pepper
1½ cups fat-free marinara sauce, heated

1 Preheat oven to 350°F. Spray large rimmed baking sheet with nonstick spray.

2 Heat oil in large nonstick skillet over medium heat. Add onion and mushrooms and cook, stirring occasionally, until vegetables are tender, about 10 minutes. Add garlic and cook, stirring constantly, until fragrant, 30 seconds. Transfer to large bowl; let cool 5 minutes.

3 Add beef, ½ cup tomato sauce, bread crumbs, egg whites, Worcestershire, basil, oregano, salt, and pepper to bowl and stir just until blended.

4 Transfer mixture to baking sheet and form into 4 × 9-inch loaf. Spread remaining ½ cup tomato sauce over top. Bake until instant-read thermometer inserted into center of loaf registers 160°F, about 1 hour. Let stand 5 minutes before slicing. Cut into 12 slices. Divide slices among 6 serving plates; top each serving with ¼ cup marinara sauce.

PER SERVING (2 slices meat loaf and ¼ cup sauce): 259 Cal, 9 g Total Fat, 3 g Sat Fat, 0 g Trans Fat, 64 mg Chol, 866 mg Sod, 18 g Carb, 3 g Fib, 27 g Prot, 65 mg Calc.

PointsPlus value: **6.**

cook's note

A combination of steamed green beans and yellow wax beans make a colorful side dish for the meat loaf.

crown roast of pork with cranberry-rice pilaf

Serves 12

PORK

1 (12-rib) crown roast of pork, trimmed and
   prepared by butcher (about 5 ½ pounds)
4 garlic cloves, minced
1 tablespoon minced fresh thyme
1 tablespoon minced fresh rosemary
1½ teaspoons kosher salt
1 teaspoon black pepper

PILAF

2 teaspoons olive oil
1 small onion, chopped
1 celery stalk, chopped
1 carrot, chopped
1 garlic clove, minced
3 cups reduced-sodium chicken broth
1 cup brown and wild rice blend
½ cup pearl barley
¼ teaspoon salt
¼ teaspoon black pepper
½ cup dried cranberries
¼ cup chopped fresh flat-leaf parsley

1 Preheat oven to 375°F. Line large roasting pan with foil; spray foil with nonstick spray. Sprinkle pork all over with garlic, thyme, rosemary, salt, and pepper and place in pan (if necessary, fit small ovenproof bowl into center of roast to help keep its circular shape). Wrap tips of bones in foil to prevent burning. Roast pork for 1 hour 15 minutes.

2 Meanwhile, to make pilaf, heat oil in large saucepan over medium heat. Add onion, celery, carrot, and garlic and cook, stirring occasionally, until vegetables are softened, 5 minutes. Add broth, rice blend, barley, salt, and pepper; bring to boil. Reduce heat and simmer, covered, until liquid is absorbed and grains are tender, about 45 minutes. Add cranberries, cover, and set aside 10 minutes. Add parsley and fluff with fork.

3 Remove pork from oven; remove bowl (if used). Mound pilaf in center of pork and return to oven; roast until instant-read thermometer inserted into pork without touching bone registers 145°F, 25–30 minutes longer.

4 Using 2 spatulas, transfer roast to platter. Loosely cover with foil and let stand 20 minutes. Remove and discard foil and string used to tie roast. Carve pork between ribs and serve with pilaf.

PER SERVING (1 chop and ½ cup pilaf): 324 Cal, 11 g Total Fat, 4 g Sat Fat, 0 g Trans Fat, 79 mg Chol, 466 mg Sod, 24 g Carb, 3 g Fib, 31 g Prot, 28 mg Calc.
***PointsPlus* value: 8.**

cook's note

Crown roasts usually need to be special ordered, so call or stop by your butcher or your supermarket's meat department several days ahead to make your request.

roasted pork tenderloin with apple-raisin sauce

Serves 4

1 (1-pound) pork tenderloin, trimmed
½ teaspoon salt
¼ teaspoon black pepper
2 teaspoons minced fresh thyme
2 Granny Smith apples, cored, each cut into 8 wedges

¾ cup apple cider
2 tablespoons fruit chutney (such as fig or apple)
½ cup golden raisins
1 large shallot, minced

1 Preheat oven to 400°F.

2 Spray large ovenproof skillet with nonstick spray and set over medium-high heat. Sprinkle tenderloin with salt and pepper; place in skillet and cook, turning occasionally, until browned on all sides, about 5 minutes. Sprinkle pork with 1 teaspoon thyme.

3 Place apples around pork and transfer skillet to oven. Roast until an instant-read thermometer inserted into center of tenderloin registers 145°F, about 10 minutes. Transfer pork to cutting board, cover loosely with foil, and let stand 10 minutes.

4 Meanwhile, set skillet over medium-high heat; add cider, chutney, raisins, and shallot to apples. Cook, scraping up any browned bits on bottom of skillet, until juices are slightly thickened, about 6 minutes. Stir in remaining 1 teaspoon thyme. Cut pork into 8 slices and serve with sauce.

PER SERVING (2 slices pork and ½ cup sauce): 262 Cal, 4 g Total Fat, 1 g Sat Fat, 0 g Trans Fat, 45 mg Chol, 370 mg Sod, 37 g Carb, 3 g Fib, 22 g Prot, 32 mg Calc.

PointsPlus value: *7.*

cook's note

For this dish, the sauce is prepared in the same ovenproof skillet where the pork baked. Be careful when you make the sauce and don't inadvertently grasp the hot skillet handle without a mitt.

thyme-crusted roast pork loin with apricot-port sauce

Serves 6

1 (1½-pound) boneless center-cut pork loin,
    trimmed
1 teaspoon dried thyme
1 teaspoon salt
¼ teaspoon black pepper
1 onion, chopped

1 carrot, chopped
2 cups reduced-sodium chicken broth
⅔ cup ruby port
¼ cup apricot preserves
½ cup chopped dried apricots
1 tablespoon unsalted butter

1. Preheat oven to 400°F. Place rack in roasting pan and spray rack with nonstick spray.

2. Sprinkle pork with ¾ teaspoon thyme, ¾ teaspoon salt, and pepper and place on rack in roasting pan. Put onion, carrot, broth, and port in roasting pan.

3. Roast pork for 30 minutes. Brush pork with preserves and roast until instant-read thermometer inserted into center of pork registers 145°F, about 15 minutes. Transfer pork to cutting board, cover loosely with foil, and let stand 10 minutes.

4. Meanwhile, to make sauce, strain pan juices through sieve into small saucepan. Discard solids. Add apricots and remaining ¼ teaspoon thyme to saucepan; bring to boil. Boil 1 minute. Remove pan from heat; swirl in butter and remaining ¼ teaspoon salt. Cut pork into 12 slices and serve with sauce.

PER SERVING (2 slices pork with 3 tablespoons sauce): 313 Cal, 10 g Total Fat, 4 g Sat Fat, 0 g Trans Fat, 72 mg Chol, 485 mg Sod, 23 g Carb, 2 g Fib, 26 g Prot, 50 mg Calc.

PointsPlus value: *7.*

**Thyme-Crusted Roast Pork Loin
with Apricot-Port Sauce**

Grilled Pork Tenderloin with Pineapple-Basil Relish and Chili-Lime Corn on the Cob, page 299

grilled pork tenderloin with pineapple-basil relish

Serves 6

¼ cup plus 2 tablespoons lime juice
4 tablespoons chopped fresh basil
1 jalapeño pepper, seeded and minced
2 garlic cloves, minced
¼ teaspoon salt

1½ pounds pork tenderloins, trimmed
½ large pineapple, peeled, cored, and diced
½ cup diced red bell pepper
¼ cup diced red onion
⅛ teaspoon cayenne pepper

1 Combine ¼ cup lime juice, 2 tablespoons basil, jalapeño, garlic, and salt in zip-close plastic bag; add tenderloins. Squeeze out air and seal bag; turn to coat pork. Refrigerate, turning bag occasionally, 1 hour.

2 Meanwhile, to make salsa, combine pineapple, bell pepper, onion, cayenne, remaining 2 tablespoons lime juice, and remaining 2 tablespoons basil in medium bowl. Cover and refrigerate.

3 Spray grill rack with nonstick spray; preheat grill to medium heat or prepare medium fire. Remove pork from marinade and place on grill rack; discard marinade. Cover grill and cook pork 10 minutes. Turn, cover, and cook until well marked and instant-read thermometer inserted into center of tenderloins registers 145°F, about 10 minutes longer. Let stand 10 minutes. Cut tenderloins into 24 thin slices and serve with salsa.

PER SERVING (4 slices pork and ½ cup salsa): 172 Cal, 4 g Total Fat, 1 g Sat Fat, 0 g Trans Fat, 45 mg Chol, 75 mg Sod, 13 g Carb, 2 g Fib, 22 g Prot, 22 mg Calc.
PointsPlus value: *4.*

cook's note

To make it a meal, fresh watermelon wedges are the perfect finish to this hearty dinner.

grilled pork tenderloin with lime-tamarind sauce

Serves 4

¼ cup lime juice
¼ cup Asian fish sauce
2 garlic cloves, minced
2 tablespoons packed light brown sugar

2 teaspoons tamarind concentrate
1 teaspoon chili-garlic paste
1 (1-pound) pork tenderloin, trimmed
2 tablespoons chopped fresh cilantro

1 Whisk together lime juice, fish sauce, garlic, sugar, tamarind, and chili-garlic paste in small bowl until smooth. Transfer half of lime juice mixture to large zip-close plastic bag; add pork. Squeeze out air and seal bag; turn to coat pork. Refrigerate, turning bag occasionally, about 30 minutes. Reserve remaining marinade.

2 Spray grill rack with nonstick spray and preheat grill to medium-high or prepare medium-high fire.

3 Remove pork from marinade; discard marinade. Place on grill rack and grill, turning frequently, until instant-read thermometer inserted into center of pork registers 145°F, about 20 minutes. Transfer to cutting board, cover loosely with foil, and let stand 10 minutes. Cut pork into 16 slices. Stir cilantro into remaining marinade and serve with pork.

PER SERVING (4 slices pork with 1 tablespoon sauce): 149 Cal, 4 g Total Fat, 1 g Sat Fat, 0 g Trans Fat, 45 mg Chol, 962 mg Sod, 7 g Carb, 0 g Fib, 22 g Prot, 18 mg Calc.

PointsPlus value: **4.**

cook's note

Look for tamarind concentrate in Asian or Middle Eastern food stores or specialty supermarkets. Tamarind is the fruit pod of a tall shade tree native to Asia and its flavor is a complex mix of sweet and sour.

mushroom-smothered rosemary pork chops

Serves 4

4 (¼-pound) boneless center-cut pork loin
   chops, trimmed
¾ teaspoon salt
½ teaspoon black pepper
2 garlic cloves, minced

2 teaspoons minced fresh rosemary
2 teaspoons olive oil
1 pound cremini mushrooms, quartered
⅓ cup reduced-sodium chicken broth
1 teaspoon whole grain mustard

1 Sprinkle pork chops with ½ teaspoon salt and ¼ teaspoon pepper; rub with 1 clove of garlic and 1 teaspoon rosemary.

2 Heat 1 teaspoon of oil in large skillet over medium heat. Add pork to skillet and cook until instant-read thermometer inserted into side of chops registers 145°F, 2–3 minutes per side. Transfer to platter; keep warm.

3 Add remaining 1 teaspoon oil to skillet. Add mushrooms, remaining 1 clove of garlic, remaining 1 teaspoon rosemary, remaining ¼ teaspoon salt, and remaining ¼ teaspoon pepper. Cook, stirring occasionally, until mushrooms begin to soften, 5 minutes. Add broth and cook until most of liquid evaporates and mushrooms are tender, about 3 minutes longer. Remove from heat and stir in mustard.

4 Divide pork chops among 4 plates; top evenly with mushrooms.

PER SERVING (1 pork chop with ½ cup mushrooms): 173 Cal, 8 g Total Fat, 2 g Sat Fat, 0 g Trans Fat, 47 mg Chol, 553 mg Sod, 6 g Carb, 1 g Fib, 20 g Prot, 31 mg Calc.
PointsPlus value: **4.**

cook's note

To make it a meal, serve with these homey chops with steamed green beans and mashed potatoes (1 pound of red-skinned potatoes, cooked and mashed with salt and pepper to taste will increase the per-serving *PointsPlus* value by *2*).

pork chops and rice with mole sauce

Serves 6

3 dried pasilla chile peppers, seeded
2½ cups boiling water
6 (¼-pound) boneless center-cut pork loin
  chops, trimmed
1 teaspoon salt
¼ teaspoon black pepper
2 teaspoons olive oil
1 onion, chopped
3 garlic cloves, peeled

2 large plum tomatoes, chopped
½ teaspoon dried oregano
½ teaspoon ground cumin
¼ teaspoon cinnamon
1 cup reduced-sodium chicken broth
1 ounce semisweet chocolate, chopped
3 cups hot cooked white rice
2 tablespoons chopped fresh cilantro

1 Heat large deep skillet over medium-high heat. Add pasilla chiles and toast 30 seconds on each side. Transfer to bowl and cover with boiling water; let stand 20 minutes. Drain and discard liquid. Transfer chiles to blender.

2 Meanwhile, sprinkle pork with ½ teaspoon of salt and black pepper. Heat 1 teaspoon oil in same skillet over medium-high heat. Add pork chops and cook until browned, about 2 minutes per side. Transfer pork to plate; set aside.

3 Add remaining 1 teaspoon oil to same skillet. Add onion and garlic and cook, stirring often, until onion is golden, 4–5 minutes. Stir in tomatoes and cook until softened, about 3 minutes. Add oregano, cumin, cinnamon, and remaining ½ teaspoon salt; cook until fragrant, about 30 seconds. Add tomato mixture and broth to blender with chiles; puree.

4 Transfer puree to same skillet; cook, stirring often, until thickened, about 8 minutes. Add chocolate; stir until melted, 1–2 minutes. Add pork chops and turn to coat with sauce. Simmer until pork is cooked through, 6–8 minutes.

5 Divide rice evenly among 6 plates; top with pork and sauce. Sprinkle with cilantro.

PER SERVING (1 pork chop, ¼ cup sauce, and ½ cup rice): 289 Cal, 10 g Total Fat, 3 g Sat Fat, 0 g Trans Fat, 47 mg Chol, 521 mg Sod, 30 g Carb, 2 g Fib, 20 g Prot, 33 mg Calc.
PointsPlus value: **7.**

brown sugar–dijon glazed ham with sweet potatoes

Serves 4

3 large sweet potatoes (about ¾
    pound each)
2 tablespoons packed light brown sugar

2 tablespoons Dijon mustard
4 (3-ounce) slices reduced-sodium lean
    deli ham

1 Spray grill rack with nonstick spray and preheat grill to medium-high heat or prepare medium-high fire.

2 Put potatoes in medium saucepan and add enough water to cover. Bring to boil over high heat; reduce heat and simmer, covered, just until almost tender, 20–25 minutes. Drain. When cool enough to handle, peel potatoes and quarter lengthwise.

3 Combine sugar and mustard in small bowl. Brush sugar mixture on both sides of ham slices. Spray potatoes with nonstick spray. Place potatoes on grill rack and grill, turning, until browned and tender, about 6 minutes. Meanwhile, place ham on grill rack and grill until heated through and browned, 1 minute on each side.

PER SERVING (1 slice ham and 3 sweet potato wedges): 254 Cal, 5 g Total Fat, 2 g Sat Fat, 0 g Trans Fat, 45 mg Chol, 952 mg Sod, 32 g Carb, 3 g Fib, 20 g Prot, 50 mg Calc.
PointsPlus value: **6.**

cook's note
Thoroughly coat the grill rack with nonstick spray so that the sugary glaze on the ham doesn't stick to the grill.

balsamic-sorghum glazed ham

Serves 12

¾ cup balsamic vinegar
2 tablespoons sorghum syrup
1 (3-pound) low-sodium lean boneless ham

1 Preheat oven to 350°F. Line medium baking pan with foil and spray foil with nonstick spray.

2 To make glaze, combine vinegar and syrup in small saucepan; bring to boil over medium-high heat. Boil until mixture is reduced and syrupy, about 10 minutes.

3 Place ham, cut side down, in pan. Spoon glaze over ham. Bake, uncovered, until ham is heated through and instant-read thermometer registers 140°F, about 30 minutes. Transfer to cutting board and cover loosely with foil. Let stand 10 minutes. Cut into twelve (½-inch-thick) slices.

PER SERVING (1 slice glazed ham): 158 Cal, 4 g Total Fat, 2 g Sat Fat, 0 g Trans Fat, 55 mg Chol, 846 mg Sod, 10 g Carb, 0 g Fib, 19 g Prot, 9 mg Calc.

PointsPlus value: *4.*

cook's note

Sorghum syrup is a sweet Southern staple with a rich amber color and mild caramel flavor. It's available in supermarkets regionally, in natural foods stores, and from online sources. You can substitute 1 tablespoon honey and 1 tablespoon molasses for the sorghum syrup in this recipe with good results.

Balsamic-Sorghum Glazed Ham and Spicy Coconut Basmati Rice with Black-Eyed Peas, page 317

prosciutto and arugula pizza

Serves 6

2 teaspoons olive oil
8 plum tomatoes, chopped
¼ teaspoon salt
⅛ teaspoon black pepper
1 tablespoon balsamic vinegar
2 tablespoons chopped fresh basil

1 pound prepared fresh or thawed frozen
   pizza dough
8 thin slices prosciutto, cut into 1-inch strips
   (about 2 ounces)
¾ cup shredded fontina cheese
3 cups baby arugula

1. Place oven rack on bottom rung of oven. Preheat oven to 450°F.

2. Heat oil in large nonstick skillet over medium heat. Add tomatoes, salt, and pepper; cook, stirring frequently, until most of liquid has evaporated, about 10 minutes. Stir in vinegar and cook 1 minute longer. Remove from heat and stir in basil.

3. Spray 10½ × 15½-inch jelly-roll pan with nonstick spray. With floured hands, stretch and press pizza dough onto bottom of pan. Spread tomato sauce onto dough. Top crust evenly with prosciutto. Sprinkle evenly with fontina.

4. Bake on bottom rack of oven until crust is golden and cheese is melted, 15–20 minutes. Top with arugula and cut into 6 squares.

PER SERVING (1 square): 296 Cal, 11 g Total Fat, 4 g Sat Fat, 0 g Trans Fat, 22 mg Chol, 622 mg Sod, 37 g Carb, 3 g Fib, 11 g Prot, 108 mg Calc.

PointsPlus value: **8.**

bratwursts and sauerkraut braised in beer

Serves 4

4 (3-ounce) fully
   cooked smoked
   low-fat bratwursts,
   each cut diagonally
   into thirds
1 onion, thinly sliced
½ teaspoon caraway
   seeds (optional)
⅛ teaspoon black
   pepper
1 ripe pear, cut into
   chunks
1 (16-ounce) bag
   sauerkraut, rinsed
   and drained well
1 cup amber or dark
   beer

1 Spray large nonstick skillet with nonstick spray and set over medium heat. Add bratwursts and cook until browned on all sides, about 5 minutes. Transfer to plate. To same skillet, add onion, caraway seeds, if using, and pepper; cook until onion is lightly browned, 6–8 minutes, stirring occasionally. Add pear and cook until softened, 3–4 minutes longer.

2 Add sauerkraut and beer to skillet; bring to boil, lower heat, and simmer until most liquid has evaporated, 10–15 minutes, stirring occasionally. Return bratwursts to skillet and cook until heated through, about 5 minutes.

PER SERVING (3 pieces bratwurst and ¾ cup sauerkraut mixture): 217 Cal, 12 g Total Fat, 4 g Sat Fat, 0 g Trans Fat, 48 mg Chol, 839 mg Sod, 16 g Carb, 2 g Fib, 13 g Prot, 24 mg Calc.

PointsPlus value: *7.*

how to
braise

To cook meats or poultry by browning on the stovetop then slowly baking or simmering in liquid.

what you need

A Dutch oven or a large pot that has a tight-fitting lid and can go from stovetop to oven.

how it's done

Heat a small amount of oil in a Dutch oven over medium-high heat until the oil is hot (2 teaspoons of oil is enough for a large pot). Season the meat and add it to the pot. Wait 1 to 2 minutes for a brown crust to develop; then turn to brown it on all sides. Add enough cooking liquid to reach about halfway up the meat and scrape the pot to release the browned bits from the bottom.

Cover and simmer or bake at 350°F until tender, about 1 hour for poultry and 2 to 3 hours for beef, pork, or lamb.

Grilled Rack of Lamb with Lemon-Mint Crust and Asparagus with Chopped Egg and Dill, page 284

grilled rack of lamb with lemon-mint crust

Serves 6

1 garlic clove
1 slice whole wheat bread
2 tablespoons lightly packed fresh mint
    leaves
2 tablespoons lightly packed fresh flat-leaf
    parsley leaves

Grated zest of 1 lemon
1 tablespoon olive oil
2 (6-rib) racks of lamb, trimmed and
    frenched by butcher
½ teaspoon salt
½ teaspoon black pepper

1 Put garlic in food processor and pulse until chopped. Add bread, mint, parsley, and lemon zest; pulse until finely chopped. Pour oil through feed tube and pulse until combined; set aside.

2 Spray grill rack with nonstick spray; preheat grill to medium high or prepare medium-high fire.

3 Sprinkle lamb all over with salt and pepper. Place on grill rack and grill, turning once, until well browned, about 5 minutes per side. Transfer lamb to platter. Press herb mixture evenly on meaty (rounded) side of lamb racks; lightly spray herb mixture with nonstick spray. Return lamb, herb side up, to grill and cook until instant-read thermometer inserted into center of each rack (not touching bone) registers 145°F, about 10 minutes. (Do not turn lamb.)

4 Transfer lamb to cutting board and cover loosely with foil. Let stand 10 minutes, then slice between each bone, making 12 chops.

PER SERVING (2 chops): 224 Cal, 10 g Total Fat, 3 g Sat Fat, 0 g Trans Fat, 87 mg Chol, 249 mg Sod, 3 g Carb, 1 g Fib, 28 g Prot, 31 mg Calc.

PointsPlus value: *5.*

cook's note
Serve the lamb with purchased seeded crescent rolls from your local bakery (a 1-ounce crescent roll will add *3 PointsPlus* value to each serving).

pan-seared lamb chops with baby artichokes

Serves 4

1 pound baby artichokes (about 6), tough outer leaves discarded, each cut lengthwise in half
4 (5-ounce) bone-in loin lamb chops, about 1 inch thick, trimmed
¾ teaspoon salt
¼ teaspoon black pepper

2 garlic cloves, minced
1 cup reduced-sodium chicken broth
2 tablespoons chopped fresh flat-leaf parsley
1 teaspoon grated lemon zest
1 tablespoon lemon juice

1 Bring large pot of water to boil over high heat. Add artichokes, reduce heat, and simmer until small knife inserted into bottom of an artichoke goes in easily, 10–15 minutes. Drain and keep warm.

2 Meanwhile, sprinkle lamb with ½ teaspoon salt and pepper. Spray large skillet with nonstick spray and set over medium-high heat. Add lamb and cook until instant-read thermometer inserted into side of each chop registers 145°F, about 5 minutes per side. Transfer to plate and keep warm.

3 Add garlic to skillet and cook, stirring constantly, until fragrant, 30 seconds. Add broth and cook, scraping up browned bits on bottom of skillet. Boil until broth has reduced to ½ cup, about 5 minutes. Stir in artichokes, parsley, lemon zest and juice, and remaining ¼ teaspoon salt.

4 Place chops on 4 plates. With slotted spoon, transfer artichokes evenly to plates. Drizzle chops and artichokes with pan juices.

PER SERVING (1 lamb chop and 3 artichoke halves): 163 Cal, 5 g Total Fat, 2 g Sat Fat, 0 g Trans Fat, 52 mg Chol, 667 mg Sod, 10 g Carb, 7 g Fib, 19 g Prot, 32 mg Calc.

PointsPlus value: *4.*

cook's note

To make it a meal, whole wheat orzo pasta is the perfect accompaniment for soaking up the pan juices (½ cup cooked whole wheat orzo per serving will increase the *PointsPlus* value by *2*).

spice-rubbed lamb chops with grape tomato–couscous

Serves 2

½ cup reduced-sodium chicken broth
2 teaspoons olive oil
½ cup whole wheat couscous
2 scallions, thinly sliced
½ cup grape tomatoes, halved
1 tablespoon chopped fresh cilantro
1 teaspoon grated lemon zest
1 tablespoon lemon juice

1 garlic clove, minced
¼ teaspoon ground cumin
¼ teaspoon ground coriander
¼ teaspoon black pepper
⅛ teaspoon salt
2 (¼-pound) bone-in loin lamb chops, trimmed

1 Bring broth and 1 teaspoon oil to boil in small saucepan. Stir in couscous and scallions; remove from heat, cover, and let stand 5 minutes. Add tomatoes, cilantro, and lemon zest and juice and fluff with a fork.

2 Meanwhile, combine garlic, cumin, coriander, pepper, salt, and remaining 1 teaspoon oil in small bowl. Rub both sides of lamb chops with mixture.

3 Spray ridged grill pan with nonstick spray and set over medium-high heat. Place lamb on pan and cook, turning occasionally, until instant-read thermometer inserted into side of chop registers 145°F, 6–8 minutes. Transfer chops to 2 plates; divide couscous evenly between plates.

PER SERVING (1 lamb chop and ½ cup couscous): 369 Cal, 10 g Total Fat, 2 g Sat Fat, 1 g Trans Fat, 45 mg Chol, 345 mg Sod, 48 g Carb, 8 g Fib, 24 g Prot, 66 mg Calc.

PointsPlus value: *9.*

Maple-Glazed Grilled Chicken, page 153 and Green Beans with Feta and Mint, page 289

MAIN DISHES
poultry

rosemary-lemon roasted chicken with sweet potatoes

Serves 8

3 large sweet potatoes, peeled and cut into
 ½-inch chunks
1 onion, chopped
2 teaspoons olive oil
3 teaspoons chopped fresh rosemary

1 teaspoon salt
½ teaspoon black pepper
1 (4-pound) whole chicken, split in half
2 teaspoons grated lemon zest
2 tablespoons lemon juice

1 Preheat oven to 350°F. Spray large roasting pan with nonstick spray.

2 Add sweet potatoes and onion to roasting pan; drizzle with oil. Sprinkle with 1 teaspoon rosemary, ¼ teaspoon salt, and ¼ teaspoon pepper. Toss to combine and arrange in single layer around edge of pan.

3 Rub underneath skin of chicken with lemon zest and remaining 2 teaspoons rosemary, ¾ teaspoon salt, and ¼ teaspoon pepper. Place chicken in center of pan.

4 Bake, stirring vegetables once, until vegetables are tender and instant-read thermometer inserted into thigh registers 165°F, about 1 hour. Transfer chicken to cutting board and let stand 10 minutes before carving. Remove and discard skin before eating. Stir lemon juice into vegetables.

PER SERVING (⅛ of chicken with about ½ cup vegetables): 250 Cal, 8 g Total Fat, 2 g Sat Fat, 0 g Trans Fat, 81 mg Chol, 398 mg Sod, 16 g Carb, 3 g Fib, 28 g Prot, 45 mg Calc.
***PointsPlus* value: 6.**

cook's note

If you want to add more vegetables to this dish, you can add carrots, turnips, or rutabagas, peeled and cut into ½-inch chunks along with the sweet potatoes.

wine-braised chicken with wild mushrooms

Serves 6

3 (¾-pound) bone-in chicken breast halves,
    skinned and cut crosswise in half
1 teaspoon salt
¼ teaspoon black pepper
2 (4-ounce) packages assorted sliced fresh
    wild mushrooms (such as oyster, baby
    bella, and shiitake)

1 small onion, chopped
½ cup dry white wine
1 cup reduced-sodium chicken broth
1 tablespoon all-purpose flour
2 teaspoons chopped fresh sage or
    ½ teaspoon dried

1. Preheat oven to 375°F.

2. Sprinkle chicken with ¾ teaspoon salt and 1/8 teaspoon pepper. Spray Dutch oven with nonstick spray and set over medium-high heat. Add chicken and cook until browned, about 2 minutes per side. Transfer to plate.

3. Add mushrooms and onion to skillet and cook, stirring frequently, until vegetables are softened, about 5 minutes. Add wine and cook until liquid is almost evaporated, about 3 minutes.

4. Whisk together broth and flour in bowl until smooth. Stir broth mixture into vegetable mixture; bring to boil. Stir in sage and remaining ¼ teaspoon salt and 1/8 teaspoon pepper. Return chicken and any accumulated juices to Dutch oven.

5. Cover and bake until chicken is cooked through, about 35 minutes.

PER SERVING (1 chicken breast half with ⅓ cup mushroom sauce): 191 Cal, 4 g Total Fat, 1 g Sat Fat, 0 g Trans Fat, 76 mg Chol, 469 mg Sod, 5 g Carb, 1 g Fib, 30 g Prot, 26 mg Calc.
PointsPlus value: **5.**

cook's note
Wild mushrooms give this recipe complex flavor and interesting texture, but if all you've got are white button mushrooms, the dish will still taste great.

sweet-and-spicy chicken with apricot quinoa

Serves 4

PILAF

2 teaspoons canola oil
¼ cup diced onion
1 garlic clove, minced
½ teaspoon ground cumin
2 cups reduced-sodium chicken broth
1 cup quinoa, rinsed
3 dried apricot halves, diced
2 tablespoons chopped fresh flat-leaf
   parsley

CHICKEN

¼ cup sweet chili sauce
2 teaspoons grated lime zest
1 teaspoon lime juice
4 (¼-pound) skinless boneless chicken
   breasts
½ teaspoon salt
Lime wedges

1 To make pilaf, heat oil in medium saucepan over medium-high heat. Add onion, garlic, and cumin. Cook, stirring constantly, until fragrant, about 30 seconds. Add broth, quinoa, and apricots; bring to boil. Reduce heat and simmer, covered, until quinoa is tender and liquid is absorbed, about 20 minutes. Remove from heat; stir in parsley.

2 Meanwhile, to make chicken, stir together chili sauce, lime zest, and lime juice in small bowl. Sprinkle chicken with salt. Spray large skillet with nonstick spray and set over medium-high heat. Add chicken and cook, turning frequently and basting with chili sauce mixture, until chicken is cooked through, about 6 minutes. Serve chicken with pilaf and lime wedges.

PER SERVING (1 chicken breast and ¾ cup pilaf): 357 Cal, 8 g Total Fat, 1 g Sat Fat, 0 g Trans Fat, 63 mg Chol, 615 mg Sod, 38 g Carb, 4 g Fib, 32 g Prot, 51 mg Calc.

PointsPlus value: **9.**

cook's note

If you buy dried apricot halves just for this recipe and you're not sure what to do with the leftovers, they make a great snack when you're craving something sweet (4 dried apricot halves have a *PointsPlus* value of *1*).

middle eastern chicken and pita salad

Serves 4

3 teaspoons olive oil
4 (¼-pound) skinless boneless chicken
    breasts
½ teaspoon salt
¼ teaspoon black pepper
¼ cup reduced-sodium chicken broth
1 teaspoon grated lemon zest
2 tablespoons lemon juice

1 garlic clove, minced
½ teaspoon ground cumin
½ teaspoon ground coriander
2 (6-inch) whole wheat pita breads
6 cups torn romaine lettuce
½ English (seedless) cucumber, thinly sliced
1 cup cherry tomatoes, halved
½ cup loosely packed fresh mint leaves

1 Heat 1 teaspoon oil in large nonstick skillet over medium heat. Sprinkle chicken with ¼ teaspoon salt and 1/8 teaspoon pepper. Place in skillet and cook, turning occasionally, until cooked through, 8–10 minutes. Transfer chicken to cutting board and let cool slightly; cut into thin slices.

2 Meanwhile, to make dressing, whisk together broth, lemon zest and juice, garlic, ¼ teaspoon cumin, ¼ teaspoon coriander, and remaining ¼ teaspoon salt and 1/8 teaspoon pepper in large bowl.

3 Preheat broiler.

4 Lightly spray one side of each pita bread with olive oil nonstick spray, then sprinkle lightly with remaining ¼ teaspoon coriander and ¼ teaspoon cumin. Arrange pita bread on broiler rack and broil 6 inches from heat until crisp, about 1 minute per side. Let pita bread cool slightly, then cut into bite-size pieces.

5 Add chicken, pita, lettuce, cucumber, tomatoes, and mint to dressing and toss to coat.

PER SERVING (about 1¾ cups): 283 Cal, 9 g Total Fat, 2 g Sat Fat, 0 g Trans Fat, 70 mg Chol, 549 mg Sod, 22 g Carb, 5 g Fib, 30 g Prot, 66 mg Calc.
***PointsPlus* value: 7.**

cook's note

This recipe is perfect for using any small amounts of fresh vegetables you might have on hand. See what's in the fridge—you can add sliced radishes, red onion, bell pepper, or zucchini to the salad.

asian chicken noodle soup

Serves 4

4 ounces rice noodles
2 cups reduced-sodium chicken broth
2 tablespoons reduced-sodium soy sauce
2 teaspoons grated peeled fresh ginger
1 garlic clove, minced
½ teaspoon chili-garlic paste

4 (5-ounce) skinless boneless chicken
   breasts, thinly sliced
1 medium yellow squash, halved lengthwise
   and sliced
4 ounces snow peas, trimmed and halved
2 tablespoons chopped fresh cilantro

1 Cook rice noodles according to package directions; drain.

2 Meanwhile, combine broth, soy sauce, ginger, garlic, and chili-garlic paste in large skillet; bring to boil. Add chicken; return to simmer. Simmer, covered, for 10 minutes. Add yellow squash and peas and cook uncovered until chicken is cooked through and vegetables are crisp-tender, 5 minutes longer.

3 Divide noodles among 4 bowls. Top each bowl of noodles evenly with chicken, vegetable mixture, and broth. Sprinkle with cilantro.

PER SERVING (1 bowl): 321 Cal, 5 g Total Fat, 1 g Sat Fat, 0 g Trans Fat, 88 mg Chol, 649 mg Sod, 30 g Carb, 2 g Fib, 36 g Prot, 52 mg Calc.
PointsPlus value: *8.*

cook's note

Chili-garlic paste adds a definite spicy kick to this soup. If you have young children, you can leave it out and let everyone add this fiery condiment to their own taste at the table.

Asian Chicken Noodle Soup

basil-garlic grilled chicken with cucumber-tomato salad

Serves 4

⅓ cup lemon juice
¼ cup chopped fresh basil
1 tablespoon olive oil
2 garlic cloves, minced
4 (5-ounce) skinless boneless chicken
   breasts

1 teaspoon ground cumin
¾ teaspoon salt
2 cups grape tomatoes, halved
2 scallions, thinly sliced
1 medium cucumber, peeled and diced
   (about 1½ cups)

1 Spray grill rack with nonstick spray. Preheat grill to medium high or prepare medium-high fire.

2 Combine lemon juice, 2 tablespoons basil, oil, and garlic in medium bowl. Transfer 3 tablespoons of mixture to zip-close plastic bag; add chicken and cumin. Squeeze out air and seal bag; turn to coat chicken. Refrigerate, turning bag occasionally, about 30 minutes. Reserve remaining marinade.

3 Remove chicken from marinade; discard marinade. Sprinkle chicken with ½ teaspoon salt. Place chicken on grill rack and grill, turning frequently, until chicken is cooked through, 8–10 minutes.

4 Meanwhile, to make salad, add tomatoes, scallions, cucumber, remaining 2 tablespoons basil, and remaining ¼ teaspoon salt to reserved marinade and toss to coat. Serve chicken with salad.

PER SERVING (1 chicken breast with about ¾ cup salad): 244 Cal, 8 g Total Fat, 2 g Sat Fat, 0 g Trans Fat, 88 mg Chol, 536 mg Sod, 7 g Carb, 2 g Fib, 34 g Prot, 44 mg Calc.
PointsPlus value: **6.**

cook's note

To make it a meal, grill fresh nectarines for dessert. Halve and pit nectarines and lightly spray with nonstick spray. Place on the grill rack, and grill, turning once, until softened, about 4 minutes.

chicken salad with creamy goat cheese–dill dressing

Serves 6

⅓ cup fat-free mayonnaise
¼ cup crumbled goat cheese
3 tablespoons plain fat-free yogurt
2 teaspoons grated lemon zest
2 teaspoons lemon juice
2 tablespoons chopped fresh dill
6 (5-ounce) skinless boneless chicken
   breasts

½ teaspoon salt
⅛ teaspoon black pepper
4 cups torn romaine lettuce
4 radishes, thinly sliced
3 plum tomatoes, quartered
1 yellow bell pepper, seeded and
   thinly sliced
½ cucumber, peeled, seeded, and sliced

1 To make dressing, whisk together mayonnaise, goat cheese, yogurt, lemon zest, and lemon juice in medium bowl until smooth; stir in 1 tablespoon dill. Cover and refrigerate until ready to serve.

2 Sprinkle chicken with remaining 1 tablespoon dill, salt, and pepper. Spray large nonstick skillet with nonstick spray and set over medium heat. Add chicken and cook, turning occasionally, until browned and cooked through, about 8 minutes. Transfer chicken to cutting board; let stand about 5 minutes, then cut each breast into thin slices.

3 Put lettuce, radishes, tomatoes, bell pepper, and cucumber in large bowl and toss to combine. Divide lettuce mixture among 6 plates. Top salads with chicken and drizzle with dressing.

PER SERVING (1½ cups salad with 1 chicken breast and 3 tablespoons dressing): 233 Cal, 7 g Total Fat, 2 g Sat Fat, 0 g Trans Fat, 92 mg Chol, 415 mg Sod, 7 g Carb, 2 g Fib, 35 g Prot, 64 mg Calc.
PointsPlus value: **6.**

cook's note

You can make this dish a day ahead. To do so, make the dressing, cover, and refrigerate. Cook the chicken, let cool, cover, and refrigerate. Prepare the fresh ingredients for the salad and store in zip-close plastic bags. When you're ready to serve, it will take just a few minutes to assemble the salads.

**Chicken and Vegetable Kebabs
with Minted Rice Pilaf**

chicken and vegetable kebabs with minted rice pilaf

Serves 4

RICE

1 teaspoon olive oil
1 onion, finely chopped
1 cup brown basmati rice
2¼ cups reduced-sodium chicken broth
¼ cup dried currants
½ teaspoon ground coriander
¼ teaspoon salt
1 tablespoon chopped fresh mint

KEBABS

2 tablespoons lemon juice
2 teaspoons paprika
1 teaspoon ground cumin
1 teaspoon ground coriander
1 pound skinless boneless chicken breasts,
    cut into 1-inch chunks
2 small zucchini, thickly sliced
1 yellow bell pepper, cut into 1-inch pieces
1 medium red onion, cut into 1-inch pieces
1 cup cherry tomatoes
½ teaspoon salt

1　To make rice, heat oil in medium saucepan over medium-high heat. Add onion and cook, stirring frequently, until softened, 3–5 minutes. Add rice and cook, stirring constantly, until lightly toasted, 2–3 minutes. Add broth, currants, coriander, and salt; bring to boil. Reduce heat and simmer, covered, until rice is tender, 40–45 minutes. Remove saucepan from heat. Let stand 10 minutes, then fluff rice with fork and stir in mint; keep warm.

2　Meanwhile, spray grill rack with nonstick spray. Preheat grill to medium- high or prepare medium-high fire.

3　To make kebabs, stir together lemon juice, paprika, cumin, and coriander in large bowl; add chicken, zucchini, bell pepper, onion, and tomatoes and toss to coat.

4　Thread chicken and vegetables separately onto eight (8-inch) metal skewers; sprinkle with salt. Place skewers on grill rack and grill, turning frequently, until chicken is cooked through and vegetables are tender, 8–10 minutes. Serve with rice pilaf.

PER SERVING (1 chicken skewer, 1 vegetable skewer, and ¾ cup rice): 388 Cal, 7 g Total Fat, 2 g Sat Fat, 0 g Trans Fat, 70 mg Chol, 724 mg Sod, 47 g Carb, 7 g Fib, 33 g Prot, 56 mg Calc.

PointsPlus value: *9.*

crispy chicken strips with buttermilk dipping sauce

Serves 6

¼ cup light sour cream
3 tablespoons reduced-fat mayonnaise
3 tablespoons low-fat buttermilk
1 small garlic clove, minced
1½ teaspoons apple cider vinegar
¾ teaspoon salt
3 cups cornflakes

¼ cup all-purpose flour
½ teaspoon chili powder
1 large egg
2 large egg whites
1½ pounds skinless boneless chicken
    breast, cut into 30 (¼-inch-thick) strips

1 Preheat oven to 375°F. Spray large baking sheet with nonstick spray.

2 Whisk together sour cream, mayonnaise, buttermilk, garlic, vinegar, and ¼ teaspoon salt in small bowl. Cover and refrigerate until ready to serve.

3 Put cornflakes in food processor or blender and pulse to make fine crumbs; transfer to shallow bowl. In medium bowl, combine flour, chili powder, and remaining ½ teaspoon salt. Whisk together egg and egg whites in third bowl. Add chicken strips to flour mixture and toss to coat. Working with one strip at a time, shake off excess flour, dip in egg mixture, then dredge in cornflakes. Place coated strips on prepared baking sheets.

4 Spray chicken strips lightly with nonstick spray. Bake 7 minutes; turn with tongs, then bake until golden and cooked through, 7–8 minutes longer. Serve warm with sauce.

PER SERVING (5 chicken strips and 1½ tablespoons sauce): 269 Cal, 8 g Total Fat, 2 g Sat Fat, 0 g Trans Fat, 108 mg Chol, 560 mg Sod, 18 g Carb, 1 g Fib, 29 g Prot, 40 mg Calc.

PointsPlus value: *7.*

cook's note

Turn this dish into a salad. Serve the chicken on a bed of mixed greens, plum tomato wedges, and cucumber slices, and use the dipping sauce as a dressing.

chicken, black bean, and corn chili

Serves 6

2 teaspoons canola oil
1 pound skinless boneless chicken breasts, cut into 1-inch pieces
1 large onion, chopped
1 large green bell pepper, diced
2 garlic cloves, minced
1 tablespoon chili powder
2 teaspoons ground cumin
1 (15½-ounce) can black beans, rinsed and drained

1 (14½-ounce) can diced tomatoes with mild green chiles
1 (8-ounce) can tomato sauce
¾ cup frozen corn kernels, thawed
½ cup reduced-sodium chicken broth
Chopped fresh cilantro
Thinly sliced scallions

1 Heat oil in large saucepan over medium-high heat. Add chicken and cook, stirring often, until lightly browned, about 5 minutes. Add onion and bell pepper and cook, stirring often, until vegetables are softened, about 5 minutes. Add garlic, chili powder, and cumin and cook, stirring constantly, until fragrant, 30 seconds.

2 Stir in black beans, tomatoes, tomato sauce, corn, and chicken broth; bring to boil. Reduce heat and simmer, partially covered, until chili is slightly thickened, about 20 minutes. Ladle into 6 bowls; sprinkle with cilantro and scallions.

PER SERVING (1¼ cups): 241 Cal, 5 g Total Fat, 1 g Sat Fat, 0 g Trans Fat, 47 mg Chol, 599 mg Sod, 27 g Carb, 8 g Fib, 24 g Prot, 94 mg Calc.

PointsPlus value: *6.*

cook's note

To make it a meal, a salad flavored with cilantro and lime is the perfect partner. Toss together 8 cups of baby lettuces, a handful of whole cilantro leaves, 4 plum tomatoes cut into wedges, the grated zest and juice of 1 lime, and salt and pepper to taste.

braised chicken with white beans and tomatoes

Serves 4

4 (5-ounce) skinless bone-in chicken thighs
½ teaspoon salt
¼ teaspoon black pepper
2 teaspoons olive oil
2 large shallots, chopped
3 garlic cloves, minced

1 (14½-ounce) can diced tomatoes
½ cup reduced-sodium chicken broth
1 (15½-ounce) can cannellini (white kidney) beans, rinsed and drained
1 tablespoon minced fresh thyme
2 teaspoons grated lemon zest

1 Sprinkle chicken with salt and pepper. Heat 1 teaspoon oil in Dutch oven over medium-high heat. Add chicken and cook, turning once, until browned, about 6 minutes. Transfer to plate. Add remaining 1 teaspoon oil to Dutch oven. Add shallots and cook, stirring occasionally, until softened, about 5 minutes. Add garlic and cook, stirring constantly, until fragrant, 30 seconds.

2 Add tomatoes and broth; bring to boil, stirring to scrape browned bits from bottom of pot. Add chicken, beans, and thyme. Reduce heat and simmer, covered, until chicken is tender and cooked through, about 20 minutes. Stir in lemon zest.

PER SERVING (1 chicken thigh with about 1 cup bean mixture): 295 Cal, 10 g Total Fat, 3 g Sat Fat, 0 g Trans Fat, 56 mg Chol, 719 mg Sod, 25 g Carb, 6 g Fib, 27 g Prot, 94 mg Calc.

PointsPlus value: *7.*

maple-glazed grilled chicken

Serves 6

¼ cup ketchup
2 tablespoons apple cider vinegar
2 tablespoons maple syrup
1 tablespoon paprika
1½ tablespoons ground cumin

1½ teaspoons chili powder
¾ teaspoon salt
½ teaspoon black pepper
6 bone-in chicken drumsticks or thighs
    (about 1¾ pounds), trimmed

1 Spray grill rack with nonstick spray; preheat grill to medium heat or prepare medium fire.

2 For glaze, combine ketchup, vinegar, and maple syrup in small bowl. For spice rub, combine paprika, cumin, chili powder, salt, and pepper in another small bowl. Rub spice rub under skin of chicken.

3 Place chicken on grill rack, cover grill, and grill 8 minutes. Turn, cover, and grill 8 minutes longer. Turn, brush chicken with half of glaze, and grill 3 minutes. Turn, brush chicken with remaining glaze, and grill until instant-read thermometer inserted into thickest part of chicken pieces without touching bone registers 165°F, about 3 minutes longer. Remove skin before eating.

PER SERVING (1 drumstick): 111 Cal, 3 g Total Fat, 1 g Sat Fat, 0 g Trans Fat, 65 mg Chol, 256 mg Sod, 4 g Carb, 0 g Fib, 17 g Prot, 24 mg Calc.

PointsPlus value: *3.*

cook's note

Chicken drumsticks and thighs are an excellent choice for grilling. They have more flavor than mild-tasting white meat. And since they have more fat than chicken breasts, they stay moist and succulent on the grill.

chicken braised with coffee

Serves 4

4 (5-ounce) skinless bone-in chicken thighs
½ teaspoon salt
⅛ teaspoon black pepper
1 medium onion, halved and sliced
1 fennel bulb, halved lengthwise and sliced
2 garlic cloves, thinly sliced

1 teaspoon chili powder
1 teaspoon dried oregano
1 teaspoon packed brown sugar
¾ cup strong brewed coffee
2 teaspoons red-wine vinegar

1 Sprinkle chicken with salt and pepper. Spray large deep nonstick skillet with nonstick spray and set over medium heat. Add chicken and cook, turning once, until browned, about 6 minutes. Transfer to plate.

2 Add onion, fennel, garlic, chili powder, oregano, and brown sugar to skillet and stir to blend. Reduce heat to low, cover, and cook, stirring occasionally, until vegetables are tender, 8 minutes. Add coffee and vinegar and bring to boil.

3 Place chicken on top of onion mixture. Reduce heat to low, cover, and simmer 10 minutes. Turn chicken and simmer until tender and cooked through, about 10 minutes more.

PER SERVING (1 chicken thigh and 3 tablespoons sauce): 172 Cal, 8 g Total Fat, 2 g Sat Fat, 0 g Trans Fat, 57 mg Chol, 355 mg Sod, 6 g Carb, 1 g Fib, 20 g Prot, 44 mg Calc.
PointsPlus value: **4.**

cook's note

If you don't have brewed coffee for this recipe, it's fine to use instant coffee or espresso. Stir together 2 teaspoons of instant coffee granules or 1 teaspoon of instant espresso granules and ¾ cup hot tap water to substitute for the brewed coffee.

chicken chili with black beans and sweet potato

Serves 6

½ pound habanero and green chile chicken sausage, halved lengthwise and sliced
1 pound skinless boneless chicken thighs, cut into 1-inch pieces
1 large onion, chopped
2 red or green bell peppers, chopped
3 garlic cloves, minced
2 tablespoons chili powder
1 tablespoon ground cumin
¼ teaspoon salt

1 large sweet potato, peeled and cut into ¾-inch chunks
1 (28-ounce) can diced tomatoes
1 (15½-ounce) can black beans, rinsed and drained
1 (14½-ounce) can low-sodium chicken broth
¼ cup tomato paste
6 tablespoons shredded reduced-fat sharp Cheddar cheese

1. Spray Dutch oven with nonstick spray and set over medium-high heat. Add sausage and cook, stirring occasionally, until browned, about 6 minutes. Transfer to plate.

2. Add chicken to Dutch oven and cook, stirring, until browned, about 8 minutes. Stir in onion and cook until softened, about 5 minutes. Stir in bell peppers, garlic, chili powder, cumin, and salt. Cook, stirring, until fragrant, about 1 minute. Add sausage, sweet potato, tomatoes, beans, broth, and tomato paste; bring to boil. Reduce heat, cover, and simmer 30 minutes, stirring occasionally. Uncover and simmer until potato is tender and chili thickens slightly, about 15 minutes longer.

3. Ladle chili into 6 bowls; sprinkle evenly with cheese.

PER SERVING (1⅔ cups chili and 1 tablespoon cheese): 378 Cal, 13 g Total Fat, 4 g Sat Fat, 0 g Trans Fat, 71 mg Chol, 955 mg Sod, 34 g Carb, 10 g Fib, 33 g Prot, 189 mg Calc.
PointsPlus value: **9.**

cook's note

Habanero and green chile chicken sausage is fully cooked, so all you have to do is brown it. If you can't find it, you can substitute turkey sausage. If you use turkey sausage, remove the casings, and cook it as directed in step 1, stirring with a wooden spoon to break up the sausage.

chicken and black bean tostadas

Serves 4

1 teaspoon canola oil
1 large onion, chopped
2 garlic cloves, minced
2 teaspoons chili powder
1 teaspoon ground cumin
⅛ teaspoon salt
1 (14½-ounce) can diced tomatoes
1 (15½-ounce) can no-salt-added black
   beans, rinsed and drained

1 cup shredded cooked chicken breast
8 (6-inch) tostada shells
2 cups shredded romaine lettuce
1 large tomato, chopped
1 cup fat-free salsa
Lime wedges

1 Heat oil in large nonstick skillet over medium heat. Add onion and garlic; cook, stirring frequently, until golden, about 7 minutes. Add chili powder, cumin, and salt; cook, stirring constantly, until fragrant, about 1 minute.

2 Add canned tomatoes, beans, and chicken; bring to boil. Reduce heat and simmer, stirring occasionally, until thickened, 10–12 minutes.

3 Spoon about 1/3 cup of chicken mixture onto each tostada shell. Top with lettuce and tomato and serve with salsa and lime wedges.

PER SERVING (2 tostadas and ¼ cup salsa): 412 Cal, 12 g Total Fat, 4 g Sat Fat, 0 g Trans Fat, 29 mg Chol, 935 mg Sod, 57 g Carb, 13 g Fib, 23 g Prot, 137 mg Calc.
PointsPlus value: **10.**

cook's note

Instead of making tostadas, you can put the chicken mixture and toppings inside corn or flour tortillas to make soft tacos.

Chicken and Black Bean Tostadas

buying and using a rotisserie chicken

When time is tight, a rotisserie chicken is a cook's secret weapon. You can carve the bird and serve it with some purchased side dishes for an instant dinner, or use the meat to make superfast soups, salads, and sandwiches. Follow these tips for purchasing and using one of the best ever kitchen time-savers.

- Shop at a busy store where it's obvious they sell a lot of rotisserie chicken. Bustling stores will roast chickens throughout the day and you'll have a better chance of getting a freshly roasted bird.

- Look for stores that use a time stamp on the package to tell you what time the bird came out of the oven. Most stores pull chickens off the shelf after 2 to 3 hours and use the meat to prepare foods for their deli.

- If there's no time stamp, look for smooth evenly golden skin. Shriveled or very dark skin can indicate the bird is overcooked and dry. If you see the attendant removing chickens from the rotisserie while you are shopping, by all means, ask for one. Some stores even make an announcement on the loudspeaker when fresh chickens are just coming out of the oven.

- If you're concerned about extra sodium, ask if the store marinates the chicken in a brine solution and if they use any salt in seasoning the chicken before cooking.

- Before carving rotisserie chicken or using it in recipes, remove and discard the skin to save *PointsPlus* value.

- For safety, always refrigerate any unused chicken within 2 hours of purchasing and use within 4 days.

- To make a chicken sandwich wrap from pantry staples, toss together ¾ cup cooked shredded skinless chicken breast, ¼ cup thinly sliced celery, 2 tablespoons thinly sliced scallion, 2 tablespoons plain fat-free Greek yogurt, a squeeze of lemon juice, and salt and pepper to taste. Top a medium flour tortilla with lettuce leaves, top with the chicken mixture, and roll up. *PointsPlus* value: *7*.

- For a 10 minute chicken and rice soup, bring 1½ cups reduced-sodium chicken broth to a boil in a small saucepan. Add ¾ cup cooked diced skinless chicken breast, ¼ cup cooked brown rice, and 1 thinly sliced scallion; return to a boil. Stir in a handful of baby spinach leaves and cook until wilted. Season to taste with salt and pepper. *PointsPlus* value: *6*.

- Use rotisserie chicken in these recipes to make them even quicker:

    Chicken Pot Pies with Cornbread Crust, page 161

    Chicken and Black Bean Tostadas, page 156

    Walnut Chicken Salad with Broccoli, page 159

    Quick Chicken Fried Rice with Tomatoes and Cilantro, page 266

walnut chicken salad with broccoli

Serves 4

3 cups fresh small broccoli florets
2 tablespoons light sour cream
1 tablespoon reduced-fat mayonnaise
1 tablespoon apple cider vinegar
1 teaspoon honey
¼ teaspoon salt

⅛ teaspoon black pepper
1 cup shredded cooked chicken breast
1 McIntosh apple, chopped
1 scallion, thinly sliced
2 tablespoons golden raisins
2 tablespoons chopped toasted walnuts

1 Bring medium saucepan of water to boil. Add broccoli and cook just until crisp-tender, 3 minutes. Drain. Rinse under cold running water until cool and drain. Pat dry on paper towels.

2 Whisk together sour cream, mayonnaise, vinegar, honey, salt, and pepper in medium bowl. Add broccoli, chicken, apple, scallion, and raisins; toss to coat. Cover and refrigerate until chilled, at least 2 hours and up to 4 hours. Sprinkle with walnuts just before serving.

PER SERVING (1¼ cups): 169 Cal, 6 g Total Fat, 1 g Sat Fat, 0 g Trans Fat, 33 mg Chol, 261 mg Sod, 17 g Carb, 3 g Fib, 13 g Prot, 57 mg Calc.

PointsPlus value: *4.*

Chicken Pot Pies with Cornbread Crust

chicken pot pies with cornbread crust

Serves 6

2 cups reduced-sodium chicken broth
2 teaspoons chopped fresh thyme or
   1 teaspoon dried
½ pound carrots, cut into ½-inch slices
½ pound turnips, peeled and cut into 1-inch
   chunks
3 celery stalks, cut into ½-inch slices
¾ pound green beans, cut into 2-inch
   lengths
1 cup frozen pearl onions, thawed
¾ cup all-purpose flour
3 cups shredded cooked chicken breast

¼ cup light sour cream
2 tablespoons chopped fresh flat-leaf
   parsley
¾ teaspoon salt
½ teaspoon black pepper
¾ cup yellow cornmeal
1½ teaspoons baking powder
½ teaspoon baking soda
1 cup fat-free buttermilk
1 large egg
1½ tablespoons canola oil

1 Preheat oven to 400°F. Spray six (2-cup) ramekins or baking dishes with nonstick spray.

2 To make filling, combine broth and thyme in Dutch oven and bring to boil over high heat. Add carrots, turnips, and celery; reduce heat and simmer 8 minutes. Add green beans and onions; simmer until vegetables are crisp-tender, about 4 minutes. Using slotted spoon, transfer vegetables to bowl and reserve.

3 Whisk ¼ cup flour into broth mixture until blended and bring to boil. Reduce heat and simmer, whisking constantly, until thickened, about 4 minutes. Stir in reserved vegetables, chicken, sour cream, parsley, ½ teaspoon salt, and pepper. Spoon filling into ramekins.

4 To make topping, whisk together cornmeal, remaining ½ cup flour, baking powder, baking soda, and remaining ¼ teaspoon salt in large bowl. Whisk buttermilk, egg, and oil in small bowl until blended. Add buttermilk mixture to cornmeal mixture, stirring to make a smooth batter. Spoon batter evenly over filling. Place pot pies on baking sheet. Bake until crust is golden brown and filling is bubbly, about 25 minutes.

PER SERVING (1 pot pie): 408 Cal, 10 g Total Fat, 3 g Sat Fat, 0 g Trans Fat, 98 mg Chol, 913 mg Sod, 49 g Carb, 6 g Fib, 31 g Prot, 204 mg Calc.

PointsPlus value: *10.*

cuban chicken picadillo

Serves 6

2 teaspoons olive oil
1 pound ground skinless chicken breast
1 onion, chopped
2 garlic cloves, minced
2 red bell peppers, chopped
1 tablespoon chili powder

¼ teaspoon cinnamon
6 pimiento-stuffed green olives, thinly
  sliced
1 (14½-ounce) can diced tomatoes
¼ cup golden raisins

1 Heat oil in large nonstick skillet over medium heat. Add chicken, onion, and garlic; cook, breaking up chicken with wooden spoon, until browned, about 8 minutes. Add bell peppers, chili powder, and cinnamon; cook, stirring constantly, until fragrant, about 3 minutes.

2 Add olives, tomatoes, and raisins to skillet; bring to boil. Reduce heat and simmer, covered, stirring occasionally, 10 minutes.

PER SERVING (⅔ cup): 169 Cal, 5 g Total Fat, 1 g Sat Fat, 0 g Trans Fat, 47 mg Chol, 224 mg Sod, 13 g Carb, 3 g Fib, 19 g Prot, 48 mg Calc.

PointsPlus value: **4.**

cook's note

Serve the picadillo with tortillas (a medium-size flour tortilla for each serving will increase the *PointsPlus* value by *2*).

roasted turkey breast with herbed gravy

Serves 10

2 tablespoons plus 1 teaspoon chopped
    fresh sage
1 tablespoon plus 1 teaspoon chopped
    fresh thyme
1 tablespoon butter, softened

½ teaspoon salt
¼ teaspoon black pepper
1 (4½-pound) turkey breast with ribs
4 cups reduced-sodium chicken broth
2 tablespoons all-purpose flour

1   Preheat oven to 375°F. Spray large roasting pan with nonstick spray.

2   Stir together 2 tablespoons sage, 1 tablespoon thyme, butter, salt, and pepper in small bowl. Loosen skin around turkey breast by running your fingers between skin and meat, starting at tips of breast halves. Once skin is loosened, spread herb mixture under skin and pat skin back in place.

3   Place turkey breast in pan. Pour 1½ cups of broth into pan. Roast turkey until instant-read thermometer inserted into center registers 165°F, about 2 hours. Transfer turkey breast to cutting board, cover loosely with foil, and let stand 10 minutes.

4   Meanwhile, to make gravy, pour pan juices into measuring cup and skim off any fat; return juices to pan. Whisk remaining 2½ cups broth and flour in small bowl until smooth; add to roasting pan. Add remaining 1 teaspoon sage and 1 teaspoon thyme to pan. Set pan over two burners over medium-high heat; cook, whisking constantly, until mixture comes to boil. Reduce heat and simmer, whisking occasionally, until gravy has reduced to 2 cups, about 3 minutes.

5   Discard ribs and skin from turkey breast. Cut turkey into 20 slices and serve with gravy.

PER SERVING (2 slices turkey and about 3 tablespoons gravy): 195 Cal, 3 g Total Fat, 1 g Sat Fat, 0 g Trans Fat, 108 mg Chol, 536 mg Sod, 2 g Carb, 0 g Fib, 39 g Prot, 31 mg Calc.

PointsPlus value: *5.*

honey-brined turkey with homemade gravy

Serves 12, plus leftovers

1 cup honey
¾ cup kosher salt
5 bay leaves
8 cups boiling water
1 (12-pound) turkey, giblets reserved for
    another use
Pear and Sage Stuffing (optional; see recipe
    page 310)

2 teaspoons canola oil
½ teaspoon salt
¾ teaspoon black pepper
1¾ cups reduced-sodium chicken broth
2 tablespoons all-purpose flour

1 Combine honey, kosher salt, bay leaves, and boiling water in large stockpot and stir until salt is dissolved. Let cool to room temperature; add turkey and enough cold water to just cover turkey. Refrigerate at least 4 hours or overnight.

2 Place oven rack in bottom third of oven. Preheat oven to 450°F. Remove turkey from brine, rinse under cold running water, and place on rack in roasting pan. Pat dry inside and out with paper towels. Tuck wing tips under bird. Spoon stuffing (if using) into cavity of turkey, filling it no more than two-thirds full. Tie turkey legs together with kitchen string. Rub skin with oil and sprinkle with salt and pepper. Pour ¾ cup broth into bottom of pan; roast turkey 20 minutes. Reduce oven temperature to 350°F. Roast until instant-read thermometer inserted into thickest part of thigh registers 165°F, about 2 hours longer. (During last 30 minutes of cooking, bake any leftover stuffing in baking dish sprayed with nonstick spray alongside turkey.) Transfer turkey to platter and let stand 30 minutes.

3 To make gravy, pour drippings and juices from roasting pan into fat separator or glass measuring cup. Spoon 1½ tablespoons of fat into small saucepan; discard remaining fat. Place saucepan over medium heat. Stir in flour; cook, stirring, 2 minutes. Add remaining 1 cup broth to pan juices to yield 1½ cups total; whisk broth mixture into flour mixture. Cook, whisking often, until gravy is thickened, 4–5 minutes.

4 Discard turkey skin; carve breast and thigh meat into 24 slices; save drumsticks and wings for another use. Serve turkey slices with gravy and stuffing.

PER SERVING (2 slices turkey without skin and 2 tablespoons gravy): 194 Cal, 4 g Total Fat, 1 g Sat Fat, 0 g Trans Fat, 114 mg Chol, 484 mg Sod, 2 g Carb, 0 g Fib, 34 g Prot, 26 mg Calc.

PointsPlus value: **4.**

Honey-Brined Turkey with Homemade Gravy and Pear and Sage Stuffing, page 310

roast

To cook foods in an uncovered roasting pan in the oven.

what you need

For roasting meats and poultry, a roasting pan with a rack that fits inside the pan and an instant-read thermometer so you'll know when they are done. For vegetables, a shallow, rimmed baking pan.

how it's done

Trim any visible fat from meats. Leave the skin on poultry to preserve moisture, but remove it before eating. Cut vegetables into uniform-size pieces for even cooking. Season all foods before roasting and toss vegetables with a small amount of oil. Meats and poultry do not need oil.

Meats and poultry generally roast at temperatures between 350°F and 375°F (larger meats roast at lower temperatures) and vegetables at 400°F or 425°F. Poultry should be cooked until an instant-read thermometer reaches 165°F when inserted into the center of the thigh. Beef and pork should reach 145°F when a thermometer is inserted in the center and should stand for at least 3 minutes before carving.

orange-rosemary glazed turkey breast

Serves 8

4 teaspoons minced fresh rosemary	2 teaspoons olive oil
2 garlic cloves, minced	2 cups water
1 teaspoon salt	½ cup orange marmalade
½ teaspoon black pepper	2 tablespoons orange juice
1 (4-pound) boneless turkey breast, skin removed	1 tablespoon Dijon mustard

1 Preheat oven to 350°F. Spray rack with nonstick spray and set in roasting pan.

2 Combine 2 teaspoons rosemary, garlic, salt, and pepper in small bowl. Rub turkey all over with oil; rub with rosemary mixture. Place on rack and pour water into roasting pan. Roast until instant-read thermometer inserted into thickest part of breast registers 140°F, about 1 hour 15 minutes.

3 Meanwhile, stir together marmalade, orange juice, mustard, and remaining 2 teaspoons rosemary in small bowl until smooth.

4 When turkey reaches 140°F, remove from oven and brush with one-third of orange glaze. Return to oven and roast 10 minutes. Brush again with one-third of glaze, return to oven, and roast 5 minutes. Brush with remaining glaze and roast until instant-read thermometer inserted into thickest part of breast registers 165°F, 5–10 minutes longer. Let stand 10 minutes; carve into 24 thin slices.

PER SERVING (3 slices): 271 Cal, 3 g Total Fat, 1 g Sat Fat, 0 g Trans Fat, 118 mg Chol, 421 mg Sod, 18 g Carb, 1 g Fib, 43 g Prot, 28 mg Calc.

PointsPlus* value: *7.

lemon-basil turkey cutlets

Serves 4

1 large lemon	2 teaspoons light butter
2 tablespoons all-purpose flour	1 shallot, diced
¼ teaspoon salt	½ cup reduced-sodium chicken broth
¼ teaspoon black pepper	Pinch sugar
4 (¼-pound) turkey breast cutlets	2 tablespoons thinly sliced fresh basil

1 Grate zest from lemon; set aside. Cut away all white pith from lemon and cut into sections; set aside.

2 On sheet of wax paper, combine flour, salt, and pepper. Lightly coat turkey with flour mixture.

3 Spray large nonstick skillet with nonstick spray and set over medium heat. Add turkey and cook, turning once, until golden brown and almost cooked through, about 3 minutes. Transfer to plate.

4 Add butter and shallot to skillet; cook, stirring often, until shallot is softened, 5 minutes. Add broth and sugar to skillet; bring to boil. Add turkey, lemon zest, and lemon sections to skillet; simmer until turkey is cooked through, about 2 minutes longer. Transfer turkey to 4 serving plates. Add basil to skillet and stir to combine; spoon sauce evenly over turkey.

PER SERVING (1 turkey cutlet with about 1½ tablespoons sauce): 146 Cal, 2 g Total Fat, 1 g Sat Fat, 0 g Trans Fat, 78 mg Chol, 279 mg Sod, 3 g Carb, 1 g Fib, 28 g Prot, 28 mg Calc.

PointsPlus value: *3.*

Baked Turkey Sausage and Rice Arancini

baked turkey sausage and rice arancini

Serves 4

1 (5¼-ounce) package boil-in-the-bag
   brown rice
½ pound Italian-style turkey sausage,
   casings removed
1 onion, finely chopped
½ cup fat-free mozzarella cheese,
   finely diced

3 tablespoons grated Parmesan cheese
3 large egg whites
1 tablespoon water
½ cup plain dried bread crumbs
1 cup fat-free marinara sauce, heated

1. Preheat oven to 425°F. Spray large baking sheet with nonstick spray.

2. Cook rice according to package directions; transfer to large bowl.

3. Spray large nonstick skillet with nonstick spray and set over medium heat. Add sausage and onion; cook, breaking sausage apart with wooden spoon, until sausage is no longer pink and onion is tender, about 6 minutes. Stir sausage mixture into rice. Let cool to room temperature. Stir in mozzarella, Parmesan, and 2 egg whites.

4. Whisk together remaining egg white and water in medium bowl. Place bread crumbs on sheet of wax paper. With wet hands, shape rice mixture into 8 balls, using about 1/3 cup for each. Dip balls, one at a time, into egg white mixture, then gently roll in crumbs to coat.

5. Place balls on baking sheet; lightly spray with nonstick spray. Bake, turning occasionally, until arancini are browned and heated through, about 20 minutes. Serve with marinara sauce.

PER SERVING (2 balls and ¼ cup sauce): 396 Cal, 11 g Total Fat, 3 g Sat Fat, 0 g Trans Fat, 58 mg Chol, 978 mg Sod, 48 g Carb, 4 g Fib, 28 g Prot, 271mg Calc.

PointsPlus value: *10.*

cook's note

Serve the arancini with a simple salad of baby arugula tossed with lemon juice and salt and pepper to taste.

turkey sloppy joes

Serves 6

1 pound ground skinless turkey breast
1 large onion, diced
2 green bell peppers, chopped
3 garlic cloves, minced
2 teaspoons ground cumin

¾ cup fat-free marinara sauce
½ cup chili sauce
⅛ teaspoon cayenne pepper
6 whole wheat sandwich rolls, split and
toasted

1 Spray large nonstick skillet with nonstick spray and set over medium heat. Add turkey and cook, breaking it up with wooden spoon, until no longer pink, about 5 minutes. Add onion, bell peppers, and garlic; cook, stirring, until vegetables are softened, 5 minutes. Add cumin and cook, stirring constantly, until fragrant, 1 minute.

2 Add marinara sauce, chili sauce, and cayenne, stirring to combine; bring mixture to simmer. Reduce heat to low and simmer, covered, stirring occasionally, until thickened, about 12 minutes. Spoon ¾ cup of turkey mixture onto bottom of each roll. Cover with tops of rolls.

PER SERVING (1 sandwich): 233 Cal, 2 g Total Fat, 1 g Sat Fat, 0 g Trans Fat, 51 mg Chol, 617 mg Sod, 29 g Carb, 4 g Fib, 24 g Prot, 89 mg Calc.

PointsPlus value: **6.**

cook's note
Top the sandwiches with thinly sliced cabbage for extra crunch and color.

cornish hens with spinach-apple stuffing

Serves 4

1 tablespoon maple syrup
2 teaspoons butter, melted
2 (1¼-pound) Cornish game hens, skinned
½ teaspoon dried thyme
½ teaspoon salt
¼ teaspoon black pepper

1 (10-ounce) package frozen chopped
    spinach, thawed and squeezed dry
1 large Gala apple, peeled and chopped
¼ cup slivered almonds, toasted
2 tablespoons golden raisins
2 tablespoons thinly sliced scallions

1. Preheat oven to 350°F. Place rack in roasting pan.

2. Stir together maple syrup and butter in small bowl. Rub hens with ¼ teaspoon of thyme, ¼ teaspoon of salt, and 1/8 teaspoon of pepper.

3. Stir together spinach, apple, almonds, raisins, scallions, remaining ¼ teaspoon thyme, remaining ¼ teaspoon salt, and remaining 1/8 teaspoon pepper in medium bowl. Spoon half of stuffing into cavity of each hen. Tie legs of each hen together with kitchen string.

4. Place hens on rack in roasting pan. Brush hens with syrup mixture. Bake until instant-read thermometer inserted into a thigh registers 165°F, about 1 hour.

5. Transfer hens to cutting board, cover loosely with foil and let stand 5 minutes. Pour pan juices into measuring cup and skim off any fat. Cut each hen in half and serve with pan juices.

PER SERVING (½ stuffed hen with 2 teaspoons pan juices): 280 Cal, 11 g Total Fat, 3 g Sat Fat, 0 g Trans Fat, 122 mg Chol, 429 mg Sod, 18 g Carb, 4 g Fib, 30 g Prot, 120 mg Calc.
PointsPlus value: *7.*

cook's note

While the hens bake, why not bake some sweet potatoes to serve alongside? One medium baked sweet potato per serving will increase the *PointsPlus* value by *4.*

Spaghetti with Mussels, Clams, and Shrimp, page 201

MAIN DISHES
seafood

mustard and herb–crusted salmon

Serves 6

1 slice whole wheat bread, crust removed
¼ cup chopped fresh flat-leaf parsley
2 tablespoons minced fresh chives
1 tablespoon grated lemon zest
1 (1½-pound) salmon fillet, skin on

½ teaspoon salt
⅛ teaspoon black pepper
1½ tablespoons spicy brown mustard
Lemon wedges

1 Preheat oven to 450°F. Line large baking sheet with foil; spray foil with nonstick spray.

2 Put bread in food processor and pulse to make coarse crumbs. Transfer to medium bowl and stir in parsley, chives, and lemon zest.

3 Place salmon, skin side down, on foil. Sprinkle with salt and pepper and spread with mustard. Sprinkle bread crumb mixture over mustard, pressing lightly to help it adhere.

4 Roast until fish is just opaque in center, 20–25 minutes. Cut evenly into 6 pieces and serve with lemon wedges.

PER SERVING (1 piece): 148 Cal, 4 g Total Fat, 1 g Sat Fat, 0 g Trans Fat, 59 mg Chol, 341 mg Sod, 3 g Carb, 1 g Fib, 23 g Prot, 28 mg Calc.

PointsPlus value: *3.*

cook's note

A large 1½-pound salmon fillet makes a beautiful presentation, but if you have trouble finding a large fillet, you can use six (4-ounce) fillets instead. You will need to reduce the roasting time to 12 to 15 minutes.

steamed salmon with yogurt sauce

Serves 4

4 (5-ounce) salmon
    fillets
2 teaspoons grated
    lemon zest
1 small garlic clove,
    minced
½ teaspoon ground
    cumin
¼ teaspoon black
    pepper

½ cup plain fat-free
    Greek-style yogurt
1 tablespoon chopped
    fresh dill
1 tablespoon minced
    scallion
6 large Boston lettuce
    leaves
½ teaspoon salt

1 Place salmon, skin side down, on large plate; sprinkle with 1 teaspoon lemon zest, garlic, cumin, and pepper. Cover and refrigerate 30 minutes.

2 Meanwhile, to make sauce, stir together yogurt, dill, scallion, and remaining 1 teaspoon lemon zest in small bowl. Cover and refrigerate until ready to serve.

3 Arrange lettuce leaves in bottom of large steamer basket. Sprinkle salmon with salt and arrange skin side down on top of lettuce. Set steamer basket in large skillet over 1 inch of boiling water. Cover tightly and steam just until fish is opaque in center, 6–8 minutes. Serve salmon with sauce. Discard lettuce leaves.

PER SERVING (1 salmon fillet with 2 tablespoons sauce): 253 Cal, 5 g Total Fat, 1 g Sat Fat, 0 g Trans Fat, 66 mg Chol, 443 mg Sod, 7 g Carb, 1 g Fib, 31 g Prot, 96 mg Calc.

PointsPlus value: **5.**

how to
steam

To cook food in a basket above simmering water in a covered saucepan.

what you need

A collapsible steamer basket and a saucepan with a tight-fitting lid or a large pot with a steamer basket insert. You can also steam food in a tiered bamboo steamer set inside a wok or skillet of boiling water.

how it's done

Pour about 1 inch of water into a large pot and bring to a boil. There should be enough water to cook the food without boiling away quickly, but not so much that the water touches the food.

Place the food in the basket, carefully set it over the water, and cover the pot. Adjust the heat so that the water is gently bubbling. Cook the food to the desired degree of doneness. Vegetables such as green beans or snow peas should be crisp and brightly colored. Potatoes or winter squash should be fork-tender. Fish and shellfish should be opaque, and chicken should be cooked through.

grilled salmon with honey-lime fruit salad

Serves 4

2 tablespoons minced red onion
2 tablespoons lime juice
2 teaspoons honey
1 small garlic clove, minced
1 teaspoon olive oil
½ teaspoon salt

¼ teaspoon black pepper
4 (5-ounce) salmon fillets
4 cups mixed baby salad greens
1 ripe pear, thinly sliced
1 apple, thinly sliced

1 Spray grill rack with nonstick spray. Preheat grill to medium high or prepare medium-high fire.

2 To make dressing, whisk together onion, lime juice, honey, garlic, oil, ¼ teaspoon salt, and 1/8 teaspoon pepper in large bowl.

3 Sprinkle salmon with remaining ¼ teaspoon salt and remaining 1/8 teaspoon pepper. Place on grill rack and grill, turning once, until salmon is just opaque in center, about 4 minutes per side.

4 Add greens, pear, and apple to dressing and toss to coat. Divide salad and salmon evenly among 4 plates.

PER SERVING (1 salmon fillet with 1½ cups salad): 284 Cal, 9 g Total Fat, 2 g Sat Fat, 0 g Trans Fat, 93 mg Chol, 399 mg Sod, 18 g Carb, 4 g Fib, 31 g Prot, 59 mg Calc.

PointsPlus value: *7.*

Grilled Salmon with Honey-Lime Fruit Salad

buying sustainable seafood

If you want to make the best choices for the environment when you're at the seafood counter, it pays to be aware of what fisheries authorities recommend.

Some species of fish are in decline and it's best to avoid them so they can recover. Other species are caught using methods that result in a large by-catch of other marine life. Farmed fish is a good option, but only if it is farmed where strict environmental standards are the norm (mostly in the United States and Canada). When buying wild-caught seafood, shop at a market that displays sustainability ratings to ensure that you are buying species that are not overfished or that are not caught in ways that harm other marine life.

Here are the latest recommendations on what to buy and what to avoid from the Monterey Bay Aquarium Seafood Watch, a program that offers scientifically based advice to help consumers choose seafood that is fished or farmed in ways that do not harm the environment. For more information and pocket guides to sustainable seafood for each region of the country, visit their website at seafoodwatch.org.

BUY	AVOID
Catfish U.S. farmed	**Chilean Seabass**
Clams Farmed	**Cod** U.S. Atlantic and Canadian
Cod U.S. Pacific cod	**Mahi Mahi** Imported
Crab U.S. Dungeness crab	**Red Snapper**
Flounder U.S. wild-caught flounder, fluke, or sole	**Shrimp** Imported
Grouper U.S. or Gulf of Mexico red grouper	**Swordfish** Imported
Halibut U.S. wild-caught Pacific	**Orange Roughy**
Monkfish U.S. wild-caught	**Tuna** Bluefin
Mussels Farmed	
Salmon Wild-caught Alaskan, Coho farmed in tank systems	
Scallops Farmed	
Shrimp U.S. or Canadian wild-caught or farmed	
Striped Bass U.S. wild-caught or farmed	
Swordfish U.S. wild-caught	
Tilapia U.S. or Ecuadorian farmed farmed	
Trout Rainbow U.S. farmed	
Tuna U.S. bigeye, tongol, or yellowfin	

pan-seared salmon with lemon lentils

Serves 4

1 teaspoon olive oil
1 onion, chopped
1 carrot, chopped
2 garlic cloves, minced
3 cups reduced-sodium chicken broth
1 cup green (French) lentils, picked over
   and rinsed

½ teaspoon salt
¼ teaspoon black pepper
4 (5-ounce) salmon fillets
¼ cup chopped fresh flat-leaf parsley
1 teaspoon grated lemon zest
1 tablespoon lemon juice

1 Heat oil in medium saucepan over medium-high heat. Add onion and carrot and cook, stirring occasionally, until vegetables have softened, about 5 minutes. Add garlic, and cook, stirring constantly, until fragrant, 30 seconds.

2 Add broth, lentils, ¼ teaspoon salt, and 1/8 teaspoon pepper; bring to boil. Reduce heat and simmer, covered, until lentils are tender and liquid is absorbed, about 25 minutes. Remove saucepan from heat; keep warm.

3 Meanwhile, spray large skillet with nonstick spray and set over medium-high heat. Sprinkle salmon with remaining ¼ teaspoon salt and remaining 1/8 teaspoon pepper. Place salmon in skillet and cook until just opaque in center, about 4 minutes per side.

4 Stir parsley, lemon zest, and lemon juice into lentils; divide evenly among 4 plates. Place salmon on top of lentils.

PER SERVING (1 salmon fillet and ¾ cup lentils): 426 Cal, 12 g Total Fat, 3 g Sat Fat, 0 g Trans Fat, 80 mg Chol, 794 mg Sod, 33 g Carb, 9 g Fib, 46 g Prot, 77 mg Calc.

PointsPlus value: *10.*

asian marinated grilled tuna with zucchini salad

Serves 4

2 tablespoons rice vinegar
1 tablespoon lime juice
1 tablespoon reduced-sodium
   vegetable broth
1 tablespoon canola oil
1½ teaspoons reduced-sodium soy sauce

½ teaspoon minced garlic
¼ teaspoon salt
4 (5-ounce) tuna steaks
2 medium zucchini (about 1 pound)
1 scallion, thinly sliced
2 tablespoons chopped fresh cilantro

1 Whisk together vinegar, lime juice, broth, canola oil, soy sauce, garlic, and 1/8 teaspoon salt in large bowl. Transfer 2 tablespoons of mixture to zip-close plastic bag; add tuna. Squeeze out air and seal bag; turn to coat tuna. Refrigerate, turning bag occasionally, for 30 minutes. Reserve remaining marinade.

2 Spray large grill pan with nonstick spray and set over medium-high heat. Remove tuna from marinade; discard marinade in bag. Pat tuna dry with paper towels; sprinkle with remaining 1/8 teaspoon salt. Place tuna in pan and grill until just opaque in center, about 4 minutes per side.

3 Meanwhile, use vegetable peeler to cut zucchini into thin lengthwise slices. Add zucchini, scallion, and cilantro to marinade in bowl; toss to coat. Using slotted spoon, divide zucchini among 4 serving plates. Top zucchini with tuna; drizzle tuna with any marinade remaining in bowl.

PER SERVING (1 tuna steak and ¾ cup zucchini): 256 Cal, 11 g Total Fat, 2 g Sat Fat, 1 g Trans Fat, 54 mg Chol, 285 mg Sod, 4 g Carb, 1 g Fib, 34 g Prot, 32 mg Calc.
PointsPlus value: **6.**

cook's note

To make it a meal, soba noodles are a flavorful and satisfying side dish (1 cup cooked soba noodles per serving will increase the *PointsPlus* value by **3**).

grilled tuna niçoise salad with basil-balsamic dressing

Serves 4

⅓ cup plain low-fat yogurt
¼ cup chopped shallots
1 tablespoon balsamic vinegar
1 tablespoon olive oil
1½ teaspoons lemon juice
⅛ plus ¼ teaspoon salt
⅛ plus ¼ teaspoon black pepper

2 tablespoons chopped fresh basil
¾ pound small red new potatoes
½ pound fresh green beans, trimmed
4 (5-ounce) tuna steaks
2 small heads Bibb lettuce, leaves separated
1 cup cherry tomatoes, halved
8 pitted brine-cured niçoise olives

1 Combine yogurt, shallots, vinegar, oil, lemon juice, 1/8 teaspoon salt, and 1/8 teaspoon pepper in blender; puree. Transfer to small bowl; stir in basil. Cover and refrigerate until chilled, at least 2 hours or up to 1 day.

2 Combine potatoes with enough cold water to cover in large saucepan; bring to boil over medium-high heat. Reduce heat and simmer until tender, 15–20 minutes. With slotted spoon, transfer potatoes to plate. Let stand to cool. Return water to boil. Add green beans and cook until crisp-tender, about 4 minutes. Drain in colander, then rinse under cold running water to stop cooking; set aside.

3 Spray large grill pan with nonstick spray and set over medium-high heat. Sprinkle tuna with remaining ¼ teaspoon salt and ¼ teaspoon pepper. Place tuna in pan and grill until browned on outside but still pink in center, 3–4 minutes per side.

4 Arrange lettuce leaves on 4 plates. Cut potatoes into quarters; arrange on lettuce. Top with beans, tomatoes, and olives. Place tuna steak on each salad; drizzle evenly with dressing.

PER SERVING (1 plate): 365 Cal, 12 g Total Fat, 3 g Sat Fat, 0 g Trans Fat, 55 mg Chol, 366 mg Sod, 27 g Carb, 5 g Fib, 38 g Prot, 130 mg Calc.
***PointsPlus* value: 9.**

cook's note
This creamy balsamic dressing tastes great on mixed green salads or sliced tomato and cucumber salad.

pan-seared tuna with citrus-avocado salsa

Serves 4

4 (5-ounce) tuna steaks
½ teaspoon ground cumin
⅛ teaspoon black pepper
2 ruby grapefruits, peeled and cut into sections

1 small avocado, peeled, pitted, and cut into ½-inch pieces
2 scallions, thinly sliced
¼ cup chopped fresh flat-leaf parsley
½ teaspoon salt

1 Place tuna on plate; sprinkle with cumin and pepper. Cover and refrigerate 30 minutes.

2 Meanwhile, to make relish, place grapefruit sections in medium bowl; break into small pieces using 2 forks. Stir in avocado, scallions, and parsley.

3 Spray large skillet with nonstick spray and set over medium-high heat. Sprinkle tuna with salt. Place tuna in pan and cook until well browned and just slightly pink in center, 3 minutes per side. Serve tuna with salsa.

PER SERVING (1 tuna steak and about ½ cup salsa): 279 Cal, 11 g Total Fat, 2 g Sat Fat, 0 g Trans Fat, 90 mg Chol, 485 mg Sod, 13 g Carb, 5 g Fib, 34 g Prot, 75 mg Calc.
PointsPlus value: **7.**

cook's note

Tuna steaks develop a delicious browned crust when cooked in a skillet over medium-high heat. Make sure the skillet is hot before adding the tuna so the fish will brown quickly without overcooking.

Pan-Seared Tuna with Citrus-Avocado Salsa

striped bass with cucumber-cantaloupe salsa

Serves 4

1 cup diced cantaloupe
½ seedless (English) cucumber, peeled and chopped
¼ cup diced red bell pepper
1 jalapeño pepper, seeded and minced
2 tablespoons diced red onion

1 tablespoon fresh lime juice
1 tablespoon chopped fresh cilantro
4 (5-ounce) striped bass fillets
¼ teaspoon salt
⅛ teaspoon black pepper

1 To make salsa, gently stir together cantaloupe, cucumber, bell pepper, jalapeño, onion, lime juice, and cilantro in medium bowl.

2 Spray large skillet with nonstick spray and set over medium heat. Sprinkle bass with salt and pepper. Place bass in skillet and cook until just opaque in center, about 4 minutes on each side. Serve bass with salsa.

PER SERVING (1 fillet with ½ cup salsa): 161 Cal, 3 g Total Fat, 1 g Sat Fat, 0 g Trans Fat, 114 mg Chol, 114 mg Sod, 5 g Carb, 1 g Fib, 26 g Prot, 31 mg Calc.
PointsPlus value: **4.**

cook's note

To make it a meal, prepare a simple orzo side dish. Stir 1 tablespoon chopped fresh mint, the grated zest and juice of 1 lime, and salt and pepper to taste into 2 cups hot cooked whole wheat orzo (½ cup of cooked whole wheat orzo will increase the *PointsPlus* value by *2*).

five-spice catfish with pineapple-pepper stir-fry

Serves 4

½ cup orange juice
2 tablespoons reduced-sodium soy sauce
¾ teaspoon cornstarch
4 (5-ounce) catfish fillets
2 teaspoons five-spice powder
¼ teaspoon salt

1 large red bell pepper, cut into
   ¾-inch pieces
1½ cups fresh pineapple chunks
2 scallions, thinly sliced
1 jalapeño pepper, seeded and minced
2 tablespoons chopped fresh cilantro

1 Whisk together orange juice, soy sauce, and cornstarch in small bowl.

2 Sprinkle catfish with five-spice powder and salt.

3 Spray large nonstick skillet with nonstick spray and set over medium heat. Add bell pepper and cook, stirring occasionally, until softened, 2 minutes. Add pineapple, scallions, and jalapeño; cook, stirring, until bell pepper is crisp-tender and pineapple begins to brown, about 1 minute. Transfer to medium bowl.

4 Wipe out skillet and spray with nonstick spray. Add catfish and cook until browned and just opaque throughout, about 3 minutes per side. Place 1 fillet on each of 4 plates.

5 Return bell pepper mixture to skillet. Re-whisk orange juice mixture and add to skillet. Cook, stirring constantly, until sauce comes to boil and thickens slightly, about 1 minute. Remove from heat and stir in cilantro. Spoon bell pepper mixture evenly onto plates.

PER SERVING (1 catfish fillet and ¾ cup bell pepper mixture): 254 Cal, 10 g Total Fat, 2 g Sat Fat, 0 g Trans Fat, 84 mg Chol, 570 mg Sod, 16 g Carb, 2 g Fib, 25 g Prot, 40 mg Calc.

PointsPlus value: *6.*

cook's note
Serve the catfish and vegetables with brown rice (½ cup cooked brown rice per serving will increase the *PointsPlus* value by *3*).

blackened cajun catfish

Serves 4

2 teaspoons paprika
1 teaspoon cracked black pepper
½ teaspoon onion powder
½ teaspoon salt
¼ teaspoon cayenne pepper

¼ teaspoon dried thyme, crushed
4 (5-ounce) catfish fillets
2 teaspoons canola oil
Lemon wedges

1. Stir together paprika, black pepper, onion powder, salt, cayenne, and thyme in small bowl. Place catfish in large shallow dish; sprinkle with spice mixture. Cover and refrigerate 15 minutes.

2. Heat oil in large skillet over medium-high heat. Add fish to skillet and cook until just opaque in center, 3 minutes per side. Serve with lemon wedges.

PER SERVING (1 fillet): 210 Cal, 12 g Total Fat, 2 g Sat Fat, 0 g Trans Fat, 84 mg Chol, 448 mg Sod, 1 g Carb, 1 g Fib, 24 g Prot, 19 mg Calc.

PointsPlus value: **5.**

tilapia with puttanesca sauce

Serves 4

2 teaspoons olive oil
1 medium onion, chopped
½ red bell pepper, diced
1 (14½-ounce) can diced tomatoes
6 Kalamata olives, pitted and chopped
1 tablespoon capers, rinsed

Pinch red pepper flakes
4 (¼-pound) tilapia fillets
¼ teaspoon salt
⅛ teaspoon black pepper
2 tablespoons chopped fresh flat-leaf parsley

1. Heat oil in medium skillet over medium heat. Add onion and bell pepper and cook, stirring occasionally, until vegetables are softened, 5 minutes. Stir in tomatoes, olives, capers, and pepper flakes and bring to boil. Reduce heat and simmer until sauce thickens slightly, about 8 minutes.

2. Meanwhile, sprinkle tilapia with salt and pepper. Spray large nonstick skillet with nonstick spray and set over medium heat. Add tilapia and cook until just opaque throughout, about 3 minutes on each side. Spoon sauce evenly onto 4 plates, top each with a fillet, and sprinkle with parsley.

PER SERVING (1 tilapia fillet and about ½ cup sauce): 175 Cal, 5 g Total Fat, 1 g Sat Fat, 0 g Trans Fat, 50 mg Chol, 455 mg Sod, 8 g Carb, 2 g Fib, 25 g Prot, 61 mg Calc.

PointsPlus value: **4.**

sautéed tilapia with spinach and grapes

Serves 4

1 teaspoon olive oil
2 shallots, chopped
2 garlic cloves, minced
1 tablespoon water
2 (10-ounce) bags fresh spinach
½ teaspoon salt

¼ teaspoon black pepper
1 cup seedless red grapes
2 teaspoons red-wine vinegar
4 (¼-pound) tilapia fillets
½ teaspoon ground coriander
½ teaspoon ground cumin

1 Heat oil in large skillet over medium-high heat. Add shallots and cook, stirring occasionally, until shallots have softened, about 5 minutes. Add garlic and cook, stirring frequently, until fragrant, about 30 seconds.

2 Increase heat to high. Add water, then add spinach, in batches, ¼ teaspoon salt, and 1/8 teaspoon pepper, stirring just until each batch wilts. Add grapes and cook, stirring occasionally, until just heated through, about 2 minutes. Stir in vinegar.

3 Meanwhile, sprinkle tilapia with coriander, cumin, remaining ¼ teaspoon salt, and remaining 1/8 teaspoon pepper. Spray large nonstick skillet with nonstick spray and set over medium heat. Add tilapia and cook until just opaque throughout, about 3 minutes per side. Spoon spinach evenly onto 4 plates, top each with a fillet.

PER SERVING (1 tilapia filet and 1 cup spinach mixture): 196 Cal, 4 g Total Fat, 1 g Sat Fat, 0 g Trans Fat, 50 mg Chol, 460 mg Sod, 15 g Carb, 4 g Fib, 28 g Prot, 169 mg Calc.
PointsPlus value: **5.**

cook's note

To make it a meal, a quick-cooking side dish of whole-wheat angel hair pasta will be delicious (½ cup of cooked whole-wheat angel hair pasta will increase the *PointsPlus* value by *2*).

lemon cod and potato casserole

Serves 4

1¼ pounds red potatoes, sliced
1 large fennel bulb, halved and sliced
    crosswise
1 medium onion, halved and sliced
3 garlic cloves, thinly sliced
1½ teaspoons olive oil

½ teaspoon salt
¼ teaspoon black pepper
4 (5-ounce) cod fillets
2 teaspoons grated lemon zest
1 tablespoon drained capers
Lemon wedges

1 Preheat oven to 425°F. Spray large shallow baking dish with nonstick spray.

2 Place potatoes, fennel, onion, garlic, oil, ¼ teaspoon salt, and pepper in baking dish; toss to coat. Roast, stirring twice, until potatoes are almost tender, about 30 minutes.

3 Arrange cod fillets on top of potato mixture; sprinkle with lemon zest, remaining ¼ teaspoon salt, and capers. Roast until cod is just opaque throughout, about 20 minutes. Serve with lemon wedges.

PER SERVING (1 cod fillet and about 1 cup vegetables): 276 Cal, 2 g Total Fat, 0 g Sat Fat, 0 g Trans Fat, 61 mg Chol, 493 mg Sod, 34 g Carb, 5 g Fib, 30 g Prot, 81 mg Calc.
PointsPlus value: **7.**

cook's note

To make it a meal, end with a serving of sweet fresh blueberries for dessert.

halibut and asparagus with tarragon gremolata

Serves 4

4 (5-ounce) halibut fillets
3 teaspoons grated lemon zest
2 garlic cloves, minced
2 tablespoons chopped fresh tarragon

½ teaspoon salt
¼ teaspoon black pepper
1 pound asparagus, trimmed
2 teaspoons olive oil

1. Place halibut in large shallow dish; sprinkle with 1½ teaspoons lemon zest and half of garlic. Cover and refrigerate for 15 minutes.

2. Spray broiler rack with nonstick spray; preheat broiler.

3. Meanwhile, to make gremolata, stir together tarragon, remaining 1½ teaspoons lemon zest, and remaining garlic in small bowl.

4. Sprinkle halibut with ¼ teaspoon salt and 1/8 teaspoon pepper. Place on prepared broiler rack. Place asparagus on broiler rack; spray lightly with nonstick spray. Sprinkle with remaining ¼ teaspoon salt and 1/8 teaspoon pepper; toss to coat. Broil 5 minutes. Turn asparagus; broil until fish is just opaque in center and asparagus is crisp-tender, 3–4 minutes longer.

5. Place asparagus on serving platter; drizzle with oil, and toss to coat. Sprinkle fish and asparagus with gremolata.

PER SERVING (1 fish fillet and about 5 asparagus spears): 159 Cal, 4 g Total Fat, 1 g Sat Fat, 0 g Trans Fat, 66 mg Chol, 387 mg Sod, 3 g Carb, 2 g Fib, 26 g Prot, 35 mg Calc.

PointsPlus value: *4.*

cook's note

To make it a meal, add even more healthful veggies with a salad of baby arugula tossed with thinly sliced fresh fennel bulb, lemon zest and juice, and salt and pepper to taste.

roasted swordfish with tomatoes and olives

Serves 6

4 plum tomatoes, cut into quarters
1 red onion, cut into ¼-inch wedges
6 Kalamata olives, pitted and chopped
2 garlic cloves, minced
2 teaspoons olive oil

½ teaspoon salt
6 (5-ounce) swordfish steaks
¼ teaspoon black pepper
¼ cup dry white wine
2 tablespoons chopped fresh basil

1 Preheat oven to 400°F. Spray medium shallow roasting pan with nonstick spray.

2 Combine tomatoes, onion, olives, garlic, oil, and ¼ teaspoon salt in large bowl.

3 Arrange swordfish in single layer in roasting pan. Sprinkle with pepper and remaining ¼ teaspoon salt. Scatter tomato mixture around swordfish. Drizzle with wine. Roast until tomatoes have softened and fish is opaque in center, 25–30 minutes. Sprinkle with basil.

PER SERVING (1 swordfish steak with ⅓ cup tomato mixture): 212 Cal, 10 g Total Fat, 2 g Sat Fat, 0 g Trans Fat, 80 mg Chol, 328 mg Sod, 4 g Carb, 1 g Fib, 25 g Prot, 22 mg Calc.

PointsPlus value: *5.*

cook's note
Instead of swordfish, you can use halibut or cod in this recipe.

shrimp, chorizo, and rice stew

Serves 4

2 teaspoons olive oil
1 (¼-pound) low-fat chorizo sausage,
    chopped
1 large onion, chopped
1 celery stalk, chopped
2 garlic cloves, minced
½ cup long-grain white rice
1 teaspoon paprika

3 cups water
1 (14½-ounce) can no-added-salt diced
    tomatoes
½ teaspoon dried thyme
1 pound medium peeled and deveined
    shrimp
¼ cup chopped fresh flat-leaf parsley

1. Heat oil in Dutch oven over medium-high heat. Add chorizo, onion, celery, and garlic; cook, stirring frequently, until vegetables have softened, about 3 minutes. Add rice and paprika; cook, stirring frequently, until rice is lightly toasted, about 2 minutes.

2. Add water, tomatoes, and thyme; bring to boil. Reduce heat and simmer, covered, until rice is tender, about 15 minutes.

3. Add shrimp and return to boil. Reduce heat and simmer, covered, until shrimp are just opaque in center, about 5 minutes. Stir in parsley.

PER SERVING (generous 2 cups): 293 Cal, 7 g Total Fat, 1 g Sat Fat, 0 g Trans Fat, 191 mg Chol, 986 mg Sod, 30 g Carb, 3 g Fib, 27 g Prot, 139 mg Calc.
PointsPlus value: **7.**

cook's note

Chorizo is a spicy cured pork sausage popular in Spain, Mexico, and South America. The flavor will vary depending on the producer, but it's always guaranteed to give any dish a smoky peppery kick.

curried shrimp and mango salad

Serves 4

½ cup plain low-fat Greek yogurt
1 garlic clove, minced
1 tablespoon lemon juice
1 teaspoon curry powder
Pinch cayenne pepper
¾ pound cooked peeled and deveined
    medium shrimp

1 large mango, peeled, pitted, and chopped
2 scallions, thinly sliced
½ English (seedless) cucumber, thinly sliced
2 tablespoons chopped fresh cilantro
1 large head Bibb lettuce, separated
    into leaves

1 Stir together yogurt, garlic, lemon juice, curry powder, and cayenne in large bowl. Add shrimp, mango, scallions, cucumber, and cilantro; stir to combine. Cover and refrigerate at least 2 hours and up to 6 hours.

2 Divide lettuce among 4 serving plates; top evenly with shrimp salad.

PER SERVING (1 plate): 218 Cal, 3 g Total Fat, 1 g Sat Fat, 0 g Trans Fat, 212 mg Chol, 958 mg Sod, 21 g Carb, 3 g Fib, 28 g Prot, 170 mg Calc.

PointsPlus value: **5.**

cook's note

Use spicy greens, like arugula or watercress, instead of the Bibb lettuce to add more zing to this salad.

spicy shrimp salad with creamy herb dressing

Serves 4

⅓ cup low-fat buttermilk
3 tablespoons fresh flat-leaf parsley
2 tablespoons fresh basil
1 scallion, thinly sliced
1 tablespoon lemon juice
1 tablespoon olive oil
⅛ teaspoon black pepper
1 pound peeled and deveined medium
  shrimp

2 teaspoons no-salt Cajun seasoning
6 cups chopped romaine lettuce
1 red bell pepper, chopped
1 cup frozen corn kernels, thawed
1 cup grape tomatoes, halved
½ English (seedless) cucumber, chopped

1 To make dressing, puree buttermilk, parsley, basil, scallion, lemon juice, oil, and pepper in blender. Cover and refrigerate at least 2 hours or up to 3 days. Stir before serving.

2 Spray broiler rack with nonstick spray and preheat broiler.

3 Toss together shrimp and Cajun seasoning in medium bowl until coated evenly. Place shrimp on broiler rack and broil 5 inches from heat until just opaque in center, about 3 minutes per side.

4 Combine lettuce, bell pepper, corn, tomatoes, and cucumber in large bowl; add 3 tablespoons dressing and toss to coat. Divide salad evenly among 4 serving plates; top with shrimp. Drizzle with remaining dressing.

PER SERVING (1 plate): 211 Cal, 6 g Total Fat, 1 g Sat Fat, 0 g Trans Fat, 175 mg Chol, 819 mg Sod, 19 g Carb, 5 g Fib, 23 g Prot, 147 mg Calc.
PointsPlus value: **5.**

cook's note

Make a double batch of this creamy dressing and use it as a dip for fresh vegetables.

hot-and-sour seafood soup

Serves 6

2 (14½-ounce) cans reduced-sodium
    chicken broth
1¾ cups cold water
2 heads baby bok choy, stems thinly sliced,
    leaves chopped, separated
¼ pound shiitake mushrooms, stems
    removed, caps thinly sliced
1 red bell pepper, chopped
3 tablespoons apple cider vinegar

1 tablespoon reduced-sodium soy sauce
2 teaspoons chili-garlic paste
1 tablespoon cornstarch
1 pound cod, tilapia, or catfish fillets, cut
    into 1-inch pieces
4 ounces bay scallops
3 scallions, thinly sliced
1½ teaspoons Asian (dark) sesame oil

1 Bring broth and 1½ cups water to boil in large saucepan over high heat. Stir in bok choy stems, mushrooms, bell pepper, vinegar, soy sauce, and chili-garlic paste. Return to boil; reduce heat and simmer 5 minutes. Stir in bok choy leaves; simmer 3 minutes longer.

2 Stir remaining ¼ cup water and cornstarch together in small cup until smooth, then stir mixture into soup. Cook, stirring, until soup thickens slightly, about 1 minute. Stir in cod and scallops and cook just until opaque in center, about 3 minutes. Stir in scallions and sesame oil. Divide evenly among 6 soup bowls.

PER SERVING (about 1½ cups): 120 Cal, 2 g Total Fat, 0 g Sat Fat, 0 g Trans Fat, 36 mg Chol, 553 mg Sod, 6 g Carb, 1 g Fib, 19 g Prot, 61 mg Calc.

PointsPlus value: *3.*

cook's note

You can make this soup using 1¼ pounds of peeled and deveined medium shrimp instead of the cod and scallops. The cooking time will remain the same.

citrus-marinated calamari and scallop salad

Serves 6

½ pound thawed frozen calamari rings
½ pound bay scallops
1 large pink grapefruit
2 teaspoons olive oil
Zest and juice of 1 lemon

¼ teaspoon salt
⅛ teaspoon black pepper
1 fennel bulb, thinly sliced
½ small red onion, thinly sliced
2 tablespoons fresh flat-leaf parsley

1 Bring medium pot filled two-thirds full with water to gentle simmer. Add calamari and scallops and cook just until opaque, about 1 minute. Drain; rinse under cold running water and drain again. Pat dry with paper towels.

2 With knife, cut away peel and white pith from grapefruit. Working over large bowl, cut between membranes to release segments. Squeeze juice from membranes. Transfer grapefruit segments to small bowl, leaving juice behind. Whisk oil, lemon zest and juice, salt, and pepper into grapefruit juice.

3 Add calamari, scallops, fennel, onion, parsley, and grapefruit sections to grapefruit juice mixture; toss gently to coat. Cover and refrigerate at least 30 minutes or up to 8 hours.

PER SERVING (¾ cup): 107 Cal, 2 g Total Fat, 0 g Sat Fat, 0 g Trans Fat, 86 mg Chol, 259 mg Sod, 12 g Carb, 2 g Fib, 10 g Prot, 50 mg Calc.

PointsPlus* value: *3.

cook's note

To make it a meal, serve this summery salad with a refreshing wedge of cantaloupe or honeydew melon for dessert.

gingery scallop and snap pea stir-fry

Serves 4

6 ounces rice noodles
1 pound sea scallops
2 tablespoons reduced-sodium soy sauce
1 tablespoon minced peeled fresh ginger
2 cups fresh sugar snap peas, trimmed

1 orange or red bell pepper, thinly sliced
2 garlic cloves, minced
⅛ teaspoon red pepper flakes
2 teaspoons canola oil
¼ cup chopped fresh cilantro

1. Cook rice noodles according to package directions; drain and keep warm.

2. Meanwhile, toss together scallops, 1 tablespoon soy sauce, and ginger in medium bowl.

3. Spray large deep nonstick skillet with nonstick spray and set over medium heat. Add peas and bell pepper; stir-fry until crisp-tender, about 3 minutes. Stir in garlic and pepper flakes; stir-fry until fragrant, about 30 seconds. Transfer to plate.

4. Add oil to skillet. Add scallop mixture and stir-fry until scallops are browned and just opaque throughout, about 3 minutes. Add pea mixture and remaining 1 tablespoon soy sauce; stir-fry until heated through, about 1 minute longer.

5. Divide noodles among 4 serving plates; top evenly with scallop mixture. Sprinkle with cilantro.

PER SERVING (generous 1 cup scallop mixture with about ½ cup noodles): 275 Cal, 3 g Total Fat, 0 g Sat Fat, 0 g Trans Fat, 23 mg Chol, 675 mg Sod, 46 g Carb, 3 g Fib, 15 g Prot, 33 mg Calc.
PointsPlus value: *7.*

cook's note

Sugar snap peas cook in just a few minutes, so watch them carefully when you stir-fry. If overcooked, they turn a dull color and lose their appealingly crisp texture.

warm scallop salad with cucumber dressing

Serves 4

½ cup peeled, seeded, and diced cucumber
⅓ cup light mayonnaise
¼ cup plain low-fat yogurt
3 tablespoons chopped scallions
1 tablespoon lemon juice
1 teaspoon Dijon mustard

½ teaspoon salt
¼ teaspoon black pepper
6 cups baby spinach
1 cup grape or cherry tomatoes, halved
1 red or yellow bell pepper, thinly sliced
1 pound sea scallops

1 To make dressing, puree cucumber, mayonnaise, yogurt, scallions, lemon juice, mustard, ¼ teaspoon salt, and 1/8 teaspoon pepper in blender or food processor.

2 Arrange spinach, tomatoes, and bell pepper evenly on 4 serving plates.

3 Spray large heavy skillet with olive oil nonstick spray and set over medium-high heat. Pat scallops dry with paper towels. Sprinkle with remaining ¼ teaspoon salt and 1/8 teaspoon pepper. Add scallops and cook just until browned and opaque in center, 2–3 minutes per side.

4 Place scallops on top of salads; drizzle evenly with dressing.

PER SERVING (1 plate): 153 Cal, 6 g Total Fat, 1 g Sat Fat, 0 g Trans Fat, 30 mg Chol, 925 mg Sod, 12 g Carb, 3 g Fib, 15 g Prot, 94 mg Calc.

PointsPlus value: *4.*

Garlic-Ginger Steamed Clams with Pasta

garlic-ginger steamed clams with pasta

Serves 4

2 teaspoons canola oil
3 garlic cloves, minced
3 scallions, chopped
⅓ cup diced red bell pepper
2 teaspoons minced peeled fresh ginger
¼ teaspoon red pepper flakes
1 cup reduced-sodium chicken broth

3 tablespoons dry sherry
1 tablespoon reduced-sodium soy sauce
3 dozen littleneck clams, scrubbed
1 (9-ounce) package fresh angel hair pasta
3 tablespoons chopped fresh basil
   (optional)

1 Heat oil in large deep skillet over medium heat. Add garlic and cook, stirring constantly, until fragrant, about 30 seconds. Add scallions, bell pepper, ginger, and pepper flakes and cook, stirring constantly, 1 minute. Add chicken broth, sherry, and soy sauce; bring to boil.

2 Add clams and simmer, covered, until shells open, about 8 minutes. Transfer with tongs to large bowl as they open. Discard any that do not open.

3 Meanwhile, cook pasta according to package directions, omitting salt if desired.

4 Divide pasta among 4 shallow bowls; top evenly with clam mixture. Sprinkle evenly with basil, if using.

PER SERVING (about 1½ cups): 345 Cal, 5 g Total Fat, 1 g Sat Fat, 0 g Trans Fat, 75 mg Chol, 489 mg Sod, 42 g Carb, 2 g Fib, 31 g Prot, 89 mg Calc.
PointsPlus value: **9.**

cook's note

To prevent clams from overcooking and becoming tough, use a slotted spoon to remove them from the skillet as they open. Any clams that have not opened after about 8 minutes of cooking should not be eaten.

steamed mussels with oven frites

Serves 4

3 baking potatoes (about ½ pound each), each cut lengthwise into 12 wedges
3 teaspoons olive oil
½ teaspoon salt
⅛ teaspoon black pepper
1 small onion, chopped
3 garlic cloves, minced

2 teaspoons curry powder
2 large tomatoes, chopped
½ cup dry white wine
2 pounds mussels, scrubbed and debearded
¾ cup light coconut milk
¼ cup chopped fresh cilantro
Lime wedges

1 Preheat oven to 425°F. Spray large rimmed baking pan with nonstick spray.

2 Place potatoes in baking pan; drizzle with 2 teaspoons oil, sprinkle with ¼ teaspoon salt, and pepper and toss to coat. Arrange in single layer on pan with cut sides down. Bake until browned on bottom, 25 minutes. Turn potatoes onto opposite cut sides and bake until browned, 15 minutes longer.

3 Meanwhile, heat remaining 1 teaspoon oil in large deep nonstick skillet over medium heat. Add onion and cook, stirring occasionally, until softened, about 5 minutes. Add garlic and curry powder; cook, stirring constantly, until fragrant, 30 seconds. Add tomatoes, wine, and remaining ¼ teaspoon salt.

4 Increase heat to medium high; bring to boil. Add mussels. Cook, covered, until mussels open, about 4 minutes. Discard any mussels that do not open. With slotted spoon, divide mussels among 4 bowls. Add coconut milk to skillet; simmer 1 minute. Stir in cilantro. Ladle sauce evenly over mussels. Serve with potatoes and lime wedges.

PER SERVING (about 13 mussels, ½ cup sauce, and 9 potato wedges): 297 Cal, 7 g Total Fat, 2 g Sat Fat, 0 g Trans Fat, 26 mg Chol, 386 mg Sod, 42 g Carb, 5 g Fib, 17 g Prot, 83 mg Calc.

PointsPlus value: **6.**

spaghetti with mussels, clams, and shrimp

Serves 6

8 ounces whole wheat spaghetti
2 teaspoons olive oil
1 dozen mussels, scrubbed and debearded
18 littleneck clams, scrubbed
8 ounces large shrimp, peeled and deveined
1 (14½-ounce) can diced tomatoes

¼ cup water
2 garlic cloves, finely chopped
¼ teaspoon salt
¼ teaspoon red pepper flakes
2 tablespoons chopped fresh
  flat-leaf parsley

1 Prepare spaghetti according to package directions, omitting salt if desired. Drain.

2 Meanwhile, heat oil in large skillet over medium-high heat. Add mussels and clams; cover and cook until they begin to open, about 4 minutes for mussels, 3–4 minutes longer for clams. Transfer with tongs to large bowl as they open. Discard any that do not open.

3 Add shrimp to skillet and cook, stirring occasionally, just until opaque in center, about 3 minutes. Transfer to bowl with mussels and clams.

4 Add tomatoes, water, garlic, salt, and pepper flakes to skillet; bring to boil. Cook, uncovered, stirring occasionally, until sauce thickens slightly, 8–10 minutes.

5 Stir parsley into sauce. Return seafood to skillet and heat thoroughly through. Transfer spaghetti to large serving bowl. Spoon seafood and sauce over pasta and serve at once.

PER SERVING (1½ cups): 264 Cal, 4 g Total Fat, 1 g Sat Fat, 0 g Trans Fat, 89 mg Chol, 960 mg Sod, 34 g Carb, 5 g Fib, 24 g Prot, 91 mg Calc.

PointsPlus* value: *7.

cook's note

To make it a meal, finish on a light note with plain fat-free Greek yogurt topped with fresh raspberries (½ cup plain fat-free Greek yogurt per serving will increase the *PointsPlus* value by *1*).

Chickpea Stew with Mushrooms and Spinach, page 207

MAIN DISHES
vegetarian

tofu–soba noodle salad with napa cabbage

Serves 4 • Vegetarian

6 ounces soba noodles
1½ teaspoons grated orange zest
⅓ cup fresh orange juice
3 tablespoons reduced-sodium soy sauce
1½ teaspoons honey
1 teaspoon Asian (dark) sesame oil

1 garlic clove, minced
1 (14-ounce) package firm tofu, drained and
   cut into 1-inch cubes
3 cups thinly sliced Napa or green cabbage
2 scallions, thinly sliced
½ cup whole cilantro leaves

1 Cook noodles according to package directions. Drain, reserving ¼ cup cooking water. Rinse noodles in colander under cold running water; drain.

2 Meanwhile, whisk orange zest and juice, soy sauce, honey, oil, and garlic in small bowl until blended.

3 Spray large nonstick skillet with nonstick spray and set over medium heat. Add tofu and cook, without turning, until crisp and golden, about 5 minutes. With tongs, turn tofu and cook until crisp and golden on second side, about 5 minutes.

4 Re-whisk orange juice mixture, add to skillet, and bring to boil. Reduce heat to medium-low and simmer, spooning sauce over tofu frequently, about 2 minutes.

5 Combine noodles, cabbage, scallions, and cilantro in large bowl. Add tofu mixture and reserved cooking water from noodles; toss to coat.

PER SERVING (about 1½ cups): 236 Cal, 6 g Total Fat, 1 g Sat Fat, 0 g Trans Fat, 0 mg Chol, 615 mg Sod, 36 g Carb, 7 g Fib, 16 g Prot, 262 mg Calc.

PointsPlus* value: *6.

cook's note
Firm or extra-firm tofu is best for dishes like this one where the tofu needs to remain in cubes, since the dense texture keeps it from falling apart while cooking.

thai tofu and edamame stir-fry

Serves 4 • Vegetarian

½ cup light coconut milk
¼ cup reduced-sodium vegetable broth
2 teaspoons packed light brown sugar
1 teaspoon Thai red curry paste
1 teaspoon reduced-sodium soy sauce
2 teaspoons canola oil
1 small red onion, thinly sliced
2 garlic cloves, minced

1 (14-ounce) package firm tofu, drained and
  cut into 1-inch cubes
1 (10-ounce) bag frozen shelled edamame,
  thawed
2 yellow or red bell peppers, cut into
  1-inch pieces
¼ cup chopped fresh basil

1 Whisk together coconut milk, broth, brown sugar, curry paste, and soy sauce in small bowl.

2 Heat oil in large skillet over medium-high heat. Add onion and garlic; cook, stirring constantly, until fragrant, about 30 seconds. Add tofu, edamame, and bell peppers; stir-fry until bell peppers are crisp-tender, about 3 minutes.

3 Re-whisk coconut milk mixture and add to skillet. Stir-fry until liquid has thickened slightly, about 2 minutes. Remove from heat and stir in basil.

PER SERVING (1½ cups): 231 Cal, 12 g Total Fat, 2 g Sat Fat, 0 g Trans Fat, 0 mg Chol, 222 mg Sod, 19 g Carb, 6 g Fib, 17 g Prot, 267 mg Calc.

PointsPlus value: **6.**

cook's note

Serve the stir-fry with brown rice (½ cup cooked brown rice for each serving will increase the *PointsPlus* value by *3*).

stir-fry

To cook small pieces of food quickly in a small amount of oil in a wok or large skillet over medium-high heat.

what you need

A large wok or a large, deep skillet that is roomy enough to hold the food without crowding. You'll also need a wooden spoon or spatula for stirring the food.

how it's done

All ingredients should be prepared before cooking begins and placed near the stove. Foods should be thinly sliced or cut into small even-size pieces so they cook quickly and uniformly. Heat wok or large, deep skillet over medium-high heat, then add just enough canola oil to lightly coat wok (2 teaspoons oil will coat 12-inch wok).

Add the food to the wok and stir-fry, moving the pieces constantly, just until done, 3 to 5 minutes. Beef and pork can be cooked until just slightly pink in the middle, chicken should be cooked through with no pink juices, and shellfish should be opaque.

tofu and broccoli stir-fry

Serves 4 • Vegetarian

⅔ cup reduced-sodium vegetable broth
3 tablespoons reduced-sodium soy sauce
2 tablespoons mirin
1 tablespoon minced peeled fresh ginger
2 teaspoons cornstarch
½ teaspoon Asian (dark) sesame oil
½ teaspoon chili-garlic paste

2 teaspoons canola oil
6 cups small broccoli florets
1 red bell pepper, thinly sliced
3 scallions, cut into 3-inch pieces
1 (14-ounce) container extra-firm tofu, drained and cut into 1-inch chunks
¼ cup chopped fresh cilantro

1 Whisk together broth, soy sauce, mirin, ginger, cornstarch, sesame oil, and chili-garlic paste in small bowl.

2 Heat canola oil in large skillet over medium-high heat. Add broccoli, bell pepper, and scallions and cook, stirring often, until scallions are tender, about 2 minutes. Stir in tofu. Re-whisk broth mixture and add to skillet; bring to boil. Cook, stirring often, until sauce is slightly thickened, about 3 minutes. Remove from heat and stir in cilantro.

PER SERVING (1½ cups): 195 Cal, 9 g Total Fat, 1 g Sat Fat, 0 g Trans Fat, 0 mg Chol, 533 mg Sod, 18 g Carb, 5 g Fib, 15 g Prot, 253 mg Calc.

PointsPlus value: *5.*

cook's note

Use the leftover broccoli stems from preparing this recipe to make broccoli slaw. Shred them using a food processor or box grater and use in your favorite recipe.

chickpea stew with mushrooms and spinach

Serves 6 • Vegetarian

2 teaspoons olive oil
1 large leek, white part only, thinly sliced
   and well rinsed
½ pound oyster mushrooms or other wild
   mushrooms, trimmed
¼ teaspoon salt
¼ teaspoon black pepper
2 baking potatoes, peeled and cut into
   1-inch chunks

1 parsnip, peeled and cut into ½-inch slices
¾ cup baby carrots
1 small zucchini, cut into ½-inch slices
2 garlic cloves, minced
1 tablespoon tomato paste
2 cups reduced-sodium vegetable broth
1 (15½-ounce) can chickpeas, rinsed
   and drained
1 (5-ounce) bag baby spinach

1 Heat oil in large nonstick skillet over medium heat. Add leek, mushrooms, salt, and pepper and cook, stirring occasionally, until softened, 5–6 minutes.

2 Add potatoes, parsnip, carrots, zucchini, garlic, tomato paste, and broth; bring to boil. Reduce heat and simmer, covered, until vegetables are fork-tender, 20–25 minutes.

3 Add chickpeas and spinach; cook, stirring occasionally, until chickpeas are heated through and spinach is wilted, 2–3 minutes.

PER SERVING (1 cup): 220 Cal, 3 g Total Fat, 0 g Sat Fat, 0 g Trans Fat, 0 mg Chol, 411 mg Sod, 42 g Carb, 7 g Fib, 9 g Prot, 81 mg Calc.

PointsPlus value: **6.**

cook's note

To serve the stew in mini pumpkins, cut off the tops and scoop out the seeds, then spray the insides with nonstick spray. Place the pumpkin shells and lids on an oiled baking sheet and bake in a 375°F oven until they begin to soften, 20 to 30 minutes. Ladle the stew into the pumpkins and serve at once.

easy pantry minestrone

Serves 6   •   Vegetarian

2 teaspoons olive oil
2 carrots, halved lengthwise and sliced
1 celery stalk, sliced
1 onion, diced
2 garlic cloves, minced
7 cups reduced-sodium vegetable broth
1 (15½-ounce) can red kidney beans, rinsed and drained

1 (15½-ounce) can chickpeas, rinsed and drained
1 cup whole wheat macaroni or other small pasta
2 teaspoons dried basil
1 (14½-ounce) can diced tomatoes, drained
1 small zucchini, chopped
2 tablespoons refrigerated basil pesto

1 Heat oil in Dutch oven over medium-high heat. Add carrots, celery, and onion and cook, stirring occasionally, until softened, 5 minutes. Add garlic and cook, stirring constantly, until fragrant, 30 seconds.

2 Add broth, kidney beans, chickpeas, macaroni, and basil and bring to boil. Reduce heat and simmer, partially covered, 10 minutes. Stir in tomatoes and zucchini and simmer until pasta and vegetables are very tender, 10 minutes longer. Ladle into bowls and top each with 1 teaspoon pesto.

PER SERVING (1 bowl): 307 Cal, 6 g Total Fat, 1 g Sat Fat, 0 g Trans Fat, 1 mg Chol, 876 mg Sod, 53 g Carb, 10 g Fib, 14 g Prot, 120 mg Calc.

PointsPlus value: **8.**

cook's note

The zucchini adds a touch of freshness to the soup, but if you don't have any on hand, you can leave it out or substitute 2 cups chopped green cabbage or a chopped red bell pepper.

Easy Pantry Minestrone

moroccan chickpea and lentil stew

Serves 6 • Vegetarian

2 teaspoons canola oil
1 onion, diced
2 celery stalks, diced
1 teaspoon cinnamon
1 teaspoon turmeric
¾ teaspoon black pepper
8 cups reduced-sodium vegetable broth

1 (15½-ounce) can chickpeas, rinsed and drained
1 (14½-ounce) can diced tomatoes
1 cup brown lentils, picked over and rinsed
¾ cup fine egg noodles
¼ cup chopped fresh cilantro
Lemon wedges

1 Heat oil in large saucepan over medium-high heat. Add onion and celery; cook, stirring occasionally, until softened, about 5 minutes. Add cinnamon, turmeric, and pepper; cook, stirring constantly, until fragrant, 30 seconds.

2 Add broth, chickpeas, tomatoes, and lentils; bring to boil. Reduce heat and simmer, partially covered, until lentils are tender, about 30 minutes.

3 Stir in noodles and cook until tender, about 3 minutes. Remove from heat; stir in chopped cilantro. Serve with lemon wedges.

PER SERVING (1⅓ cups): 259 Cal, 4 g Total Fat, 0 g Sat Fat, 0 g Trans Fat, 4 mg Chol, 793 mg Sod, 46 g Carb, 10 g Fib, 14 g Prot, 90 mg Calc.

PointsPlus value: *7.*

cook's note

Serve the stew with warmed whole wheat pita bread (a 1-ounce whole wheat pita bread will increase the *PointsPlus* value by *2*).

green lentils and rice with caramelized onions

Serves 4 • Vegetarian

¾ cup green (French) lentils, picked over
   and rinsed
3 cups reduced-sodium vegetable broth
1 (3-inch) cinnamon stick
1¼ teaspoons ground cumin
¼ teaspoon black pepper

1 cup quick-cooking brown rice
1 large sweet onion, halved and thinly sliced
¼ cup chopped fresh flat-leaf parsley
½ cup fat-free plain yogurt
Lemon wedges

1 Combine lentils, broth, cinnamon stick, cumin, and pepper in medium saucepan; bring to boil over high heat. Reduce heat and simmer, covered, 5 minutes. Stir in rice and simmer, covered, until lentils are just tender and still hold their shape and rice has absorbed all cooking liquid, about 10 minutes. Remove saucepan from heat and let stand 3 minutes.

2 Meanwhile, spray large nonstick skillet with nonstick spray and set over medium heat. Add onion and cook, stirring frequently, until deep golden, about 15 minutes.

3 Remove and discard cinnamon stick. Spoon lentil mixture evenly on 4 plates and top with onion and yogurt. Serve with lemon wedges.

PER SERVING (¾ cup lentils and rice, ¼ cup onion, and 2 tablespoons yogurt): 250 Cal, 1 g Total Fat, 0 g Sat Fat, 0 g Trans Fat, 1 mg Chol, 346 mg Sod, 47 g Carb, 9 g Fib, 13 g Prot, 107 mg Calc.

PointsPlus value: **6.**

Cannellini Ravioli with Spinach

cannellini ravioli with spinach

Serves 4 • Vegetarian

1 cup canned cannellini (white kidney)
    beans, rinsed and drained
3 tablespoons grated Parmesan cheese
3 tablespoons part-skim ricotta cheese
1 tablespoon chopped fresh flat-leaf parsley
1 teaspoon grated lemon zest
¼ teaspoon salt
32 (3-inch) square or round wonton
    wrappers

2 teaspoons olive oil
3 garlic cloves, thinly sliced
⅛ teaspoon red pepper flakes
3 cups reduced-sodium vegetable broth
1 bunch spinach (about 1¼ pounds),
    coarsely chopped

1 To make filling, put beans in food processor and pulse until smooth. Add Parmesan, ricotta, parsley, lemon zest, and salt; process until smooth. Transfer to small bowl.

2 Lay 8 wonton wrappers out on work surface. (Cover remaining wontons with damp paper towels to prevent them from drying out.) Place 1 level tablespoon filling in center of each wonton wrapper. Brush edges of wontons with water. Top each filled wonton with another wonton, pressing edges to make tight seal. Place ravioli on baking sheet in one layer and cover with damp paper towels. Repeat with remaining filling and wonton wrappers to make a total of 16 ravioli.

3 Bring large pot of water to boil. Carefully drop ravioli into water and cook until they just begin to float, about 2 minutes; drain.

4 Meanwhile, heat oil in large skillet over medium heat. Add garlic and pepper flakes and cook until garlic is golden, about 2 minutes. Add broth and bring to boil. Add spinach and cook until wilted, 1 minute.

5 Divide ravioli evenly among 4 shallow soup bowls and ladle broth mixture evenly on top.

PER SERVING (1 bowl): 341 Cal, 6 g Total Fat, 2 g Sat Fat, 0 g Trans Fat, 13 mg Chol, 971 mg Sod, 56 g Carb, 8 g Fib, 17 g Prot, 295 mg Calc.

PointsPlus value: *9.*

whole grains

Whole grains are simple to make, and most of them don't take as long to cook as you might think. Use this chart as a handy reference for cooking your favorites or trying something new.

Grain (1 cup)	Water	Bring to a boil, then cover and simmer	Makes	PointsPlus value in ½ cup cooked serving	Fiber in ½ cup cooked serving
Barley	3 cups	30 minutes	3½ cups	2 PointsPlus value	3 grams
Bulgur	3 cups	12–15 minutes	3 cups	2 PointsPlus value	4 grams
Quinoa	2 cups	20 minutes	3 cups	3 PointsPlus value	2 grams
Brown rice	2 cups	40 minutes	3 cups	3 PointsPlus value	2 grams
Wild rice	2 cups	45 minutes	3½ cups	2 PointsPlus value	1 gram
Wheat berries	3 cups	45–60 minutes	2 cups	2 PointsPlus value	5 grams

beans, peas, and lentils

Cooking your own beans and lentils is easy and inexpensive. Dried beans do not have to soak before cooking. Soaking saves 15 to 30 minutes of cooking time, but doesn't affect the taste or texture of the beans.

To cook dried beans and lentils in water, cover them by at least 2 inches. For 1 pound of beans or lentils, add 1½ to 2 teaspoons of salt to the water at the beginning of cooking. Check often as they cook to make sure they are covered with water at all times.

One pound of dried beans or lentils will make about 5 cups once they are cooked.

Type of bean, pea, or lentil	Bring to a boil, then cover and simmer	PointsPlus value in ½ cup serving	Fiber in ½ cup serving
Black beans	1½ hours	2 PointsPlus value	7 grams
Cannellini beans	1 hour	2 PointsPlus value	5 grams
Chickpeas	2 hours	3 PointsPlus value	6 grams
Red kidney beans	2 hours	2 PointsPlus value	7 grams
Lima beans	1 hour	2 PointsPlus value	7 grams
Pinto beans	1½ hours	2 PointsPlus value	8 grams
Brown lentils	30 minutes	2 PointsPlus value	8 grams
Green split peas	30 minutes	2 PointsPlus value	8 grams

white beans and mustard greens with parmesan

Serves 4 • Vegetarian

2 teaspoons olive oil
1 onion, thinly sliced
1 tomato, chopped
2 garlic cloves, minced
6 cups trimmed and chopped mustard greens

2 (15½-ounce) cans cannellini (white kidney) beans, rinsed and drained
¾ cup reduced-sodium vegetable broth
½ teaspoon salt
⅛ teaspoon red pepper flakes
4 tablespoons grated Parmesan cheese

1 Heat oil in large skillet over medium-high heat. Add onion and cook, stirring occasionally, until softened, about 5 minutes. Add tomato and garlic; cook, stirring occasionally, until tomato is softened, about 3 minutes.

2 Add mustard, beans, broth, salt, and pepper flakes; bring to boil. Reduce heat and simmer, partially covered, until greens are tender, about 5 minutes longer.

3 Divide evenly among 4 serving plates; sprinkle each serving with 1 tablespoon Parmesan.

PER SERVING (1¼ cups): 280 Cal, 5 g Total Fat, 2 g Sat Fat, 0 g Trans Fat, 5 mg Chol, 824 mg Sod, 43 g Carb, 13 g Fib, 18 g Prot, 236 mg Calc.

PointsPlus value: *7.*

cook's note
Mustard greens lend a spicy kick to this recipe. For a milder-flavored dish, you can use kale, escarole, or Swiss chard.

chickpeas with swiss chard and grape tomatoes

Serves 6 • Vegetarian

2 teaspoons olive oil
1 onion, thinly sliced
2 garlic cloves, thinly sliced
1 teaspoon paprika
½ teaspoon ground cumin
½ teaspoon salt
⅛ teaspoon red pepper flakes
1 (14½-ounce) can reduced-sodium
    vegetable broth

2 (15½-ounce) cans chickpeas, rinsed and
    drained
2 pounds Swiss chard, tough stems
    removed and leaves coarsely chopped
2 cups grape tomatoes
Lemon wedges

1 Heat oil in large skillet over medium-high heat. Add onion and cook, stirring occasionally, until softened, about 5 minutes. Add garlic, paprika, cumin, salt, and pepper flakes and cook, stirring constantly, until fragrant, about 30 seconds.

2 Add broth, then add beans and chard, in batches, if necessary. Cook, partially covered, stirring often, until chard is tender, about 8 minutes. Add tomatoes and cook, stirring often, until tomatoes are just heated through, about 2 minutes. Serve with lemon wedges.

PER SERVING (generous 1 cup): 230 Cal, 5 g Total Fat, 1 g Sat Fat, 0 g Trans Fat, 0 mg Chol, 839 mg Sod, 39 g Carb, 10 g Fib, 12 g Prot, 138 mg Calc.

PointsPlus value: *6.*

cook's note

To make it a meal, serve the chickpeas over whole wheat couscous (½ cup cooked whole wheat couscous per serving will increase the *PointsPlus* value by *3*).

smoky sweet "baked" beans

Serves 4 • Vegetarian

2 teaspoons canola oil
1 small onion, chopped
1 green bell pepper, chopped
2 cloves garlic, minced
1 teaspoon smoked paprika
2 (15½-ounce) cans navy beans, rinsed and
   drained

¼ cup ketchup
1 tablespoon peeled grated fresh
   horseradish or prepared horseradish,
   drained
1 teaspoon packed light brown sugar

1 Heat oil in medium saucepan over medium-high heat. Add onion and bell pepper and cook, stirring occasionally, until softened, about 5 minutes. Add garlic and paprika and cook, stirring constantly, until fragrant, about 30 seconds.

2 Add beans, ketchup, horseradish, and brown sugar and bring to boil. Reduce heat and simmer until vegetables are tender and sauce has thickened, about 10 minutes.

PER SERVING (about 1 cup): 268 Cal, 3 g Total Fat, 0 g Sat Fat, 0 g Trans Fat, 0 mg Chol, 742 mg Sod, 48 g Carb, 17 g Fib, 13 g Prot, 121 mg Calc.

PointsPlus value: *6.*

cook's note

Make these baked beans the centerpiece of a summer vegetarian grilling party— with lots of vegetables on the grill and salads to serve alongside.

chickpea salad–stuffed roasted portobellos

Serves 4 • Vegetarian

4 large portobello mushrooms, stems removed
2 tablespoons red-wine vinegar
1 tablespoon olive oil
½ teaspoon dried oregano
¼ teaspoon salt
¼ teaspoon black pepper
1 (15½-ounce) can chickpeas, rinsed and drained

1 medium tomato, chopped
½ cucumber, peeled, seeded, and chopped
½ red bell pepper, chopped
2 tablespoons chopped red onion
1 garlic clove, minced
2 cups baby spinach
¼ cup crumbled feta cheese

1. Preheat oven to 400°F. Spray large rimmed baking pan with nonstick spray.

2. Scrape away black "gills" from the underside of mushrooms with the tip of small spoon; discard. Place mushrooms in pan; spray lightly with cooking spray. Roast, turning once, until mushrooms are tender, about 20 minutes. Let cool slightly.

3. Meanwhile, whisk together vinegar, oil, oregano, salt, and black pepper in large bowl. Add chickpeas, tomato, cucumber, bell pepper, onion, and garlic; stir to combine. Let stand about 10 minutes.

4. Place a mushroom, rounded side down, on each of 4 plates. Add spinach to chickpea mixture; toss to combine. Top mushrooms evenly with salad and sprinkle with feta.

PER SERVING (1 stuffed mushroom): 221 Cal, 8 g Total Fat, 2 g Sat Fat, 0 g Trans Fat, 8 mg Chol, 433 mg Sod, 28 g Carb, 7 g Fib, 11 g Prot, 113 mg Calc.
PointsPlus value: **6.**

cook's note

If you don't want to serve the mushrooms stuffed, you can thinly slice the mushrooms after they roast and cool slightly. Then, add them to the salad when you add the spinach and toss well to combine.

lentil falafel pitas

Serves 4 • Vegetarian

4 cups water
¾ cup brown lentils, picked over and rinsed
1 onion, finely chopped
1 carrot, finely chopped
¾ teaspoon salt
1 teaspoon ground coriander
1 teaspoon ground cumin
⅛ teaspoon cayenne pepper
⅓ cup plain dried bread crumbs

¼ cup chopped fresh cilantro
1 large egg white
4 (6-inch) whole wheat pitas, warmed and halved
8 leaf lettuce leaves
2 plum tomatoes, sliced
½ English (seedless) cucumber, sliced
½ cup plain fat-free yogurt

1 To make falafel, combine water, lentils, onion, carrot, and ½ teaspoon salt in medium saucepan and bring to boil over medium-high heat. Reduce heat and simmer, covered, until lentils are tender, about 30 minutes. Drain and let cool.

2 Spray broiler rack with nonstick spray and preheat broiler.

3 Combine lentil mixture, coriander, cumin, cayenne, and remaining ¼ teaspoon salt in food processor and pulse until well combined; transfer to large bowl. Add bread crumbs, cilantro, and egg white to bowl; stir to mix well. With wet hands, form mixture into 8 balls and place 1 inch apart on broiler rack. Flatten balls to form patties and spray with nonstick spray. Broil 6 inches from heat until golden brown, about 2 minutes on each side.

4 Line each pita half with lettuce leaf, fill with patties, tomatoes, and cucumber slices. Drizzle with yogurt.

PER SERVING (2 filled pita halves): 278 Cal, 3 g Total Fat, 1 g Sat Fat, 0 g Trans Fat, 1 mg Chol, 905 mg Sod, 71 g Carb, 18 g Fib, 20 g Prot, 141 mg Calc.

PointsPlus value: **9.**

indian-spiced lentils and rice

Serves 4 • Vegetarian

2 teaspoons canola oil
1 large onion, thinly sliced
2 teaspoons grated peeled fresh ginger
2 garlic cloves, minced
3 cups reduced-sodium vegetable broth
1 large tomato, chopped

½ cup white basmati rice
½ cup red lentils, picked over and rinsed
2 teaspoons garam masala
1 teaspoon ground cumin
2 tablespoons chopped fresh cilantro
Lime wedges

1 Heat oil in medium saucepan over medium heat. Add onion and cook, stirring occasionally, until onion is tender, about 8 minutes. Add ginger and garlic and cook, stirring constantly, until fragrant, 30 seconds.

2 Transfer half of onion mixture to small bowl and set aside. Add broth, tomato, rice, lentils, garam masala, and cumin to onion mixture in saucepan. Bring to boil. Reduce heat and simmer, covered, until liquid is absorbed and rice and lentils are tender, about 20 minutes. Serve topped with reserved onion mixture and cilantro. Serve with lime wedges.

PER SERVING (¾ cup): 212 Cal, 3 g Total Fat, 0 g Sat Fat, 0 g Trans Fat, 0 mg Chol, 319 mg Sod, 40 g Carb, 6 g Fib, 8 g Prot, 43 mg Calc.

PointsPlus value: **5.**

cook's note
To make it a meal, serve fresh apricot halves and unsweetened mint tea for dessert.

shiitake and barley–stuffed cabbage

Serves 4 • Vegetarian

1 cup pearl barley
3 cups water
8 large Savoy cabbage leaves
2 teaspoons canola oil
½ pound shiitake mushrooms, stems
    removed, caps sliced
1 onion, finely chopped
1 stalk celery, chopped

2 garlic cloves, minced
3 tablespoons chopped fresh flat-leaf
    parsley
¼ teaspoon salt
¼ teaspoon black pepper
2 cups fat-free marinara sauce
1 cup water
2 teaspoons apple cider vinegar

1 Combine barley and water in medium saucepan and bring to boil over medium-high heat. Reduce heat and simmer, covered, until barley is just tender, about 30 minutes; drain.

2 Meanwhile, bring large pot of water to boil. Add cabbage leaves and return to boil. Cook until cabbage is pliable, about 8 minutes; drain. Rinse cabbage under cold running water; drain and transfer to cutting board. Trim thick ribs from base of leaves and discard.

3 Preheat oven to 350°F. Spray 9 × 13-inch baking dish with nonstick spray.

4 Heat oil in medium nonstick skillet over medium heat. Add mushrooms, onion, and celery; cook, stirring frequently, until vegetables have softened, about 10 minutes. Add garlic and cook, stirring constantly, until fragrant, 30 seconds. Stir in barley, parsley, salt, and pepper. Remove skillet from heat; let cool slightly.

5 Put mushroom mixture in food processor in batches and pulse until coarsely chopped. Place 1/3 cup of filling in center of each cabbage leaf. Fold in sides of each leaf over filling and roll up.

6 Spread ½ cup of marinara sauce on bottom of baking dish. Put rolls, seam side down, in baking dish. Stir together remaining 1½ cups marinara sauce, water, and vinegar in medium bowl; pour over rolls. Cover and bake until cabbage is very soft and sauce is bubbly, about 1½ hours.

PER SERVING (2 cabbage rolls and generous ½ cup sauce): 282 Cal, 4 g Total Fat, 0 g Sat Fat, 0 g Trans Fat, 0 mg Chol, 474 mg Sod, 56 g Carb, 12 g Fib, 10 g Prot, 112 mg Calc.

PointsPlus value: *7.*

tunisian chickpea and wheat berry stew

Serves 6 • Vegetarian

1 cup wheat berries
1 tablespoon canola oil
1 onion, chopped
1 carrot, chopped
1 red bell pepper, chopped
2 garlic cloves, minced
4 cups reduced-sodium vegetable broth
1 (15½-ounce) can chickpeas, rinsed and
   drained

1 (14½-ounce) can diced tomatoes
2 tablespoons harissa
1 tablespoon curry powder
1 tablespoon ground cumin
2 teaspoons honey
6 tablespoons plain low-fat yogurt
Chopped fresh mint

1 Bring large pot of water to boil over medium-high heat; stir in wheat berries. Reduce heat and simmer, covered, until berries are tender but still chewy, 45 minutes–1 hour. Drain.

2 Meanwhile, heat oil in large saucepan over medium-high heat. Add onion, carrot, bell pepper, and garlic; cook, stirring occasionally, until vegetables have softened, about 5 minutes. Add broth, chickpeas, tomatoes, harissa, curry powder, cumin, and honey; bring to boil. Reduce heat and simmer, covered, until vegetables are very tender, about 10 minutes. Stir in wheat berries and cook until heated through, about 3 minutes.

3 Ladle stew into 6 bowls; top each bowl with 1 tablespoon yogurt and sprinkle with mint.

PER SERVING (1⅓ cups stew with 1 tablespoon yogurt): 279 Cal, 6 g Total Fat, 1 g Sat Fat, 0 g Trans Fat, 1 mg Chol, 583 mg Sod, 51 g Carb, 8 g Fib, 10 g Prot, 121 mg Calc.
PointsPlus value: **7.**

cook's note

Harissa is a spicy North African condiment made from chiles, garlic, cumin, coriander, and caraway seeds. Look for it in small jars in the ethnic foods section of large supermarkets. If you can't find it, you can substitute 2 teaspoons of Asian chili-garlic paste.

basil basmati with green beans and blue cheese

Serves 4 • Vegetarian

4 cups reduced-sodium vegetable broth
1 cup brown basmati rice
1 pound green beans, trimmed
2 teaspoons olive oil
2 shallots, thinly sliced
1 cup cherry tomatoes, halved

¼ teaspoon salt
¼ teaspoon black pepper
¼ cup chopped fresh basil
1 tablespoon grated lemon zest
2 tablespoons crumbled blue cheese
2 tablespoons toasted chopped walnuts

1 Combine broth and rice in medium saucepan; bring to boil. Reduce heat and simmer, covered, until rice is tender and liquid is absorbed, about 35 minutes.

2 Meanwhile, bring medium saucepan of water to boil. Add beans and cook just until crisp-tender, about 3 minutes. Drain.

3 Heat oil in large nonstick skillet over medium heat. Add shallots and cook, stirring occasionally, until softened and lightly browned, about 5 minutes. Add green beans, tomatoes, salt, and 1/8 teaspoon pepper; cook, stirring occasionally, just until tomatoes are heated through, 2 minutes.

4 Stir basil, lemon zest, and remaining 1/8 teaspoon pepper into rice. Divide rice evenly among 4 serving plates. Top evenly with green bean mixture. Sprinkle with blue cheese and walnuts.

PER SERVING (1 plate): 261 Cal, 7 g Total Fat, 2 g Sat Fat, 0 g Trans Fat, 3 mg Chol, 654 mg Sod, 44 g Carb, 8 g Fib, 7 g Prot, 98 mg Calc.

PointsPlus value: *7.*

cook's note

Brown basmati rice is particularly fragrant, with an aroma of toasted nuts. It's more expensive, but it's a delicious substitute for the more regular brown rice.

bulgur pilaf with apricots and feta

Serves 4 • Vegetarian

2 teaspoons canola oil
1 onion, finely chopped
1 garlic clove, minced
3 cups reduced-sodium chicken broth
1 cup bulgur
12 dried apricots, coarsely chopped

1 (3-inch) cinnamon stick
¼ teaspoon ground allspice
2 cups baby spinach
Grated zest of 1 lemon
¼ cup crumbled feta cheese
2 tablespoons pine nuts, toasted

1 Heat oil in medium saucepan over medium-high heat. Add onion and cook, stirring occasionally, until softened, about 5 minutes. Add garlic, and cook, stirring constantly until fragrant, 30 seconds.

2 Add broth, bulgur, apricots, cinnamon stick, and allspice; bring to boil. Reduce heat and simmer, covered, until liquid is absorbed and bulgur is tender, about 15 minutes. Remove saucepan from heat; remove and discard cinnamon stick. Add spinach, in batches, stirring just until wilted. Stir in lemon zest.

3 Transfer to serving bowl; sprinkle with feta and pine nuts.

PER SERVING (¾ cup): 273 Cal, 8 g Total Fat, 2 g Sat Fat, 0 g Trans Fat, 8 mg Chol, 542 mg Sod, 45 g Carb, 9 g Fib, 10 g Prot, 110 mg Calc.

PointsPlus value: **7.**

cook's note

You can use any dried fruit you have on hand in this recipe. Instead of the apricots, try chopped dried apples, figs, dates, raisins, or dried cranberries.

quinoa and butternut squash pilaf with goat cheese

Serves 4 • Vegetarian

2 teaspoons canola oil
1 onion, diced
2 celery stalks, diced
2 cups reduced-sodium vegetable broth
2 cups peeled and diced butternut squash

1 cup quinoa, rinsed
¼ cup dried cranberries
¼ cup chopped fresh flat-leaf parsley
¼ cup crumbled goat cheese
2 tablespoons chopped pecans, toasted

1 Heat oil in large saucepan over medium-high heat. Add onion and celery and cook, stirring occasionally, until softened, about 5 minutes.

2 Add broth, squash, quinoa, and cranberries; bring to boil. Reduce heat and simmer, covered, until liquid is absorbed and squash and quinoa are tender, about 15 minutes. Remove from heat; stir in parsley.

3 Divide pilaf evenly among 4 serving plates; sprinkle with goat cheese and pecans.

PER SERVING (1 cup): 293 Cal, 9 g Total Fat, 2 g Sat Fat, 0 g Trans Fat, 4 mg Chol, 272 mg Sod, 45 g Carb, 7 g Fib, 9 g Prot, 83 mg Calc.

PointsPlus value: *7.*

cook's note

In most supermarkets you will see both red and white quinoa. Either variety will work in this recipe. They both have similar flavors, though the red variety holds its shape when cooked better than the white.

easy homemade gnocchi with asparagus and tomatoes

Serves 4 • Vegetarian

1 (15-ounce) container part-skim ricotta
   cheese
½ cup whole wheat flour
4 tablespoons grated Parmesan cheese
¾ teaspoon salt
2 teaspoons olive oil
1 pound asparagus, trimmed and cut into
   2-inch lengths

2 garlic cloves, minced
2 cups cherry tomatoes, halved
⅛ teaspoon black pepper
2 tablespoons chopped fresh dill
1 tablespoon lemon juice

1   Stir together ricotta, flour, 2 tablespoons Parmesan, and ½ teaspoon salt in large bowl (the dough will be sticky).

2   Scrape dough onto lightly floured surface; divide into 4 pieces. Roll one piece into ½-inch-wide log. Cut into 1-inch pieces. Place gnocchi on lightly floured baking sheet and cover with damp paper towels. Repeat with remaining dough.

3   Heat oil in large nonstick skillet over medium heat. Add asparagus and cook, stirring frequently, until crisp-tender, about 4 minutes. Add garlic and cook, stirring constantly, until fragrant, 30 seconds. Add tomatoes, pepper, and remaining ¼ teaspoon salt and cook just until heated through, about 2 minutes longer.

4   Meanwhile, bring large pot of water to boil. Add gnocchi, in batches, dropping them in a few at a time to prevent sticking. Simmer until gnocchi just float to surface, about 2 minutes. With slotted spoon, transfer gnocchi to skillet with asparagus mixture; add dill and lemon juice and stir to combine.

5   Divide evenly among 4 serving plates and top evenly with remaining 2 tablespoons Parmesan.

PER SERVING (1½ cups): 277 Cal, 13 g Total Fat, 7 g Sat Fat, 0 g Trans Fat, 38 mg Chol, 695 mg Sod, 23 g Carb, 4 g Fib, 19 g Prot, 406 mg Calc.

PointsPlus value: **7.**

fettuccini and zucchini with no-cook tomato sauce

Serves 4 • Vegetarian

2 zucchini
½ pound whole wheat fettuccini
2 cups grape tomatoes
½ cup lightly packed fresh basil leaves
¼ cup sun-dried tomatoes (not oil-packed)
3 garlic cloves, halved

2 tablespoons walnuts, toasted
6 tablespoons grated Parmesan cheese
2 teaspoons extra-virgin olive oil
½ teaspoon salt
½ teaspoon red pepper flakes

1 Using a vegetable peeler, cut zucchini into thin lengthwise slices; set aside.

2 Cook fettuccini according to package directions, omitting salt if desired, and adding zucchini during last 2 minutes of cooking time. Drain, reserving 2 tablespoons cooking water.

3 Meanwhile, to make sauce, combine grape tomatoes, basil, sun-dried tomatoes, garlic, walnuts, 2 tablespoons Parmesan, oil, salt, and pepper flakes in blender or food processor; blend until smooth.

4 Transfer fettuccini mixture and reserved cooking water to large bowl. Add sauce and toss to coat. Sprinkle each serving with 1 tablespoon remaining Parmesan.

PER SERVING (1½ cups pasta mixture with 1 tablespoon Parmesan): 324 Cal, 9 g Total Fat, 2 g Sat Fat, 0 g Trans Fat, 7 mg Chol, 752 mg Sod, 51 g Carb, 6 g Fib, 15 g Prot, 177 mg Calc.

PointsPlus value: *9.*

linguine with stir-fried vegetables

Serves 6 • Vegetarian

6 ounces whole wheat linguine
¾ cup reduced-sodium vegetable broth
¼ cup hoisin sauce
2 teaspoons cornstarch
3 carrots, thinly sliced on the diagonal
1 red onion, halved and sliced
¼ pound shiitake mushrooms, stems removed, caps quartered
1 pound asparagus, cut into 1½-inch pieces

1 tablespoon minced peeled fresh ginger
4 garlic cloves, minced
¼ pound snow peas, trimmed and halved
¼ pound snap peas, trimmed
1 (15-ounce) can baby corn, rinsed and drained
2 tablespoons rice vinegar
2 teaspoons Asian (dark) sesame oil

1 Cook linguine according to package directions, omitting salt if desired. Drain and keep warm.

2 Meanwhile, stir together broth, hoisin sauce, and cornstarch in small bowl until smooth.

3 Spray wok or large deep skillet with nonstick spray and set over medium-high heat. Add carrots and stir-fry 1 minute. Add onion and mushrooms and stir-fry until tender, 2–3 minutes. Add asparagus and stir-fry 1 minute. Add ginger and garlic and stir-fry 30 seconds. Stir hoisin mixture and add to wok along with snow peas, snap peas, and corn. Cook until sauce simmers and thickens, about 2 minutes.

4 Remove wok from heat and stir in vinegar and oil. Transfer linguine to platter and top with vegetable mixture.

PER SERVING (1⅓ cups vegetables and ½ cup linguine): 246 Cal, 3 g Total Fat, 1 g Sat Fat, 0 g Trans Fat, 0 mg Chol, 454 mg Sod, 50 g Carb, 8 g Fib, 10 g Prot, 70 mg Calc.

PointsPlus value: **6.**

penne with vegetable bolognese

Serves 6 • Vegetarian

2 teaspoons olive oil
1 celery stalk, diced
1 carrot, diced
1 onion, diced
2 garlic cloves, minced
½ cup dry red wine
1 (28-ounce) can diced tomatoes

½ teaspoon salt
¼ teaspoon black pepper
Pinch red pepper flakes
2 tablespoons chopped fresh basil
12 ounces whole wheat penne
6 tablespoons grated Parmesan cheese

1 Heat oil in large skillet over medium heat. Add celery, carrot, and onion; cook, stirring occasionally, until vegetables are tender, about 8 minutes. Add garlic; cook, stirring constantly, until fragrant, 30 seconds. Add wine; bring to boil.

2 Add tomatoes, salt, black pepper, and pepper flakes; return to boil. Reduce heat and simmer, uncovered, until sauce has thickened, about 20 minutes. Stir basil into sauce and simmer 2 minutes longer.

3 Meanwhile, cook penne according to package directions, omitting salt if desired. Transfer pasta to serving bowl. Spoon sauce over pasta; sprinkle with Parmesan.

PER SERVING (generous 1 cup pasta with sauce and 1 tablespoon cheese): 276 Cal, 4 g Total Fat, 2 g Sat Fat, 0 g Trans Fat, 5 mg Chol, 735 mg Sod, 51 g Carb, 6 g Fib, 12 g Prot, 164 mg Calc.

PointsPlus value: **7.**

cook's note

If you make this dish in the summer, by all means use fresh tomatoes instead of the canned tomatoes. You will need about 4 cups of chopped fresh tomatoes.

pasta with spinach pesto and feta

Serves 4 • Vegetarian

1 cup packed spinach leaves
1½ cups packed fresh basil leaves
1 tablespoon pine nuts, toasted
2 tablespoons grated Parmesan cheese
1 garlic clove, chopped
¼ teaspoon salt
⅛ teaspoon black pepper

2 tablespoons reduced-sodium vegetable broth
1 tablespoon olive oil
8 ounces whole wheat fusilli
2 large tomatoes, chopped
8 Kalamata olives, pitted and halved
¼ cup crumbled feta cheese

1 To make pesto, bring small pot of water to boil. Add spinach and cook just until wilted, about 1 minute. Drain in colander and rinse under cold running water. Squeeze out excess water and place in food processor.

2 Add basil, pine nuts, Parmesan, garlic, salt, and pepper; pulse until coarsely chopped. Add broth and oil; process until smooth.

3 Meanwhile, cook fusilli according to package directions, omitting salt if desired.

4 Combine tomatoes and olives in large serving bowl. Add pasta and pesto and toss to coat. Sprinkle with feta.

PER SERVING (about 1½ cups pasta with 1 tablespoon feta): 309 Cal, 10 g Total Fat, 3 g Sat Fat, 0 g Trans Fat, 11 mg Chol, 614 mg Sod, 47 g Carb, 6 g Fib, 13 g Prot, 165 mg Calc.
PointsPlus value: **8.**

cook's note

This is a delicious pasta dish to make in the summer with farm-fresh tomatoes. When tossed with the hot pasta, the tomatoes release their juices to create a flavorful sauce.

pasta with roasted tomatoes and basil

Serves 4 • Vegetarian

6 plum tomatoes (about 1¼ pounds), halved lengthwise
2 teaspoons olive oil
½ teaspoon salt
⅛ teaspoon black pepper

2 garlic cloves, minced
8 ounces whole wheat linguine
¼ cup chopped fresh basil
¼ cup shaved Parmesan cheese

1. Preheat oven to 375°F. Spray shallow baking pan with nonstick spray.

2. Combine tomatoes, oil, salt, and pepper in large bowl and toss to coat. Arrange tomatoes, cut side up, in pan; sprinkle with garlic. Roast until tomatoes are tender and skins wrinkle, 35–40 minutes. Let cool slightly; transfer to cutting board and coarsely chop.

3. Meanwhile, cook linguine according to package directions, omitting salt if desired. Transfer to large serving bowl. Add tomatoes and basil and toss to combine. Sprinkle with Parmesan.

PER SERVING (about 1½ cups pasta with 1 tablespoon cheese): 263 Cal, 5 g Total Fat, 2 g Sat Fat, 0 g Trans Fat, 5 mg Chol, 639 mg Sod, 46 g Carb, 6 g Fib, 12 g Prot, 124 mg Calc.

PointsPlus value: **7.**

cook's note

Make a double batch of the roasted tomatoes to add to salads or sandwiches. Roasting the tomatoes concentrates their sugars, so this dish is delicious even with winter tomatoes.

warm mozzarella and tomato flatbreads

Serves 4 • Vegetarian

1 pound prepared fresh or frozen thawed pizza or bread dough

1½ cups cherry tomatoes, each quartered

1 tablespoon white balsamic vinegar

2 teaspoons olive oil

4 ounces small fresh mozzarella balls, each quartered

1½ teaspoons fresh thyme leaves

¼ teaspoon coarse sea salt

1 Preheat oven to 425°F. Spray large baking sheet with olive oil cooking spray.

2 Sprinkle work surface lightly with flour. Place dough on work surface and divide evenly into 4 pieces. With lightly floured rolling pin, roll each piece of dough into 7×4-inch oval. Transfer ovals to prepared baking sheets. Lightly spray top of dough with olive oil cooking spray. Bake until flatbreads are golden, 12–15 minutes. Transfer flatbreads to rack to cool slightly, 2–3 minutes.

3 Meanwhile, combine tomatoes, vinegar, and oil in medium bowl; toss to coat. Top warm flatbreads evenly with tomatoes and mozzarella. Sprinkle with thyme and salt and serve at once.

PER SERVING (1 flatbread): 379 Cal, 13 g Total Fat, 4 g Sat Fat, 0 g Trans Fat, 23 mg Chol, 847 mg Sod, 54 g Carb, 3 g Fib, 15 g Prot, 8 mg Calc.

PointsPlus value: *10.*

cook's note

If you have trouble stretching the dough into ovals, let it rest for 5 to 10 minutes to relax the gluten, then try again.

Stir-Fried Beef and Bok Choy Salad, page 236

20-minute main dishes

stir-fried beef and bok choy salad

Serves 4 • Ready in 20 minutes or less

2 tablespoons Asian fish sauce
1 tablespoon reduced-sodium soy sauce
2 teaspoons grated lime zest
2 teaspoons honey
2 garlic cloves, minced
1 pound beef sirloin steak, trimmed and
    thinly sliced

⅓ cup lime juice
¼ teaspoon chili-garlic paste
4 cups thinly sliced bok choy
4 cups thinly sliced Napa cabbage
2 shallots, thinly sliced

1 Combine 1 tablespoon fish sauce, soy sauce, lime zest, 1 teaspoon honey, and half of garlic in medium bowl; add beef and toss to coat.

2 To make dressing, whisk together lime juice and remaining 1 tablespoon fish sauce, 1 teaspoon honey, and remaining garlic in small bowl; stir in chili-garlic paste. Combine bok choy, cabbage, and shallots in large serving bowl.

3 Spray large deep nonstick skillet or wok with nonstick spray and set over medium heat. Add steak in two batches and stir-fry until lightly browned, about 1 minute. Add steak and reserved dressing to bok choy mixture; toss to coat.

PER SERVING (2 cups): 208 Cal, 4 g Total Fat, 1 g Sat Fat, 0 g Trans Fat, 73 mg Chol, 961 mg Sod, 9 g Carb, 2 g Fib, 33 g Prot, 163 mg Calc.

PointsPlus value: *5.*

cook's note

You can add even more flavor to this salad by tossing ¼ cup chopped fresh cilantro or mint with the bok choy mixture.

asian beef lettuce wraps

Serves 4 • Ready in 20 minutes or less

1 pound ground lean beef (7 percent fat or less)
2 celery stalks, diced
3 scallions, thinly sliced
½ cup sliced water chestnuts

3 tablespoons reduced-sodium soy sauce
1 tablespoon grated peeled fresh ginger
¼ teaspoon chili-garlic paste
¼ cup chopped fresh cilantro
8 large Boston lettuce leaves

1. Spray large skillet with nonstick spray and set over medium-high heat. Add beef and cook, breaking it apart with wooden spoon, until browned, about 3 minutes.

2. Stir in celery and cook, stirring often, until celery is crisp-tender, about 2 minutes. Add scallions, water chestnuts, soy sauce, ginger, and chili-garlic paste; cook, stirring, until heated through, about 1 minute. Stir in cilantro.

3. Divide beef mixture among lettuce leaves.

PER SERVING (2 lettuce wraps): 192 Cal, 7 g Total Fat, 3 g Sat Fat, 0 g Trans Fat, 64 mg Chol, 472 mg Sod, 8 g Carb, 2 g Fib, 24 g Prot, 40 mg Calc.

PointsPlus value: *5.*

cook's note

To make it a meal, accompany these wraps with brown rice with a sprinkle of thinly sliced scallions and chopped fresh cilantro stirred in (½ cup cooked brown rice per serving will increase the *PointsPlus* value by *3*).

moroccan-spiced beef

Serves 4 • Ready in 20 minutes or less

1 pound ground lean beef (7 percent fat
   or less)
1 medium onion, diced
1 red bell pepper, diced
2 garlic cloves, minced
1 tablespoon paprika

½ teaspoon ground allspice
¼ teaspoon ground cinnamon
½ teaspoon salt
¼ teaspoon black pepper
1 (14½-ounce) can diced tomatoes

1 Spray large skillet with nonstick spray and set over medium-high heat. Add beef, onion, bell pepper, and garlic and cook, breaking beef apart with wooden spoon, until browned, about 3 minutes.

2 Add paprika, allspice, cinnamon, salt, and black pepper and cook, stirring constantly, until fragrant, 30 seconds. Stir in tomatoes and bring to boil; cover and cook, stirring occasionally, until vegetables are tender, 5 minutes.

PER SERVING (¾ cup): 202 Cal, 7 g Total Fat, 3 g Sat Fat, 0 g Trans Fat, 64 mg Chol, 499 mg Sod, 10 g Carb, 3 g Fib, 24 g Prot, 60 mg Calc.
***PointsPlus* value: 5.**

cook's note

To make it a meal, whole wheat couscous is an authentic pairing for this dish (½ cup cooked whole wheat couscous per serving will increase the *PointsPlus* value by *3*).

grilled flank steak with brown sugar–spice rub

Serves 4   •   Ready in 20 minutes or less

1 tablespoon packed
   light brown sugar
1 teaspoon cracked
   black pepper
1 teaspoon ground
   cumin
1 teaspoon ground
   coriander

1 teaspoon paprika
Pinch cayenne pepper
2 garlic cloves, minced
1 (1-pound) flank
   steak, trimmed
¼ teaspoon salt

1. Stir together brown sugar, black pepper, cumin, coriander, paprika, cayenne, and garlic in small bowl. Sprinkle spice mixture on both sides of steak.

2. Spray grill rack with nonstick spray; preheat grill to medium or prepare medium fire.

3. Sprinkle steak with salt and place on grill rack. Grill, turning occasionally, until instant-read thermometer inserted into side of steak registers 145°F, 10–12 minutes. Transfer to cutting board and let stand 5 minutes. Cut steak on an angle against the grain into 12 slices.

PER SERVING (3 slices steak): 208 Cal, 8 g Total Fat, 3 g Sat Fat, 0 g Trans Fat, 49 mg Chol, 186 mg Sod, 6 g Carb, 2 g Fib, 27 g Prot, 45 mg Calc.

PointsPlus value: **5.**

how to
grill

To cook food on a grill rack over a charcoal or gas fire.

what you need

A charcoal or gas grill and a long-handled metal turner or tongs for turning the food. You'll also need an instant-read thermometer to establish the proper degree of doneness for meats and poultry.

how it's done

Spray the grill rack with nonstick spray before lighting the fire. Prepare a charcoal fire or preheat a gas grill. A charcoal fire is ready for cooking when the coals have a light coating of white ash. Gas grills take about 15 minutes to preheat.

Place meats and vegetables on the grill rack, and grill. Toss vegetables with a light coating of oil (1 teaspoon of oil will coat about 4 cups of vegetables) before grilling. Place delicate fish fillets and small pieces of vegetables in a grill basket to keep them intact and to prevent them from falling through the grill rack. Turn the food for even cooking and cook to the desired degree of doneness.

filet mignon with arugula and maple-balsamic glaze

Serves 4 • Ready in 20 minutes or less

¾ cup balsamic vinegar
1 tablespoon pure maple syrup
1 teaspoon extra-virgin olive oil
4 (¼-pound) filet mignons, ½ inch thick,
    trimmed

½ teaspoon salt
¼ teaspoon coarsely ground black pepper
6 cups lightly packed baby arugula

1 Combine vinegar and maple syrup in small saucepan; bring to boil over medium-high heat. Boil until mixture is reduced to syrupy glaze, about 8 minutes. Remove saucepan from heat; whisk in oil.

2 Meanwhile, spray large skillet with nonstick spray and set over medium-high heat. Sprinkle steaks with salt and pepper. Add to skillet and cook until instant-read thermometer inserted into side of each steak registers 145°F, about 4 minutes per side.

3 Divide arugula evenly among 4 plates and top each portion with a steak. Drizzle with maple-balsamic glaze and serve at once.

PER SERVING (1½ cups arugula, 1 steak, and 1 tablespoon glaze): 222 Cal, 9 g Total Fat, 3 g Sat Fat, 0 g Trans Fat, 49 mg Chol, 341 mg Sod, 5 g Carb, 1 g Fib, 27 g Prot, 62 mg Calc.

PointsPlus value: **5.**

cook's note
The maple-balsamic glaze in this recipe is great for drizzling on steak, pork tenderloin, or grilled salmon.

Filet Mignon with Arugula
and Maple-Balsamic Glaze

quick beef and vegetable chili

Serves 4 • Ready in 20 minutes or less

1 pound ground lean beef (7 percent fat
   or less)
1 small onion, diced
1 tablespoon chili powder
1 teaspoon ground cumin

½ teaspoon salt
2 (10-ounce) packages frozen succotash
1 (14½-ounce) can reduced-sodium
   chicken broth
1 (14½-ounce) can diced tomatoes

1 Spray large saucepan with nonstick spray and set over medium-high heat. Add beef and onion and cook, breaking beef apart with wooden spoon, until browned, about 3 minutes.

2 Add chili powder, cumin, and salt and cook stirring constantly, until fragrant, 30 seconds. Stir in succotash, broth, and tomatoes and bring to boil. Cover and cook, stirring occasionally, about 10 minutes.

PER SERVING (1 cup): 325 Cal, 8 g Total Fat, 3 g Sat Fat, 0 g Trans Fat, 64 mg Chol, 811 mg Sod, 35 g Carb, 7 g Fib, 31 g Prot, 87 mg Calc.

PointsPlus value: *8.*

cook's note

To make it a meal, finish this hearty chili dinner with a cool and refreshing fruit dessert. Toss together mango slices, orange segments, and grated lime zest and sprinkle with fresh chopped mint.

salsa beef and beans with polenta

Serves 4 • Ready in 20 minutes or less

1 pound ground lean beef (7 percent fat or less)
2 teaspoons salt-free Mexican seasoning
1 (15½-ounce) can no-added-salt black beans, rinsed and drained

1 (14-ounce) jar fat-free salsa
1 (16-ounce) tube refrigerated plain polenta, cut into 8 slices
½ cup shredded reduced-fat sharp Cheddar cheese

1 Spray large saucepan with nonstick spray and set over medium-high heat. Add beef and cook, breaking beef apart with wooden spoon, until browned, about 3 minutes.

2 Add Mexican seasoning and cook stirring constantly, until fragrant, 30 seconds. Stir in beans and salsa and bring to boil. Cover and cook, stirring occasionally, about 10 minutes.

3 Meanwhile, spray large nonstick skillet with nonstick spray and set over medium heat. Add polenta and cook, turning each slice once, until heated through and lightly browned, about 6 minutes.

4 Divide polenta among 4 plates; top with beef mixture. Sprinkle with cheese.

PER SERVING (1 cup beef, 2 slices polenta, and 2 tablespoons cheese): 400 Cal, 10 g Total Fat, 4 g Sat Fat, 0 g Trans Fat, 70 mg Chol, 746 mg Sod, 42 g Carb, 9 g Fib, 36 g Prot, 168 mg Calc.

PointsPlus value: *10.*

Quick Moo Shu Pork

quick moo shu pork

Serves 4 • Ready in 20 minutes or less

4 tablespoons reduced-sodium soy sauce
1 tablespoon cornstarch
½ pound pork tenderloin, cut into
   1-inch strips
3 large egg whites, lightly beaten
2 garlic cloves, minced

1 tablespoon minced peeled fresh ginger
5 cups shredded Napa cabbage
1 cup sliced white mushrooms
5 scallions, sliced
1 teaspoon Asian (dark) sesame oil
4 whole wheat tortillas, warmed

1 Whisk 2 tablespoons soy sauce and cornstarch in medium bowl until smooth; add pork and toss to coat.

2 Spray large deep nonstick skillet or wok with nonstick spray and set over medium heat. Add egg whites and stir-fry until firm, about 2 minutes. Transfer to plate.

3 Spray same pan with nonstick spray. Add pork; stir-fry until no longer pink, about 2 minutes. Add garlic and ginger; stir-fry 1 minute. Add cabbage, mushrooms, and scallions; stir-fry until cabbage starts to wilt, about 3 minutes. Add egg, remaining 2 tablespoons soy sauce, and oil and stir-fry until heated through, about 1 minute.

4 Spoon about 1 cup of pork mixture onto each tortilla and roll up to enclose filling.

PER SERVING (1 filled tortilla): 266 Cal, 6 g Total Fat, 1 g Sat Fat, 0 g Trans Fat, 37 mg Chol, 787 mg Sod, 30 g Carb, 4 g Fib, 22 g Prot, 54 mg Calc.

***PointsPlus* value: 6.**

cook's note

This dish is traditionally served inside a thin homemade pancake. Using tortillas makes the recipe quicker—and it's just as delicious.

peppered pork chops
with red-wine sauce

Serves 4 • Ready in 20 minutes or less

4 (¼-pound) boneless center-cut pork loin
    chops, about ½ inch thick, trimmed
2 teaspoons cracked black pepper
¼ teaspoon salt
2 teaspoons olive oil

½ cup dry red wine
¾ cup reduced-sodium chicken broth
1½ teaspoons whole-grain Dijon mustard
½ teaspoon tomato paste

1 Sprinkle pork chops with pepper and salt. Heat oil in large skillet over medium-high heat. Add chops and cook until an instant-read thermometer inserted into the side of a chop registers 145°F, 4 minutes per side. Transfer chops to plate.

2 Add wine to skillet; cook, scraping up all browned bits on bottom of skillet. Boil until wine has reduced to ¼ cup, about 1 minute. Add broth and cook about 2 minutes. Whisk in mustard and tomato paste; cook until sauce has thickened and reduced to about ½ cup, about 1 minute longer. Transfer chops to 4 plates and top evenly with sauce.

PER SERVING (1 pork chop and 2 tablespoons sauce): 202 Cal, 9 g Total Fat, 2 g Sat Fat, 0 g Trans Fat, 66 mg Chol, 350 mg Sod, 3 g Carb, 0 g Fib, 22 g Prot, 33 mg Calc.
***PointsPlus* value: 5.**

cook's note

Transfer leftover tomato paste to an ice cube tray and freeze. When frozen, transfer the cubes to a zip-close plastic bag and store in the freezer for up to 6 months. When you need a small amount of paste for soups or sauces, just pull out a cube.

curried pork chops with chutney sauce

Serves 4 • Ready in 20 minutes or less

1 tablespoon all-purpose flour
2 teaspoons curry powder
4 (¼-pound) boneless center-cut pork loin
     chops, about ½ inch thick, trimmed
¼ teaspoon salt

1 tablespoon canola oil
⅓ cup orange juice
¼ cup mango chutney
2 tablespoons chopped fresh cilantro
Lime wedges

1 Stir together flour and curry powder in shallow bowl. Sprinkle chops with salt; coat with flour mixture.

2 Heat oil in large skillet over medium-high heat. Add chops and cook until an instant-read thermometer inserted into the side of a chop registers 145°F, 4 minutes per side. Transfer chops to plate.

3 Add orange juice and chutney to skillet; bring to boil. Cook, stirring constantly, until sauce thickens slightly, about 3 minutes. Remove from heat; stir in cilantro. Transfer chops to 4 plates and top evenly with sauce. Serve with lime wedges.

PER SERVING (1 pork chop): 262 Cal, 12 g Total Fat, 3 g Sat Fat, 0 g Trans Fat, 72 mg Chol, 233 mg Sod, 11 g Carb, 1 g Fib, 26 g Prot, 22 mg Calc.

PointsPlus value: **7.**

pork chops with dried cherry sauce

Serves 4 • Ready in 20 minutes or less

4 (¼-pound) boneless center-cut pork loin
    chops, about ½ inch thick, trimmed
¼ teaspoon salt
⅛ teaspoon black pepper
2 teaspoons olive oil
2 shallots, diced

Pinch dried thyme
½ cup ruby port wine
⅓ cup reduced-sodium chicken broth
¼ cup dried cherries
1 tablespoon minced fresh flat-leaf parsley

1 Sprinkle chops with salt and pepper. Heat oil in large skillet over medium-high heat. Add chops and cook until an instant-read thermometer inserted into the side of a chop registers 145°F, 4 minutes per side. Transfer chops to plate.

2 Add shallots and thyme to skillet; cook, stirring, 1 minute. Add wine, broth, and cherries; bring to boil. Cook, stirring often, until sauce has reduced by half, about 3 minutes. Remove from heat and stir in parsley. Transfer chops to 4 plates and top evenly with sauce.

PER SERVING (1 pork chop and about 2 tablespoons sauce): 269 Cal, 11 g Total Fat, 3 g Sat Fat, 0 g Trans Fat, 72 mg Chol, 241 mg Sod, 14 g Carb, 1 g Fib, 26 g Prot, 25 mg Calc.
PointsPlus value: **7.**

cook's note

Instead of dried cherries, you can use raisins, dried cranberries, or chopped dried apricots in this recipe.

honey-glazed pork chops

Serves 4 • Ready in 20 minutes or less

3 tablespoons honey
2 tablespoons reduced-sodium soy sauce
1 tablespoon rice vinegar
½ teaspoon cornstarch
2 teaspoons Asian (dark) sesame oil

4 (¼-pound) boneless center-cut pork loin
   chops, about ½ inch thick, trimmed
2 scallions, thinly sliced
1 garlic clove, minced
2 tablespoons minced fresh cilantro

1 Whisk together honey, soy sauce, vinegar, and cornstarch in small bowl.

2 Heat oil in large skillet over medium-high heat. Add chops and cook until an instant-read thermometer inserted into the side of a chop registers 145°F, 4 minutes per side. Transfer chops to plate.

3 Add scallions and garlic to skillet and cook, stirring constantly, until fragrant, 30 seconds. Add honey mixture to skillet and bring to boil. Transfer chops to 4 plates and top evenly with sauce. Sprinkle with cilantro.

PER SERVING (1 pork chop and 1½ tablespoons sauce): 263 Cal, 11 g Total Fat, 3 g Sat Fat, 0 g Trans Fat, 72 mg Chol, 311 mg Sod, 15 g Carb, 0 g Fib, 25 g Prot, 15 mg Calc.

PointsPlus value: *7.*

quick pork chops parmesan

Serves 4 • Ready in 20 minutes or less

1 large egg
¼ cup Italian-seasoned dried bread crumbs
4 (¼-pound) boneless center-cut pork loin
    chops, about ½ inch thick, trimmed
¼ teaspoon salt

⅛ teaspoon black pepper
2 teaspoons olive oil
1 cup fat-free marinara sauce, heated
½ cup shredded reduced-fat mozzarella
2 tablespoons grated Parmesan cheese

1 Preheat broiler.

2 Place egg in shallow dish; lightly beat egg. Place bread crumbs in another shallow dish. Sprinkle chops with salt and pepper. Dip each chop in egg then in crumb mixture.

3 Heat oil in large nonstick skillet over medium heat. Add chops and cook until an instant-read thermometer inserted into the side of a chop registers 145°F, 4–5 minutes on each side. Transfer chops to large flameproof baking dish.

4 Top chops with marinara; sprinkle with mozzarella and Parmesan. Broil, 5 inches from heat, until cheese begins to melt, about 1 minute.

PER SERVING (1 pork chop): 328 Cal, 17 g Total Fat, 6 g Sat Fat, 0 g Trans Fat, 129 mg Chol, 664 mg Sod, 10 g Carb, 2 g Fib, 33 g Prot, 179 mg Calc.
PointsPlus value: *8.*

cook's note

Whole wheat capellini makes a quick side dish for the pork chops (⅔ cup cooked whole wheat capellini per serving will increase the *PointsPlus* value by *3*).

Quick Pork Chops Parmesan and Balsamic-Marinated Roasted Peppers with Basil, page 286

rosemary-balsamic pork chops

Serves 4   •   Ready in 20 minutes or less

4 (¼-pound) boneless center-cut pork loin
    chops, about ½ inch thick, trimmed
¼ teaspoon salt
⅛ teaspoon black pepper
2 teaspoons olive oil
2 shallots, minced

1 garlic clove, minced
½ cup reduced-sodium chicken broth
¼ cup balsamic vinegar
1 teaspoon butter
½ teaspoon minced fresh rosemary or
    ¼ teaspoon dried

1 Sprinkle chops with salt and pepper. Heat oil in large skillet over medium-high heat. Add chops and cook until an instant-read thermometer inserted into the side of a chop registers 145°F, 4 minutes per side. Transfer chops to plate.

2 Add shallots and garlic to skillet and cook, stirring constantly, until softened, about 1 minute. Add broth and vinegar; bring to boil and cook until slightly reduced, about 4 minutes. Stir in butter and rosemary. Transfer chops to 4 plates and top evenly with sauce.

PER SERVING (1 pork chop and 2 tablespoons sauce): 239 Cal, 12 g Total Fat, 4 g Sat Fat, 0 g Trans Fat, 74 mg Chol, 274 mg Sod, 5 g Carb, 0 g Fib, 26 g Prot, 19 mg Calc.
PointsPlus value: **6.**

cook's note

For a quick side dish, serve the pork chops with fresh pasta (⅓ cup cooked fresh pasta per serving will increase the *PointsPlus* value by *3*).

pork and pepper stir-fry

Serves 4 • Ready in 20 minutes or less

¾ cup reduced-sodium chicken broth
¼ cup dry sherry
3 tablespoons reduced-sodium soy sauce
1 tablespoon cornstarch
1 tablespoon chili-garlic paste
2 teaspoons canola oil

1 pound boneless center-cut pork loin
 chops, trimmed and thinly sliced
4 scallions, cut into 1-inch pieces
1 tablespoon minced peeled fresh ginger
2 red or yellow bell peppers, chopped

1 Whisk together broth, sherry, soy sauce, cornstarch, and chili-garlic paste in small bowl until smooth.

2 Heat large skillet or wok over medium-high heat. Add 1 teaspoon oil and swirl to coat pan; add pork and stir-fry until pork is cooked through, 4–5 minutes. Transfer pork to plate.

3 Heat remaining 1 teaspoon oil in same pan. Add scallions and ginger; stir-fry until fragrant, about 30 seconds. Add peppers; stir-fry until crisp-tender, about 2 minutes. Re-whisk broth mixture; add to skillet and bring to boil. Reduce heat and simmer, stirring occasionally, until sauce bubbles and thickens slightly, about 2 minutes. Add pork and cook until heated through, about 1 minute.

PER SERVING (1 cup): 228 Cal, 9 g Total Fat, 2 g Sat Fat, 0 g Trans Fat, 66 mg Chol, 735 mg Sod, 10 g Carb, 2 g Fib, 25 g Prot, 60 mg Calc.

PointsPlus value: *6.*

white bean and bacon stew

Serves 4 • *Ready in 20 minutes or less*

2 slices thick-cut bacon, cut into strips
1 small onion, halved and sliced
1 carrot, chopped
1 celery stalk, chopped
2 garlic cloves, minced
2 (15½-ounce) cans cannellini (white kidney)
    beans, rinsed and drained

1 (14½-ounce) can diced tomatoes
1 cup reduced-sodium chicken broth
1 canned anchovy fillet, minced
2 tablespoons chopped fresh thyme
¼ teaspoon black pepper

1 Cook bacon in large saucepan over medium-high heat until crisp; drain on paper towels.

2 Pour off and discard all but 2 teaspoons drippings. Add onion, carrot, and celery to skillet and cook, stirring occasionally, until softened, about 5 minutes. Add garlic and cook, stirring constantly, until fragrant, 30 seconds.

3 Add beans, tomatoes, broth, anchovy, thyme, and pepper; bring to boil. Reduce heat and simmer, covered, until vegetables are tender, about 10 minutes. Stir in bacon.

PER SERVING (1½ cups): 167 Cal, 2 g Total Fat, 1 g Sat Fat, 0 g Trans Fat, 3 mg Chol, 629 mg Sod, 27 g Carb, 7 g Fib, 12 g Prot, 101 mg Calc.

PointsPlus value: *4.*

chicken and noodles with creamy paprika sauce

Serves 4 • Ready in 20 minutes or less

3 cups wide, yolk-free whole wheat noodles
4 (5-ounce) skinless boneless chicken breasts
3 teaspoons smoked sweet paprika
½ teaspoon salt
¼ teaspoon cayenne pepper
1 teaspoon canola oil

1 large onion, diced
⅛ teaspoon ground cloves
¾ cup reduced-sodium chicken broth
½ cup reduced-fat sour cream
1½ teaspoons all-purpose flour
2 tablespoons chopped fresh flat-leaf parsley

1 Cook noodles according to package directions, omitting salt if desired; drain.

2 Meanwhile, sprinkle chicken with 2 teaspoons of paprika, salt, and cayenne. Heat oil in large nonstick skillet over medium heat. Add chicken and cook, turning once, until well browned, about 3 minutes. Transfer to plate.

3 Add onion, cloves, and remaining 1 teaspoon paprika to skillet; cook, stirring frequently, until onion is lightly browned, about 4 minutes. Add broth and cook, scraping up browned bits from bottom of pan. Whisk in sour cream and flour until blended; bring to boil. Return chicken to skillet and reduce heat to low. Cover and simmer until chicken is cooked through, about 4 minutes. With tongs, transfer chicken to plate.

4 Stir noodles into sauce in skillet and cook until heated through, about 2 minutes. Divide noodles and sauce among 4 plates and top with chicken. Sprinkle evenly with parsley.

PER SERVING (1 chicken breast with ¾ cup noodles and sauce): 345 Cal, 10 g Total Fat, 4 g Sat Fat, 0 g Trans Fat, 100 mg Chol, 565 mg Sod, 29 g Carb, 4 g Fib, 39 g Prot, 76 mg Calc.
PointsPlus value: **9.**

**Indian Chicken with
Cucumber-Mango Sauce**

indian chicken with cucumber-mango sauce

Serves 4 • Ready in 20 minutes or less

1 teaspoon grated peeled fresh ginger
1 teaspoon garam masala
½ teaspoon salt
¼ teaspoon black pepper
4 (5-ounce) skinless boneless chicken
  breasts

½ cup fat-free plain Greek yogurt
1 tablespoon honey
1 ripe mango, peeled, pitted, and diced
½ English (seedless) cucumber, diced
2 tablespoons thinly sliced fresh mint
  (optional)

1 Stir together ginger, garam masala, salt, and pepper in small dish; coat chicken evenly with spice mixture.

2 Spray large nonstick skillet with nonstick spray and set over medium heat. Add chicken and cook, turning occasionally, until cooked through, about 8 minutes.

3 Meanwhile, to make sauce, whisk together yogurt and honey in medium bowl; stir in mango, cucumber, and mint, if using. Serve chicken with sauce.

PER SERVING (1 chicken breast and about ½ cup sauce): 253 Cal, 5 g Total Fat, 1 g Sat Fat, 0 g Trans Fat, 89 mg Chol, 401 mg Sod, 16 g Carb, 1 g Fib, 34 g Prot, 94 mg Calc.

PointsPlus value: **6.**

lemon-mint chicken

Serves 4 • *Ready in 20 minutes or less*

4 (5-ounce) skinless boneless chicken
  breasts
½ teaspoon ground cumin
½ teaspoon salt
¼ teaspoon black pepper

¼ cup chopped fresh mint
1 garlic clove, minced
1 tablespoon grated lemon zest
2 teaspoons canola oil
Lemon wedges

1 Sprinkle chicken with cumin, salt, and pepper. Rub with mint, garlic, and lemon zest, pressing to adhere.

2 Heat oil in large nonstick skillet over medium heat. Add chicken and cook, turning once, until cooked through, 8–10 minutes. Serve with lemon wedges.

PER SERVING (1 chicken breast): 205 Cal, 7 g Total Fat, 1 g Sat Fat, 0 g Trans Fat, 85 mg Chol, 376 mg Sod, 2 g Carb, 1 g Fib, 32 g Prot, 28 mg Calc.

PointsPlus value: *5.*

spice-rubbed chicken with cucumber-fennel sauce

Serves 4 • Ready in 20 minutes or less

4 (5-ounce) skinless boneless chicken
   breasts
¾ teaspoon ground coriander
¾ teaspoon ground cumin
¾ teaspoon salt

¼ teaspoon black pepper
2 teaspoons olive oil
1 cup plain reduced-fat yogurt
½ English (seedless) cucumber, diced
½ fennel bulb, chopped

1 Sprinkle chicken with ½ teaspoon coriander, ½ teaspoon cumin, ½ teaspoon salt, and pepper.

2 Heat oil in large nonstick skillet over medium heat. Add chicken and cook, turning once, until cooked through, 8–10 minutes.

3 Meanwhile, stir together yogurt, cucumber, fennel, remaining ¼ teaspoon coriander, ¼ teaspoon cumin, and ¼ teaspoon salt in medium bowl. Serve chicken with sauce.

PER SERVING (1 chicken breast and ½ cup sauce): 254 Cal, 8 g Total Fat, 2 g Sat Fat, 0 g Trans Fat, 92 mg Chol, 582 mg Sod, 8 g Carb, 1 g Fib, 36 g Prot, 154 mg Calc.

PointsPlus value: **6.**

orange-basil chicken

Serves 4 • *Ready in 20 minutes or less*

4 (5-ounce) skinless boneless chicken
   breasts
½ teaspoon salt
¼ teaspoon black pepper
2 teaspoons olive oil

2 navel oranges
⅓ cup reduced-sodium chicken broth
1 teaspoon cornstarch
2 tablespoons chopped fresh basil

1 Sprinkle chicken with salt and pepper. Heat oil in large nonstick skillet over medium heat. Add chicken and cook, turning once, until cooked through, 8–10 minutes. Transfer to plate.

2 Meanwhile, grate zest from oranges; set aside. With knife, cut away peel and white pith from oranges. Working over large bowl, cut between membranes to release segments. Squeeze juice from membranes.

3 Stir together broth and cornstarch in small bowl.

4 Add broth mixture and orange segments and juice to same skillet. Cook, stirring often, until mixture comes to boil and thickens slightly, 2 minutes. Remove from heat and stir in basil and orange zest. Serve chicken with sauce.

PER SERVING (1 chicken breast and ⅓ cup sauce) 236 Cal, 7 g Total Fat, 2 g Sat Fat, 0 g Trans Fat, 88 mg Chol, 420 mg Sod, 9 g Carb, 2 g Fib, 33 g Prot, 50 mg Calc.

PointsPlus value: **6.**

chicken tacos with cilantro slaw

Serves 4 • Ready in 20 minutes or less

4 (5-ounce) skinless boneless chicken breasts
1 tablespoon chili powder
¾ teaspoon salt
2 teaspoons canola oil
1 cup coleslaw mix

½ cup whole cilantro leaves
1 tablespoon lime juice
4 (8-inch) whole wheat tortillas, warmed
¼ cup fat-free salsa
½ cup shredded reduced-fat Monterey Jack cheese

1 Sprinkle chicken with chili powder and ½ teaspoon salt. Heat oil in large nonstick skillet over medium heat. Add chicken and cook, turning once, until cooked through, 8–10 minutes. Transfer to cutting board.

2 Meanwhile, to make slaw, place coleslaw mix, cilantro, lime juice, and remaining ¼ teaspoon salt in medium bowl; toss to combine.

3 Cut chicken into thin strips. Fill tortillas evenly with chicken, slaw, salsa, and Monterey Jack.

PER SERVING (1 taco): 347 Cal, 12 g Total Fat, 4 g Sat Fat, 0 g Trans Fat, 97 mg Chol, 928 mg Sod, 21 g Carb, 4 g Fib, 39 g Prot, 144 mg Calc.

PointsPlus value: **9.**

fresh food fast

Think it's impossible to make a fresh dinner on a weeknight? Think again. With the quick, easy recipes in this chapter and these time-saving tips, you're just minutes away from a home-cooked meal.

Sharpen Up   Sharp knives and peelers get the job done faster. If your vegetable peeler is dull, replace it with a new one.

Bag It   Buy frozen veggies in bags rather than boxes. The pieces aren't stuck together so they thaw faster and you can easily take what you need for a recipe from the bag.

Buy Some Time   Pre-prepped ingredients cost a little more, but are worth it when you are in a time crunch. Prewashed salad greens, cut-up vegetables, minced garlic, shredded cheese, peeled shrimp, and rotisserie chicken will help you get dinner done faster.

Jump-Start   Steal this time-saving trick employed by television chefs: Before you begin preparing a meal, gather all your ingredients and tools and arrange them on your countertop in roughly the order in which you'll need them.

Chop Right   Chop onions, celery, or carrots for soups, casseroles, or meat loaf in a food processor.

Think Small   Foods cut into small pieces cook faster. Slice poultry, meats, and vegetables into thin slices or small cubes before cooking.

Turn Up the Heat   To bring water to a boil quickly, start with hot tap water, set the burner on the highest heat setting, and cover the pot with a lid.

Keep on Cooking   Make the most of time spent waiting for water to boil or the oven to preheat by chopping ingredients for the main dish or making a salad to serve alongside.

Clean as You Go   As you use bowls, measuring cups, and pans, wash or stack them in the dishwasher when you have a minute. This clears up counter space and saves time with final clean-up.

gingery chicken and vegetable stir-fry

Serves 4 • Ready in 20 minutes or less

⅔ cup reduced-sodium chicken broth
3 tablespoons oyster sauce
1 tablespoon reduced-sodium soy sauce
1 tablespoon cornstarch
4 teaspoons Asian (dark) sesame oil
1 pound skinless boneless chicken breasts, cut into thin strips

1 (12-ounce) package fresh stir-fry vegetables (broccoli, carrots, and sugar snap peas)
1 tablespoon grated peeled fresh ginger

1   Whisk together broth, oyster sauce, soy sauce, and cornstarch in small bowl until smooth.

2   Heat large nonstick skillet or wok over medium heat. Pour in 2 teaspoons oil and swirl to coat pan. Add chicken and stir-fry until chicken is browned and cooked through, about 4 minutes. Transfer chicken to plate.

3   Heat remaining 2 teaspoons oil in same skillet. Add vegetables and ginger; stir-fry until vegetables are crisp-tender, about 2 minutes. Add chicken to pan. Re-whisk broth mixture and add to pan. Cook, stirring constantly, until mixture bubbles and thickens, about 1 minute.

PER SERVING (¾ cup): 227 Cal, 9 g Total Fat, 2 g Sat Fat, 0 g Trans Fat, 70 mg Chol, 634 mg Sod, 9 g Carb, 3 g Fib, 28 g Prot, 43 mg Calc.
PointsPlus value: **6.**

cook's note

Look for precooked brown rice in pouches near the dry rice at the supermarket. It's a time-saver when you need a quick partner for a stir-fry (½ cup precooked brown rice per serving will increase the *PointsPlus* value by *3*).

soy-ginger-glazed chicken thighs

Serves 4 • *Ready in 20 minutes or less*

⅓ cup reduced-sodium chicken broth
3 tablespoons reduced-sodium soy sauce
2 tablespoons mirin or dry sherry
2 teaspoons grated peeled fresh ginger
1 garlic clove, minced

2 teaspoons sugar
1 teaspoon cornstarch
4 (¼-pound) skinless boneless chicken
    thighs, trimmed
½ teaspoon black pepper

1 Whisk together broth, soy sauce, mirin, ginger, garlic, sugar, and cornstarch in small bowl.

2 Sprinkle chicken thighs with pepper. Spray large nonstick skillet with nonstick spray and set over medium heat. Add chicken and cook until browned, about 2 minutes on each side. Re-whisk cornstarch mixture. Add to skillet and bring to boil. Reduce heat to medium-low and simmer, spooning sauce over chicken, until cooked through and glazed, about 6 minutes.

PER SERVING (1 chicken thigh and 1 tablespoon sauce): 209 Cal, 9 g Total Fat, 3 g Sat Fat, 0 g Trans Fat, 70 mg Chol, 507 mg Sod, 6 g Carb, 0 g Fib, 25 g Prot, 33 mg Calc.
PointsPlus value: **5.**

cook's note

Soba noodles are a quick-cooking pasta made from buckwheat. They are a perfect accompaniment to these saucy chicken thighs (1 cup cooked soba noodles per serving will increase the ***PointsPlus*** value by **3**).

spice-crusted chicken thighs

Serves 4 • Ready in 20 minutes or less

2 teaspoons grated lemon zest
1 teaspoon olive oil
1 teaspoon grated peeled fresh ginger
1 teaspoon ground coriander
¾ teaspoon ground cumin
½ teaspoon salt

¼ teaspoon black pepper
4 (¼-pound) skinless boneless chicken
   thighs, trimmed
1 tablespoon chopped fresh cilantro
Lemon wedges

1 Combine lemon zest, oil, ginger, coriander, cumin, salt, and pepper in large shallow dish. Add chicken and turn to coat.

2 Spray large nonstick skillet with nonstick spray and set over medium heat. Add chicken to skillet and cook, turning occasionally, until well browned and cooked through, about 8 minutes. Sprinkle chicken with cilantro and serve with lemon wedges.

PER SERVING (1 chicken thigh): 141 Cal, 8 g Total Fat, 2 g Sat Fat, 0 g Trans Fat, 57 mg Chol, 345 mg Sod, 1 g Carb, 1 g Fib, 16 g Prot, 18 mg Calc.

PointsPlus value: **4.**

quick chicken fried rice with tomatoes and cilantro

Serves 4 • Ready in 20 minutes or less

1 tablespoon tomato paste
1 tablespoon Asian fish sauce
3 teaspoons canola oil
2 large eggs, lightly beaten
3 scallions, thinly sliced
1 yellow or red bell pepper, diced

2 garlic cloves, minced
2 cups cooked brown rice
1½ cups diced cooked chicken breast
2 plum tomatoes, cut into wedges
1 tablespoon chopped fresh cilantro

1 Whisk together tomato paste and fish sauce in small bowl until smooth.

2 Heat large nonstick skillet or wok over medium heat. Pour in 1 teaspoon oil and swirl to coat pan; add eggs. Stir-fry until firm, about 2 minutes. Transfer eggs to plate.

3 Heat remaining 2 teaspoons oil in same pan. Add scallions, bell pepper, and garlic; stir-fry until softened, about 3 minutes. Add rice and chicken; stir-fry until heated through, about 1 minute. Add tomatoes and tomato paste mixture; stir-fry until the tomatoes are softened, about 2 minutes. Remove pan from heat; stir in eggs and cilantro.

PER SERVING (1¼ cups): 281 Cal, 9 g Total Fat, 2 g Sat Fat, 0 g Trans Fat, 149 mg Chol, 542 mg Sod, 26 g Carb, 4 g Fib, 22 g Prot, 48 mg Calc.

PointsPlus value: *7.*

tuna with ginger-mint sauce

Serves 4 • Ready in 20 minutes or less

¼ cup chopped fresh mint
3 tablespoons finely chopped scallions
1 tablespoon minced peeled fresh ginger
1 garlic clove, minced
3 tablespoons reduced-sodium chicken broth

1 tablespoon lemon juice
2 teaspoons extra-virgin olive oil
¾ teaspoon salt
4 (5-ounce) tuna steaks

1 To make sauce, stir together mint, scallions, ginger, garlic, broth, lemon juice, oil, and ¼ teaspoon salt in small bowl.

2 Sprinkle tuna with remaining ½ teaspoon salt. Spray large skillet with nonstick spray and set over medium-high heat. Place tuna in pan and cook until well browned and just slightly pink in center, 3 minutes per side. Serve tuna with sauce.

PER SERVING (1 tuna steak and 2 tablespoons sauce): 189 Cal, 4 g Total Fat, 1 g Sat Fat, 0 g Trans Fat, 66 mg Chol, 491 mg Sod, 2 g Carb, 0 g Fib, 34 g Prot, 32 mg Calc.
PointsPlus value: **4.**

cook's note

To make it a meal, serve the tuna with steamed broccoli sprinkled with lime juice and salt and pepper to taste, and finish with fresh strawberries for dessert.

**Steamed Bass and Snap Peas
with Soy-Ginger Sauce**

steamed bass and snap peas with soy-ginger sauce

Serves 4 • Ready in 20 minutes or less

4 (5-ounce) striped bass fillets, 1 inch thick
¼ teaspoon salt
2 scallions, cut into 2-inch lengths and thinly sliced lengthwise
⅛ teaspoon red pepper flakes
4 cups sugar snap peas, trimmed

2 tablespoons reduced-sodium soy sauce
1 teaspoon grated peeled fresh ginger
1½ teaspoons rice vinegar
1½ teaspoons Asian (dark) sesame oil
¼ teaspoon chili-garlic paste

1 Sprinkle bass fillets with salt and place in steamer basket; sprinkle with scallions and pepper flakes. Set steamer basket in large skillet over 1 inch of boiling water. Cover tightly and steam 5 minutes. Place peas around fish in steamer basket. Steam until fish is just opaque throughout and peas are crisp-tender, about 2 minutes longer.

2 Meanwhile, to make sauce, stir together soy sauce, ginger, vinegar, oil, and chili-garlic paste in small bowl. Serve fish and peas drizzled with sauce.

PER SERVING (1 striped bass fillet, 1 cup peas, and about 2 teaspoons sauce): 195 Cal, 5 g Total Fat, 1 g Sat Fat, 0 g Trans Fat, 117 mg Chol, 553 mg Sod, 7 g Carb, 2 g Fib, 28 g Prot, 56 mg Calc.

PointsPlus value: **4.**

roasted miso-crusted halibut

Serves 4 • Ready in 20 minutes or less

2 tablespoons white miso
2 tablespoons packed light brown sugar
4 (5-ounce) halibut fillets, about 1 inch thick
2 tablespoons thinly sliced scallions

1 Preheat oven to 425°F and spray a shallow baking dish with nonstick spray.

2 Stir together miso and brown sugar in small bowl; spread over both sides of halibut.

3 Place halibut in baking dish; sprinkle with scallions. Roast fish until just opaque in center, about 10 minutes.

PER SERVING (1 halibut fillet): 145 Cal, 1 g Total Fat, 0 g Sat Fat, 0 g Trans Fat, 54 mg Chol, 314 mg Sod, 10 g Carb, 0 g Fib, 23 g Prot, 20 mg Calc.

PointsPlus value: *3.*

cook's note

Miso is typically used to make miso soup, but it also makes a delicious, salty, mellow-flavored glaze for mild fish fillets. Look for miso in the refrigerated section of Asian markets, natural-foods stores, and large supermarkets.

shrimp and pasta with spicy marinara sauce

Serves 4 • Ready in 20 minutes or less

6 ounces whole wheat capellini
1 tablespoon olive oil
1 small onion, diced
2 garlic cloves, minced
¾ pound peeled and deveined
   medium shrimp

1 cup fat-free marinara sauce
1 cup frozen green peas
¼ teaspoon red pepper flakes
2 tablespoons chopped fresh basil

1 Cook capellini according to package directions, omitting salt if desired. Drain, reserving ¼ cup cooking water.

2 Meanwhile, heat oil in large skillet over medium-high heat. Add onion and garlic; cook, stirring, 1 minute. Add shrimp and cook, stirring often, until almost opaque in center, about 1 minute.

3 Add marinara sauce, peas, and pepper flakes to skillet; bring to boil. Reduce heat and simmer until shrimp are just opaque in center, about 2 minutes. Stir in reserved cooking water and basil. Transfer capellini to serving platter and top with shrimp and sauce.

PER SERVING (¾ cup shrimp and sauce with ¾ cup pasta): 292 Cal, 5 g Total Fat, 1 g Sat Fat, 0 g Trans Fat, 121 mg Chol, 532 mg Sod, 41 g Carb, 6 g Fib, 22 g Prot, 84 mg Calc.

PointsPlus value: **7.**

lemon-pepper shrimp and pasta

Serves 4 • Ready in 20 minutes or less

1 (9-ounce) package refrigerated fresh
    fettuccine
2 teaspoons olive oil
2 garlic cloves, minced
1 pound peeled and deveined
    medium shrimp

1 tablespoon grated lemon zest
½ teaspoon cracked black pepper
2 plum tomatoes, chopped
2 tablespoons chopped fresh
    flat-leaf parsley

1 Cook fettuccine according to package directions, omitting salt if desired. Drain, reserving ¼ cup of cooking water.

2 Meanwhile, heat oil in large skillet over medium-high heat. Add garlic and cook, stirring constantly, until golden, 1 minute. Add shrimp, lemon zest, and pepper and cook, stirring constantly, until shrimp are just opaque in center, about 3 minutes. Add tomatoes and cook until heated through, about 1 minute. Remove from heat and stir in parsley.

3 Divide pasta evenly among 4 serving plates; top evenly with shrimp mixture.

PER SERVING (1 cup pasta with ¾ cup shrimp mixture): 301 Cal, 5 g Total Fat, 1 g Sat Fat, 0 g Trans Fat, 205 mg Chol, 934 mg Sod, 36 g Carb, 2 g Fib, 27 g Prot, 95 mg Calc.

PointsPlus value: **8.**

spicy shrimp with orzo and feta

Serves 4 • Ready in 20 minutes or less

½ pound whole wheat orzo (1⅓ cups)
2 teaspoons olive oil
2 garlic cloves, minced
1 pound peeled and deveined
   medium shrimp
¼ teaspoon red pepper flakes

1 (14-ounce) jar fat-free, no-added-salt
   marinara sauce
6 Kalamata olives, pitted and chopped
2 tablespoons chopped fresh
   flat-leaf parsley
¼ cup crumbled feta

1 Cook orzo according to package directions, omitting salt. Drain and keep warm.

2 Meanwhile, heat oil in large skillet over medium-high heat. Add garlic and cook, stirring constantly, until golden, 1 minute. Add shrimp and pepper flakes and cook, stirring constantly until shrimp are just opaque in center, about 3 minutes. Using slotted spoon, transfer shrimp to plate.

3 Add marinara sauce and olives to skillet; bring to boil. Reduce heat and simmer about 5 minutes. Stir in shrimp and cook just until heated through, about 1 minute longer. Stir in parsley.

4 Divide orzo evenly among 4 serving plates; top evenly with shrimp mixture. Sprinkle with feta.

PER SERVING (about 1 cup shrimp mixture with ⅔ cup orzo): 399 Cal, 7 g Total Fat, 2 g Sat Fat, 0 g Trans Fat, 183 mg Chol, 969 mg Sod, 55 g Carb, 6 g Fib, 31 g Prot, 179 mg Calc.

PointsPlus value: *10.*

shrimp and pasta with rosemary-lemon tomato sauce

Serves 4 • Ready in 20 minutes or less

1 (9-ounce) package refrigerated fresh fettuccine or linguine
3 teaspoons olive oil
1 pound peeled and deveined medium shrimp
2 garlic cloves, minced
4 large plum tomatoes, chopped

½ cup reduced-sodium chicken broth
2 teaspoons grated lemon zest
2 teaspoons minced fresh rosemary
½ teaspoon salt
¼ teaspoon black pepper
2 tablespoons grated Parmesan cheese

1 Cook pasta according to package directions, omitting salt if desired; drain and keep warm.

2 Meanwhile, heat 2 teaspoons oil in large nonstick skillet over medium-high heat. Add shrimp and garlic; cook, stirring often, until shrimp are pink, but not cooked through, about 2 minutes. Transfer to plate.

3 Add remaining 1 teaspoon oil to skillet. Add tomatoes, broth, lemon zest, rosemary, salt, and pepper and cook until tomatoes have softened, about 2 minutes. Add shrimp and cook until just opaque in center, about 1 minute longer.

4 Divide pasta evenly among 4 serving plates; top evenly with shrimp mixture. Sprinkle with Parmesan.

PER SERVING (1 cup pasta, generous ¾ cup sauce, and 1½ teaspoons Parmesan): 330 Cal, 8 g Total Fat, 2 g Sat Fat, 0 g Trans Fat, 202 mg Chol, 806 mg Sod, 37 g Carb, 2 g Fib, 26 g Prot, 105 mg Calc.

PointsPlus value: *8.*

tuna and pasta with roasted peppers

Serves 4 • Ready in 20 minutes or less

½ pound whole wheat fusilli
1 tablespoon olive oil
2 teaspoons grated lemon zest
2 tablespoons lemon juice
¼ teaspoon salt
⅛ teaspoon black pepper
1 (7-ounce) jar roasted red peppers (not oil-packed), drained and sliced

1 (6-ounce) can solid white tuna in water, drained and flaked
1 medium zucchini, halved lengthwise and thinly sliced
3 cups baby arugula

1 Cook pasta according to package directions, omitting salt if desired. Drain. Rinse under cold water until cool and drain again.

2 Meanwhile, whisk together oil, lemon zest and juice, salt, and black pepper in large bowl. Add red peppers, tuna, zucchini, and pasta. Toss to combine. Add arugula and toss to coat.

PER SERVING (about 1½ cups): 297 Cal, 6 g Total Fat, 1 g Sat Fat, 0 g Trans Fat, 16 mg Chol, 628 mg Sod, 47 g Carb, 6 g Fib, 19 g Prot, 67 mg Calc.

PointsPlus value: **8.**

cook's note

To make it a meal, enjoy a refreshing slice of watermelon for dessert with this cool summer salad.

spicy tuna cakes with salsa

Serves 4 • Ready in 20 minutes or less

1 (6-ounce) can solid white tuna in water, drained and flaked
10 reduced-fat tortilla chips, crushed
1 (3-ounce) can chopped mild green chiles, drained
½ cup shredded reduced-fat Monterey Jack cheese

½ red bell pepper, chopped
¼ cup chopped red onion
2 large egg whites
1 tablespoon chopped fresh cilantro
2 teaspoons canola oil
½ cup fat-free salsa

1 Combine tuna, tortilla chips, chiles, cheese, bell pepper, onion, egg whites, and cilantro in medium bowl; stir to mix well. Form into 4 cakes.

2 Heat oil in large nonstick skillet over medium heat. Add cakes and cook until golden brown, about 3 minutes per side. Serve with salsa.

PER SERVING (1 tuna cake with 2 tablespoons salsa): 168 Cal, 7 g Total Fat, 2 g Sat Fat, 0 g Trans Fat, 26 mg Chol, 550 mg Sod, 10 g Carb, 2 g Fib, 16 g Prot, 124 mg Calc.

PointsPlus value: *4.*

tuna and black bean cheeseburgers

Serves 4 • Ready in 20 minutes or less

1 (15½-ounce) can black beans, rinsed
   and drained
1 (6-ounce) can solid white tuna in water,
   drained and flaked
¼ cup chopped fresh cilantro
2 tablespoons reduced-fat mayonnaise
1 tablespoon plain dried bread crumbs

1 teaspoon chili powder
4 tablespoons shredded reduced-fat
   pepper Jack cheese
4 whole wheat hamburger buns, toasted
½ cup fat-free salsa
4 leaf lettuce leaves

1. Place beans in medium bowl; mash using potato masher or fork. Add tuna, cilantro, mayonnaise, bread crumbs, and chili powder and stir to mix well. Form into 4 patties.

2. Spray large nonstick skillet with nonstick spray and set over medium heat. Add patties and spray with nonstick spray. Cook until heated through, about 3 minutes per side. Top each patty with 1 tablespoon cheese; cover and cook until cheese melts, about 1 minute longer.

3. Serve patties in buns topped with salsa and lettuce.

PER SERVING (1 burger): 316 Cal, 6 g Total Fat, 2 g Sat Fat, 0 g Trans Fat, 21 mg Chol, 949 mg Sod, 42 g Carb, 12 g Fib, 24 g Prot, 170 mg Calc.

PointsPlus value: **7.**

gnocchi and squash with red pepper–basil sauce

Serves 4 • Vegetarian • Ready in 20 minutes or less

1 (17½-ounce) package refrigerated whole wheat gnocchi
1 (12-ounce) jar roasted red peppers (not in oil), drained
½ (14-ounce) package light silken tofu
2 teaspoons olive oil

2 garlic cloves, minced
2 yellow squash, halved lengthwise and thinly sliced
¼ teaspoon black pepper
¼ cup chopped fresh basil
2 tablespoons grated Parmesan cheese

1 Cook gnocchi according to package directions, omitting salt if desired; drain and keep warm.

2 Meanwhile, combine roasted peppers and tofu in blender; process until mixture is smooth.

3 Heat oil in large skillet over medium heat. Add garlic and cook, stirring constantly, 1 minute. Add squash and pepper and cook, stirring often, until squash is crisp-tender, 2 minutes. Add roasted pepper mixture and basil to skillet; reduce heat to low and cook until heated through, about 2 minutes.

4 Divide gnocchi evenly among 4 serving plates; top evenly with sauce. Sprinkle with Parmesan.

PER SERVING (about 1½ cups pasta mixture and ½ tablespoon cheese): 299 Cal, 5 g Total Fat, 1 g Sat Fat, 0 g Trans Fat, 2 mg Chol, 921 mg Sod, 55 g Carb, 6 g Fib, 11 g Prot, 110 mg Calc.

PointsPlus value: **8.**

Garlicky Spinach and Fontina Pizza

garlicky spinach and fontina pizza

Serves 6 • Vegetarian • Ready in 20 minutes or less

2 garlic cloves, minced
2 tablespoons water
1 (8-ounce) package baby spinach
1 (10-ounce) prebaked thin whole wheat
  pizza crust

½ cup marinated artichoke hearts, rinsed,
  drained, and chopped
6 Kalamata olives, pitted and sliced
1 cup shredded fontina cheese

1 Preheat oven to 450°F. Spray baking sheet with nonstick spray.

2 Spray medium nonstick skillet with nonstick spray and set over medium heat. Add garlic and cook, stirring constantly, until fragrant, 30 seconds. Add water and spinach, in batches, if necessary, and cook, stirring constantly, until spinach wilts and liquid has evaporated, about 2 minutes.

3 Place crust on baking sheet. Top crust evenly with spinach, artichokes, and olives. Sprinkle evenly with fontina. Bake until cheese has melted, about 8 minutes. Cut into 6 wedges.

PER SERVING (1 wedge): 215 Cal, 8 g Total Fat, 4 g Sat Fat, 0 g Trans Fat, 15 mg Chol, 435 mg Sod, 26 g Carb, 5 g Fib, 12 g Prot, 270 mg Calc.

PointsPlus value: *6.*

Pear and Sage Stuffing,
page 310, and Fresh
Cranberry Sauce with
Dried Apricots, page 319

side dishes

asparagus with chopped egg and dill

Serves 6 • Vegetarian • Ready in 20 minutes or less

2 tablespoons white-wine vinegar
1 tablespoon olive oil
1 small shallot, minced
2 teaspoons Dijon mustard
¼ teaspoon salt

⅛ teaspoon black pepper
1 hard-cooked egg, peeled
1½ pounds asparagus, trimmed
1 tablespoon chopped fresh dill

1 To make dressing, whisk together vinegar, oil, shallot, mustard, salt, and pepper in small bowl.

2 Halve egg; finely chop egg white. Press yolk through coarse sieve.

3 Put asparagus in steamer basket set in large pot over 1 inch boiling water. Cover tightly and steam until spears are crisp-tender, about 4 minutes. Transfer to platter. Stir dill into dressing and spoon over asparagus; sprinkle with egg.

PER SERVING (5 asparagus spears and about 2 teaspoons dressing): 51 Cal, 3 g Total Fat, 1 g Sat Fat, 0 g Trans Fat, 31 mg Chol, 151 mg Sod, 3 g Carb, 1 g Fib, 3 g Prot, 22 mg Calc.

PointsPlus value: *1.*

grilled bell peppers with olives

Serves 6 • Vegetarian • Ready in 20 minutes or less

4 large red or yellow bell peppers or
   combination
2 tablespoons red-wine vinegar
2½ teaspoons olive oil
¼ teaspoon salt

¼ teaspoon black pepper
⅓ cup brine-cured pitted Kalamata olives,
   finely chopped
¼ cup chopped fresh flat-leaf parsley

1. Spray grill rack with nonstick spray; preheat grill to medium or prepare medium fire.

2. Cut each pepper lengthwise into 6 strips; discard stems and seeds. Lightly spray peppers with olive oil nonstick spray. Place peppers on grill rack; grill, turning once, until tender and slightly charred, 10–12 minutes.

3. Stir together vinegar, oil, salt, pepper, and olives in medium bowl. Add peppers and toss to coat. Stir in parsley.

PER SERVING (½ cup): 46 Cal, 2 g Total Fat, 0 g Sat Fat, 0 g Trans Fat, 0 mg Chol, 147 mg Sod, 6 g Carb, 2 g Fib, 1 g Prot, 12 mg Calc.

PointsPlus value: *1.*

cook's note

For a tangy counterpoint to the peppers, sprinkle them with crumbled feta cheese just before serving. Adding ⅓ cup crumbled feta cheese to the recipe will increase the per-serving *PointsPlus* value by *1.*

balsamic-marinated roasted peppers with basil

Serves 4 • Vegetarian

4 large red or yellow bell peppers or combination
1 tablespoon balsamic vinegar
2 tablespoons capers, drained and rinsed

2 teaspoons olive oil
2 garlic cloves, minced
¼ teaspoon salt
2 tablespoons chopped fresh basil

1 Preheat broiler; place peppers on baking sheet and broil 5 inches from heat, turning occasionally, until blackened on all sides, 12–15 minutes. Transfer peppers to a paper bag and fold closed; let steam 10 minutes.

2 When cool enough to handle, peel and seed peppers and cut into thick slices; transfer to medium bowl. Add vinegar, capers, oil, garlic, and salt and toss to combine. Let stand at least 15 minutes or up to 1 hour. Stir in basil just before serving.

PER SERVING (about ¾ cup): 71 Cal, 3 g Total Fat, 0 g Sat Fat, 0 g Trans Fat, 0 mg Chol, 279 mg Sod, 12 g Carb, 2 g Fib, 2 g Prot, 22 mg Calc.
PointsPlus value: **2.**

cook's note

To make it a meal, toss a serving of the peppers with 3 ounces drained water-packed tuna and serve on a bed of greens for an easy lunch (3 ounces drained water-packed tuna per serving will increase the ***PointsPlus*** value by **2**).

green beans and mushrooms with walnuts

Serves 6 • Vegetarian

1½ pounds green beans, trimmed
2 teaspoons olive oil
1 shallot, halved and thinly sliced
6 ounces cremini mushrooms, sliced

1 tablespoon minced fresh thyme
¼ teaspoon salt
⅛ teaspoon black pepper
2 tablespoons toasted walnuts, chopped

1 Bring large pot of water to boil; add beans and cook just until bright green and tender, about 5 minutes.

2 Meanwhile, heat oil in large skillet over medium heat. Add shallot and cook, stirring, until softened, about 3 minutes. Add mushrooms and cook until liquid evaporates and mushrooms begin to brown, about 6 minutes. Add beans, thyme, salt, and pepper; cook, stirring often, 2 minutes. Transfer to serving dish and sprinkle with walnuts.

PER SERVING (1 cup): 70 Cal, 3 g Total Fat, 0 g Sat Fat, 0 g Trans Fat, 0 mg Chol, 102 mg Sod, 10 g Carb, 3 g Fib, 3 g Prot, 52 mg Calc.

PointsPlus value: *2.*

cook's note

To make the green beans for serving with the Thanksgiving Dinner menu (page 380), double all the ingredients and prepare as directed using a large deep skillet.

lemon green beans with pine nuts

Serves 6 • Vegetarian

1½ pounds slender green beans or haricots verts, trimmed
3 tablespoons lemon juice
1 tablespoon olive oil
2 teaspoons Dijon mustard
½ teaspoon salt

⅛ teaspoon black pepper
2 scallions, thinly sliced
2 tablespoons chopped fresh flat-leaf parsley
2 tablespoons pine nuts, toasted

1 Bring large pot of water to boil; add beans and cook just until bright green and tender, about 3 minutes. Drain well.

2 Whisk together lemon juice, oil, mustard, salt, and pepper in large bowl. Add beans and scallions and toss to coat. Stir in parsley. Transfer to serving platter and sprinkle with pine nuts. Serve warm, at room temperature, or chilled.

PER SERVING (1 cup): 77 Cal, 5 g Total Fat, 1 g Sat Fat, 0 g Trans Fat, 0 mg Chol, 239 mg Sod, 9 g Carb, 3 g Fib, 2 g Prot, 48 mg Calc.
PointsPlus value: **2.**

cook's note

To make the green beans for serving with the Passover Dinner menu (page 379), double all the ingredients and prepare as directed.

green beans with feta and mint

Serves 6 • Vegetarian

1 pound green beans, trimmed
2 teaspoons grated lime zest
2 tablespoons lime juice
1 tablespoon olive oil
½ teaspoon salt
⅛ teaspoon black pepper
4 plum tomatoes, chopped

1 small red onion, thinly sliced
½ large seedless (English) cucumber, peeled, halved, and thinly sliced
2 tablespoons chopped fresh mint
½ cup crumbled feta cheese

1 Bring large pot of water to boil; add beans and cook just until bright green and tender, about 5 minutes. Drain beans, cool under cold running water, and drain again.

2 Whisk together lime zest and juice, oil, salt, and pepper in large bowl. Add beans, tomatoes, onion, cucumber, and mint; toss to coat. Transfer to serving platter; sprinkle with feta.

PER SERVING (1 cup): 89 Cal, 5 g Total Fat, 2 g Sat Fat, 0 g Trans Fat, 11 mg Chol, 343 mg Sod, 9 g Carb, 3 g Fib, 4 g Prot, 99 mg Calc.

PointsPlus value: **2.**

how to
boil and simmer

To cook foods such as pasta or vegetables until tender in a pot of boiling water.

what you need

A pot with a lid that is large enough to hold the food without overcrowding is all that's required.

how it's done

For pastas and quick-cooking vegetables, fill a large pot two-thirds full with water and bring to a boil. Add the food and cook, uncovered, until tender. For foods that take longer to cook, such as potatoes, beets, grains, and dried beans, add them to the pot with cold water and bring to a boil (grains and beans are usually cooked in a specific amount of water). Reduce heat, cover, and simmer until tender.

To test the food for doneness, remove a piece with a slotted spoon. Pastas should be tender, yet firm to the bite. Vegetables such as broccoli and green beans should be crisp-tender. Dense vegetables should be cooked until fork-tender. Cook grains and dried beans until they are tender, yet hold their shape.

honey-roasted carrots

Serves 2 • Vegetarian

2 cups baby carrots
1 tablespoon honey
1 teaspoon olive oil

⅛ teaspoon salt
Pinch black pepper
2 teaspoons minced fresh chives

1 Preheat oven to 425°F. Spray small baking pan with nonstick spray.

2 Combine carrots, honey, oil, salt, and pepper in medium bowl; toss to coat carrots. Spread carrots evenly in pan. Roast, stirring occasionally, until carrots are caramelized and tender, 25–30 minutes. Stir in chives.

PER SERVING (1 cup): 108 Cal, 2 g Total Fat, 0 g Sat Fat, 0 g Trans Fat, 0 mg Chol, 131 mg Sod, 21 g Carb, 3 g Fib, 1 g Prot, 28 mg Calc.

PointsPlus value: **3.**

cook's note

If you're challenged by getting your children to eat their vegetables, these irresistibly sweet carrots should win them over.

rosemary-roasted brussels sprouts and carrots

Serves 6   •   Vegetarian

½ pound peeled baby carrots, halved
   lengthwise
1 pint Brussels sprouts, halved
2 shallots, thickly sliced
2 teaspoons olive oil

2 teaspoons fresh minced rosemary
½ teaspoon salt
¼ teaspoon black pepper
1 tablespoon red-wine vinegar

1 Preheat oven to 400°F. Place carrots, Brussels sprouts, and shallots on large baking sheet. Drizzle with oil, sprinkle with rosemary, salt, and pepper, and toss to coat.

2 Roast until carrots are just tender and Brussels sprouts and shallots begin to brown, 35–40 minutes, stirring once halfway through cooking time. Toss with vinegar.

PER SERVING (scant ⅔ cup): 44 Cal, 2 g Total Fat, 0 g Sat Fat, 0 g Trans Fat, 0 mg Chol, 263 mg Sod, 7 g Carb, 2 g Fib, 1 g Prot, 23 mg Calc.

PointsPlus value: *1.*

cook's note

To make this dish for serving with the Christmas Dinner menu (page 380), double all the ingredients and prepare as directed.

italian stuffed artichokes

Serves 6 • Vegetarian

2 lemons, halved
6 large artichokes
1¼ cups multigrain croutons, crushed
¼ cup grated Parmesan cheese
¼ cup chopped fresh basil

1 tablespoon chopped fresh oregano
1 tablespoon olive oil
2 garlic cloves, minced
¼ cup reduced-sodium vegetable broth

1 Fill large nonreactive pot two-thirds full of water and bring to boil over high heat.

2 Meanwhile, squeeze lemons into large bowl of water; drop in lemon halves. One artichoke at a time, snap off and discard dark green outer leaves, leaving light green leaves exposed. With paring knife, peel tough skin from stem. Slice off and discard top 1 inch of artichoke leaves. Drop artichoke into bowl of lemon water. Repeat with remaining artichokes.

3 Put artichokes and lemon halves into boiling water; return water to boil. Reduce heat, cover, and simmer until paring knife inserted into bottom of artichokes goes in easily, about 20 minutes. Drain artichokes, cool briefly under cold running water, and drain again. Slice each artichoke in half lengthwise and use small spoon to scoop out and discard fuzzy choke and any violet-tipped leaves surrounding choke.

4 Preheat oven to 400°F. Spray 9 × 13-inch baking dish with nonstick spray. Combine croutons, Parmesan, basil, oregano, oil, and garlic in medium bowl. Fill center of each artichoke half with 1 heaping tablespoon crouton mixture; spray tops lightly with nonstick spray. Place artichoke halves in baking dish. Pour broth around artichokes. Cover with foil and roast 15 minutes. Remove foil and roast until topping is browned, 15–20 minutes longer.

PER SERVING (2 stuffed artichoke halves): 146 Cal, 4 g Total Fat, 2 g Sat Fat, 0 g Trans Fat, 2 mg Chol, 286 mg Sod, 24 g Carb, 10 g Fib, 8 g Prot, 134 mg Calc.

PointsPlus value: *4.*

roasted ratatouille

Serves 6 • Vegetarian

1½ pounds eggplant, cut into ½-inch cubes
1 pound zucchini, cut into ½-inch cubes
1 large onion, chopped
1 red bell pepper, cut into ½-inch pieces
1 tablespoon plus 2 teaspoons olive oil

¾ teaspoon salt
¼ teaspoon black pepper
3 garlic cloves, minced
1 (14½-ounce) can diced tomatoes
¼ cup chopped fresh basil

1 Place oven racks in upper third and lower third of oven. Preheat oven to 450°F. Spray 2 large baking sheets with nonstick spray.

2 Combine eggplant, zucchini, onion, and bell pepper in large bowl; drizzle with 1 tablespoon oil, sprinkle with ½ teaspoon salt and 1/8 teaspoon pepper, and toss to coat. Spread vegetables on prepared baking sheets and roast, tossing occasionally and rotating baking sheets top to bottom once, until vegetables are tender and lightly browned, about 30 minutes. Transfer to large bowl.

3 Heat remaining 2 teaspoons oil in large nonstick skillet over medium heat. Add garlic and cook, stirring constantly, until fragrant, 30 seconds. Add tomatoes and remaining ¼ teaspoon salt and 1/8 teaspoon pepper and cook, stirring occasionally, until mixture begins to thicken, about 5 minutes. Add roasted vegetables and basil; cook, stirring often, until heated through.

PER SERVING (¾ cup): 104 Cal, 4 g Total Fat, 1 g Sat Fat, 0 g Trans Fat, 0 mg Chol, 403 mg Sod, 16 g Carb, 6 g Fib, 3 g Prot, 57 mg Calc.

PointsPlus value: **3.**

cook's note

To turn this side dish into a main dish, serve the ratatouille over whole wheat pasta (1 cup cooked whole wheat linguine per serving will increase the **PointsPlus** value by **4**).

roasted eggplant, tomato, and mozzarella stacks

Serves 4 • Vegetarian

1 large eggplant
½ teaspoon salt
¼ teaspoon black pepper
2 tablespoons white-wine vinegar
1 tablespoon olive oil
1 tablespoon reduced-sodium vegetable broth or water

½ teaspoon Dijon mustard
1 large tomato, ends trimmed, cut into 8 slices
12 large fresh basil leaves
8 tablespoons shredded part-skim mozzarella cheese

1 Preheat oven to 400°F. Spray large rimmed baking sheet with nonstick spray.

2 Trim both ends off eggplant and cut into 12 rounds. Arrange eggplant on baking sheet in one layer and spray lightly with nonstick spray; sprinkle with ¼ teaspoon salt and 1/8 teaspoon pepper. Roast, turning once, until lightly browned, about 20 minutes. Let cool slightly.

3 To make dressing, whisk together vinegar, oil, broth, mustard, and remaining ¼ teaspoon salt and 1/8 teaspoon pepper in small bowl.

4 To assemble stacks, place 4 of largest eggplant slices on platter. Drizzle evenly with 1 tablespoon dressing; top each with 1 slice of tomato and 1 basil leaf. Sprinkle each with 1 tablespoon mozzarella. Repeat layering once. Top each stack with 1 slice of eggplant, drizzle evenly with remaining 2 tablespoons dressing and top with remaining basil leaves.

PER SERVING (1 eggplant stack): 129 Cal, 7 g Total Fat, 2 g Sat Fat, 0 g Trans Fat, 8 mg Chol, 415 mg Sod, 12 g Carb, 6 g Fib, 6 g Prot, 128 mg Calc.

PointsPlus value: *3.*

Roasted Eggplant, Tomato, and Mozzarella Stacks

creamed collards

Serves 8 • Vegetarian

3 teaspoons olive oil
2 Vidalia or other sweet onions, thinly sliced
4 garlic cloves, chopped
2 large bunches collard greens, tough stems removed and discarded, leaves coarsely chopped (about 16 cups)
½ cup water

¾ teaspoon salt
2 tablespoons all-purpose flour
2 cups fat-free milk
¼ teaspoon ground nutmeg
4 slices turkey bacon, coarsely chopped, and cooked until crisp

1 Heat 1 teaspoon oil in large skillet over medium-high heat. Add onions and garlic and cook, stirring occasionally, until soft, 6–8 minutes. Add collards to skillet a few handfuls at a time, stirring and allowing leaves to wilt slightly before adding more. Add water and ½ teaspoon salt; bring to boil. Reduce heat and simmer, covered, until collards have softened, about 15 minutes.

2 Meanwhile, heat remaining 2 teaspoons oil in medium saucepan over medium-high heat. Add flour and cook, stirring constantly, 1 minute. Whisk in milk, nutmeg, and remaining ¼ teaspoon salt; bring to boil. Reduce heat and simmer, whisking occasionally, until mixture thickens, about 5 minutes. Remove saucepan from heat, cover, and set aside.

3 Add milk mixture to collards. Reduce heat and simmer, covered, stirring occasionally, until collards are fork-tender, 35–40 minutes. Transfer to serving bowl; sprinkle with bacon.

PER SERVING (¾ cup): 91 Cal, 4 g Total Fat, 1 g Sat Fat, 0 g Trans Fat, 8 mg Chol, 341 mg Sod, 11 g Carb, 3 g Fib, 5 g Prot, 184 mg Calc.
***PointsPlus* value: 2.**

oven-roasted kale with caramelized onions

Serves 6 • Vegetarian

2 (¾-pound) bunches kale, tough stems
  removed and discarded, leaves
  thinly sliced
4 teaspoons olive oil
½ teaspoon salt

⅛ teaspoon black pepper
1 large onion, thinly sliced
4 garlic cloves, thinly sliced
¼ teaspoon red pepper flakes
2 teaspoons balsamic vinegar

1 Preheat oven to 450°F. Spray large baking sheet with nonstick spray.

2 Toss kale in large bowl with 2 teaspoons oil, ¼ teaspoon salt, and pepper. Transfer to baking sheet and roast, stirring once halfway through cooking time, until edges of kale begin to brown, about 10 minutes.

3 Meanwhile, heat remaining 2 teaspoons oil in large nonstick skillet over medium heat. Add onion, garlic, pepper flakes, and remaining ¼ teaspoon salt. Cook, stirring occasionally, until onions are golden, 10–15 minutes. Stir in vinegar and cook 1 minute. Add kale and cook, stirring, until hot, about 1 minute longer.

PER SERVING (1 cup): 73 Cal, 4 g Total Fat, 1 g Sat Fat, 0 g Trans Fat, 0 mg Chol, 223 mg Sod, 10 g Carb, 3 g Fib, 3 g Prot, 97 mg Calc.

PointsPlus value: 2.

cook's note

To add more color and flavor to this dish, add 1 large tomato, chopped, when you add the kale in step 3.

almost-instant side dishes

If you're at a loss for what to serve with quick-cooking main dishes to turn them into a full meal with minimal effort, here are some super-fast options (all done in 20 minutes or less):

Israeli couscous

Precooked brown rice (find it in pouches near the dry rice)

Quick-cooking brown rice and barley

Quinoa

Refrigerated fresh pasta, such as linguine and fettuccine

Refrigerated whole wheat gnocchi

Rice noodles

Soba noodles

Whole wheat capellini (angel hair) pasta

Whole wheat couscous

Whole wheat orzo

Or try fresh vegetables that require minimal prep and cook quickly, such as:

Asparagus

Bell Peppers

Broccoli

Broccolini

Prewashed Spinach

Yellow Squash

Zucchini

Or frozen plain vegetables, such as:

Cauliflower florets

Corn

Green Beans

Green Peas

Sugar Snap Peas

chili-lime corn on the cob

Serves 6 · Vegetarian · Ready in 20 minutes or less

4 ears corn, each cut into thirds
1 tablespoon lime juice
1½ teaspoons olive oil
¼ teaspoon ground cumin

½ teaspoon salt
1 teaspoon chili powder
¼ cup whole cilantro leaves
Lime wedges

1 Bring large pot of lightly salted water to boil. Add corn; cover pot and boil corn 2 minutes.

2 Meanwhile, whisk together lime juice, oil, cumin, and salt in small dish.

3 Drain corn, place on serving platter; brush with lime juice mixture. Sprinkle with chili powder and cilantro. Serve with lime wedges.

PER SERVING (2 pieces of corn): 64 Cal, 2 g Total Fat, 0 g Sat Fat, 0 g Trans Fat, 0 mg Chol, 206 mg Sod, 12 g Carb, 2 g Fib, 2 g Prot, 3 mg Calc.

PointsPlus value: *2.*

grill-roasted fingerling potatoes

Serves 6 • Vegetarian

1½ pounds fingerling or other small
    potatoes, each halved lengthwise
1 small sweet onion, halved and
    thinly sliced

2 teaspoons olive oil
½ teaspoon salt
¼ teaspoon black pepper
¼ cup chopped fresh chives

1 Spray grill rack with nonstick spray; preheat grill to medium or prepare medium fire.

2 Combine potatoes, onion, oil, salt, and pepper in medium bowl and toss to coat. Using 18-inch-wide heavy-duty foil, layer two 20 × 18-inch sheets on top of each other to make double thickness. Spray top sheet of foil with nonstick spray. Place potato mixture in center of foil. Fold foil into packet, making a tight seal.

3 Place packet on grill rack and cook, turning occasionally, until potatoes are fork-tender, about 25 minutes. Open packet carefully (steam will escape), transfer potato mixture to bowl, and toss with chives.

PER SERVING (⅔ cup): 106 Cal, 2 g Total Fat, 0 g Sat Fat, 0 g Trans Fat, 0 mg Chol, 204 mg Sod, 21 g Carb, 2 g Fib, 3 g Prot, 19 mg Calc.

PointsPlus value: **3.**

warm potato salad with mustard dressing

Serves 4 • Vegetarian

1¼ pounds red potatoes
2 teaspoons olive oil
1 red onion, halved and thinly sliced
2 tablespoons apple cider vinegar
2 tablespoons Dijon mustard

2 tablespoons water
¼ teaspoon salt
¼ teaspoon black pepper
2 tablespoons chopped fresh
   flat-leaf parsley

1 Put potatoes in medium saucepan and add enough water to cover by 1 inch; bring to boil. Reduce heat, cover, and simmer just until potatoes are fork-tender, 13–15 minutes. Drain potatoes and set aside until cool enough to handle. Cut warm potatoes into ½-inch chunks.

2 Meanwhile, heat oil in medium skillet over medium heat. Add onion and cook, stirring occasionally, until tender, about 6 minutes. Stir in vinegar, mustard, water, salt, and pepper; bring to boil. Remove skillet from heat, add potatoes, and stir gently with rubber spatula until coated. Transfer to serving bowl; add parsley and toss to combine.

PER SERVING (½ cup): 171 Cal, 3 g Total Fat, 0 g Sat Fat, 0 g Trans Fat, 0 mg Chol, 334 mg Sod, 32 g Carb, 3 g Fiber, 4 g Prot, 24 mg Calc.

PointsPlus value: *4.*

cook's note

To make it a meal, add a chopped hard-cooked egg to a serving of the potato salad, and serve it on a bed of greens for a satisfying lunch (1 large hard-cooked egg per serving will increase the *PointsPlus* value by *2*).

mashed potatoes with leeks and garlic

Serves 4 • Vegetarian

2 teaspoons olive oil
2 large leeks, white and pale green part,
    thinly sliced
2 cups reduced-sodium vegetable broth
1 pound baking potatoes, peeled and cut in
    1-inch cubes

3 garlic cloves, chopped
3 tablespoons fat-free milk
¼ teaspoon black pepper

1 Heat oil in large saucepan over medium-high heat. Add leeks and ¼ cup broth. Simmer, stirring occasionally, until leeks are softened and liquid has evaporated, about 6 minutes.

2 Add potatoes, garlic, and remaining 1¾ cups broth; bring to boil. Reduce heat and simmer, partially covered, until potatoes are fork-tender and most of liquid is absorbed, about 20 minutes. Remove saucepan from heat; stir in milk and pepper. Coarsely mash potatoes.

PER SERVING (¾ cup): 159 Cal, 3 g Total Fat, 1 g Sat Fat, 0 g Trans Fat, 0 mg Chol, 204 mg Sod, 29 g Carb, 4 g Fib, 5 g Prot, 73 mg Calc.

PointsPlus value: **4.**

cook's note

Cooking the potatoes in broth adds rich flavor to the finished dish. If you prefer, you can use chicken broth instead of vegetable broth.

parsnip and potato mash with chives

Serves 6 • Vegetarian

1¼ pounds parsnips (about 8), peeled and
    cut into 1-inch slices
¾ pound Yukon Gold potatoes (about 4),
    peeled and cubed

¼ cup fat-free milk
½ teaspoon salt
¼ teaspoon black pepper
1 tablespoon minced fresh chives

1 Put parsnips and potatoes in large pot and add enough water to cover by 1 inch; bring to boil over high heat. Reduce heat and simmer until vegetables are very tender, about 20 minutes.

2 Drain vegetables and transfer to large bowl. Add milk, salt, and pepper and coarsely mash. Stir in chives.

PER SERVING (½ cup): 134 Cal, 0 g Total Fat, 0 g Sat Fat, 0 g Trans Fat, 0 mg Chol, 215 mg Sod, 30 g Carb, 5 g Fib, 3 g Prot, 50 mg Calc.

PointsPlus value: **3.**

cook's note

To make this side dish for serving with the Christmas Dinner menu (page 380), double all the ingredients and prepare as directed.

potato-turnip latkes

Serves 6 • Vegetarian

½ cup fat-free sour cream
1 tablespoon grated peeled fresh
   horseradish or prepared horseradish,
   drained
1 pound russet potatoes, peeled and
   shredded
1 (¼-pound) turnip, peeled and shredded

½ small onion, shredded
1 large egg, lightly beaten
2 tablespoons all-purpose flour
½ teaspoon salt
¼ teaspoon black pepper
3 teaspoons canola oil
Chopped chives

1 Combine sour cream and horseradish in small bowl; cover and refrigerate.

2 Combine potatoes, turnip, onion, egg, flour, salt, and pepper in large bowl; mix well. Form potato mixture into 12 disks, each about 2½ inches in diameter.

3 Heat 1½ teaspoons oil in large nonstick skillet over medium heat. Place 6 latkes in skillet and cook until browned and cooked through, 3–4 minutes per side; lower heat if latkes brown too quickly. Transfer to platter. Repeat with remaining oil and potato mixture. Sprinkle with chives and serve immediately with sour cream mixture.

PER SERVING (2 latkes and 2 teaspoons sour cream): 136 Cal, 4 g Total Fat, 0 g Sat Fat, 0 g Trans Fat, 38 mg Chol, 248 mg Sod, 22 g Carb, 2 g Fib, 4 g Prot, 550 mg Calc.

PointsPlus value: **4.**

Potato-Turnip Latkes

honey-glazed sweet potato fries

Serves 4 • Vegetarian

4 medium sweet potatoes, peeled
2 teaspoons canola oil
2 tablespoons lemon juice

1 tablespoon honey
¼ teaspoon salt

1 Preheat oven to 400°F. Line large rimmed baking sheet with foil; spray with nonstick spray.

2 Halve potatoes lengthwise and cut each piece lengthwise into thirds. Place on baking sheet; drizzle with oil and toss to coat. Arrange in single layer on pan with cut sides down. Roast until browned on bottom, 12–15 minutes. Turn potatoes onto opposite cut sides and roast until browned, 10 minutes longer.

3 To make glaze, stir together lemon juice, honey, and salt in small bowl. Brush potatoes with glaze and roast, turning and basting, until potatoes are tender, 6–8 minutes longer.

PER SERVING (6 wedges): 140 Cal, 2 g Total Fat, 0 g Sat Fat, 0 g Trans Fat, 0 mg Chol, 189 mg Sod, 28 g Carb, 4 g Fib, 2 g Prot, 45 mg Calc.

PointsPlus value: *3.*

maple-orange mashed sweet potatoes

Serves 6 • Vegetarian

2 pounds sweet potatoes (3 medium),
    peeled and quartered
2 teaspoons grated orange zest
⅓ cup orange juice

1 tablespoon pure maple syrup
1 tablespoon unsalted butter
¼ teaspoon cinnamon
½ teaspoon salt

1 Put potatoes in large saucepan and cover with cold water; bring to boil. Reduce heat and simmer until potatoes are very tender, about 20 minutes.

2 Drain potatoes and transfer to large bowl. Add orange zest and juice, maple syrup, butter, cinnamon, and salt and coarsely mash.

PER SERVING (½ cup): 115 Cal, 2 g Total Fat, 1 g Sat Fat, 0 g Trans Fat, 5 mg Chol, 230 mg Sod, 23 g Carb, 3 g Fib, 2 g Prot, 43 mg Calc.

PointsPlus value: *3.*

cook's note

To make the sweet potatoes for serving with the Thanksgiving Dinner menu (page 380), double all the ingredients and prepare as directed using a large Dutch oven.

root vegetable and apple slaw

Serves 4 • Vegetarian

⅓ cup apple cider vinegar
2½ teaspoons sugar
½ teaspoon salt
½ teaspoon celery seeds
⅛ teaspoon red pepper flakes
2 cups thinly sliced red cabbage

2 celery stalks, thinly sliced
2 large carrots, shredded
2 parsnip roots, peeled and shredded
2 Granny Smith apples, unpeeled, cored
   and cut into matchstick strips

1 Whisk together vinegar, sugar, salt, celery seeds, and pepper flakes in medium bowl until sugar dissolves. Add cabbage, celery, carrots, and parsnips; toss to coat. Cover and refrigerate at least 1 hour or overnight.

2 Stir in apples just before serving.

PER SERVING (1 cup): 112 Cal, 1 g Total Fat, 0 g Sat Fat, 0 g Trans Fat, 0 mg Chol, 339 mg Sod, 28 g Carb, 6 g Fib, 2 g Prot, 60 mg Calc.

PointsPlus value: *3.*

cook's note

The combination of tart apples, sweet carrots, and peppery parsnip root makes this flavorful recipe a refreshing change from ordinary slaw.

celery root salad

¼ cup reduced-fat mayonnaise
2 teaspoons Dijon mustard
¼ teaspoon salt
¼ teaspoon black pepper

1½ pounds celeriac (celery root), peeled
    and shredded
2 tablespoons chopped fresh
    flat-leaf parsley

Whisk together mayonnaise, mustard, salt, and pepper in large bowl; add celeriac and parsley and stir to combine. Serve at once, or cover and refrigerate up to 1 day.

PER SERVING (¾ cup): 111 Cal, 4 g Total Fat, 1 g Sat Fat, 0 g Trans Fat, 4 mg Chol, 508 mg Sod, 17 g Carb, 3 g Fib, 3 g Prot, 79 mg Calc.

PointsPlus value: *3.*

cook's note

If you like the robust flavor of whole grain mustard, it's a delicious option for using in this recipe.

pear and sage stuffing

Serves 12

12 slices (½ pound) reduced-calorie whole
    grain sandwich bread, diced
1 tablespoon olive oil
1 tablespoon unsalted butter
5 celery stalks, thinly sliced
3 firm-ripe pears, cored and diced
1 large onion, diced

2 tablespoons minced fresh sage or
    2 teaspoons dried
½ teaspoon salt
1 teaspoon black pepper
2 cups reduced-sodium chicken broth
½ cup chopped fresh flat-leaf parsley

1　Preheat oven to 250°F. Place bread on large baking sheet and bake until dried, about
20 minutes. Transfer to large bowl.

2　Increase oven temperature to 350°F. Spray 9 × 13-inch baking dish with nonstick spray.

3　Heat oil and butter in large skillet over medium-high heat until butter has melted.
Add celery, pears, onion, sage, salt, and pepper; cook, stirring frequently, until pears are
softened, 7–8 minutes. Add celery mixture to bowl with bread; toss to combine. Add
broth and parsley and toss again.

4　Spoon stuffing into prepared baking dish. Bake until browned and crisp on top, about
30 minutes.

PER SERVING (¾ cup): 92 Cal, 3 g Total Fat, 1 g Sat Fat, 0 g Trans Fat, 3 mg Chol, 234 mg Sod,
16 g Carb, 4 g Fib, 3 g Prot, 37 mg Calc.
PointsPlus value: *2.*

cook's note

You can use this stuffing to stuff the Honey-Brined Turkey with Homemade Gravy,
page 164. To do so, prepare the stuffing through step 3, spoon the stuffing into
the turkey, and bake the turkey at once. This recipe makes about 9 cups, enough
to stuff a turkey up to 16 pounds; any extra stuffing can be baked in a baking dish
sprayed with nonstick spray during the last 30 minutes of baking the turkey.

asparagus-mushroom matzo farfel

Serves 6

2 teaspoons olive oil
1 onion, chopped
½ pound sliced mixed mushrooms
½ teaspoon salt
½ pound asparagus, trimmed and cut into
    1-inch pieces
½ cup frozen peas

3 garlic cloves, finely chopped
¼ teaspoon dried thyme
2 cups whole wheat matzo farfel
½ cup reduced-sodium chicken broth
2 large eggs, lightly beaten
1 large egg white, lightly beaten
¼ teaspoon black pepper

1 Preheat oven to 350°F. Spray 1½-quart baking dish with nonstick spray.

2 Heat oil in large nonstick skillet over medium heat. Add onion, mushrooms, and ¼ teaspoon salt; cook, stirring occasionally, until vegetables are tender, about 10 minutes. Add asparagus, peas, garlic, and thyme; cook, stirring occasionally, until peas are bright green, 3–4 minutes.

3 Transfer vegetable mixture to large bowl. Add farfel and broth; stir until well combined. Add eggs, egg white, pepper, and remaining ¼ teaspoon salt and stir to combine.

4 Spoon mixture into baking dish. Bake until lightly browned and instant-read thermometer inserted into center registers 160°F, 25–30 minutes. Let cool 10 minutes, then cut into 6 squares.

PER SERVING (1 square): 142 Cal, 4 g Total Fat, 1 g Sat Fat, 0 g Trans Fat, 71 mg Chol, 249 mg Sod, 21 g Carb, 4 g Fib, 8 g Prot, 30 mg Calc.

PointsPlus value: *4.*

cook's note

To make this side dish for serving with the Passover Dinner menu (page 379), double all the ingredients and prepare as directed, baking in a 3-quart baking dish. Cut the casserole into 12 squares.

noodle kugel with dates and apricots

Serves 6 • Vegetarian

6 ounces wide, yolk-free noodles
3 large eggs, lightly beaten
8 ounces fat-free cottage cheese
½ cup fat-free milk
2 tablespoons reduced-fat sour cream
¼ cup pitted dates, sliced

¼ cup dried apricots, sliced
4 tablespoons sugar
⅛ teaspoon ground nutmeg
⅛ teaspoon salt
1 cup cornflakes, crushed
1 tablespoon unsalted butter, melted

1 Preheat oven to 350°F. Spray 1½-quart baking dish with nonstick spray.

2 Cook noodles according to package directions, omitting salt if desired; drain well.

3 Meanwhile, combine eggs, cottage cheese, milk, sour cream, dates, apricots, 3 tablespoons sugar, nutmeg, and salt in large bowl and whisk until well mixed. Add noodles and stir to combine.

4 Transfer to prepared baking dish. Stir together cornflakes, melted butter, and remaining 1 tablespoon sugar in small bowl; sprinkle over noodle mixture. Bake until edges are lightly browned and knife inserted into center comes out clean, 35–40 minutes. Let stand 10 minutes; cut into 6 squares. Serve warm or at room temperature.

PER SERVING (1 square): 293 Cal, 6 g Total Fat, 3 g Sat Fat, 0 g Trans Fat, 103 mg Chol, 353 mg Sod, 47 g Carb, 2 g Fib, 13 g Prot, 87 mg Calc.

PointsPlus value: *8.*

grilled zucchini and couscous with fresh herb sauce

Serves 6   •   Vegetarian

¼ cup dried currants
1⅓ cups water
¾ teaspoon salt
¼ teaspoon black pepper
1 cup whole wheat couscous
2 teaspoons grated orange zest
2 pounds zucchini, trimmed and cut on
diagonal into ½-inch slices

5 teaspoons olive oil
1½ cups lightly packed fresh basil leaves
¼ cup lightly packed fresh mint leaves
⅓ cup orange juice
1 tablespoon lemon juice

1. Spray grill rack with nonstick spray; preheat grill to medium or prepare medium fire.

2. Combine currants, water, ¼ teaspoon salt, and 1/8 teaspoon pepper in medium saucepan; bring to boil over medium-high heat. Stir in couscous; remove pan from heat, cover, and let stand 5 minutes. Stir in orange zest, cover again, and set aside.

3. Place zucchini in large bowl; drizzle with 2 teaspoons oil, sprinkle with ¼ teaspoon remaining salt, and toss to coat. Place zucchini on grill rack; grill until browned and tender, about 4 minutes per side.

4. Combine basil, mint, orange juice, lemon juice, and remaining 3 teaspoons oil, ¼ teaspoon salt, and 1/8 teaspoon pepper in blender; puree. Spoon couscous onto serving platter, top with zucchini slices, and drizzle with herb sauce.

PER SERVING (½ cup couscous, ½ cup squash, and 1½ tablespoons sauce): 226 Cal, 5 g Total Fat, 1 g Sat Fat, 0 g Trans Fat, 0 mg Chol, 395 mg Sod, 42 g Carb, 8 g Fib, 8 g Prot, 66 mg Calc.

PointsPlus value: *6.*

lemon-saffron israeli couscous

Serves 6 • Vegetarian

2 teaspoons olive oil
2 shallots, finely chopped
1 small red bell pepper, finely chopped
2 garlic cloves, finely chopped
1 (8.8-ounce) package Israeli couscous (1¾ cups)
1 teaspoon ground coriander

¼ teaspoon saffron threads, lightly crushed
2 cups reduced-sodium vegetable broth
½ teaspoon salt
¼ teaspoon black pepper
2 tablespoons minced fresh flat-leaf parsley
2 teaspoons grated lemon zest
1 tablespoon lemon juice

1 Heat oil in large saucepan over medium-high heat. Add shallots and bell pepper; cook, stirring occasionally, until vegetables have softened, 5 minutes. Add garlic and cook, stirring constantly, until fragrant, about 30 seconds.

2 Add couscous and cook, stirring, until lightly toasted, about 1 minute. Stir in coriander and saffron. Add broth, salt, and pepper; bring to boil. Reduce heat to medium low, cover, and simmer until liquid is absorbed and couscous is tender, 8–10 minutes. Remove from heat and stir in parsley and lemon zest and juice.

PER SERVING (generous ½ cup): 188 Cal, 2 g Total Fat, 0 g Sat Fat, 0 g Trans Fat, 0 mg Chol, 347 mg Sod, 36 g Carb, 3 g Fib, 6 g Prot, 23 mg Calc.

PointsPlus value: *5.*

barley-asparagus pilaf

Serves 4

2 cups reduced-sodium chicken broth
½ cup pearl barley
1½ teaspoons olive oil
1 small onion, thinly sliced
2 garlic cloves, minced
½ pound asparagus, trimmed and cut into
　　1-inch pieces

½ teaspoon salt
¼ teaspoon black pepper
1 tablespoon refrigerated basil pesto
1 tablespoon grated lemon zest
1 tablespoon lemon juice

1 Bring broth to boil in medium saucepan. Add barley and return to boil. Reduce heat and simmer, covered, until barley is tender, 30–35 minutes; drain.

2 Heat oil in large nonstick saucepan over medium heat. Add onion and cook, stirring occasionally, until softened, 5 minutes. Add garlic and cook, stirring constantly, until fragrant, about 30 seconds.

3 Add barley, asparagus, salt, and pepper. Cook, stirring occasionally, until asparagus is crisp-tender, 3–4 minutes. Remove from heat and stir in pesto and lemon zest and juice.

PER SERVING (¾ cup): 149 Cal, 4 g Total Fat, 1 g Sat Fat, 0 g Trans Fat, 1 mg Chol, 607 mg Sod, 24 g Carb, 5 g Fib, 5 g Prot, 47 mg Calc.

PointsPlus value: *4.*

louisiana rice pilaf

Serves 4

1 teaspoon canola oil
¼ pound cremini mushrooms, chopped
¼ cup chopped onion
¼ cup chopped celery
¼ cup chopped green bell pepper
1 garlic clove, finely chopped

½ teaspoon Cajun seasoning
½ teaspoon dried oregano
¾ cup quick-cooking brown rice
1¼ cups reduced-sodium chicken broth
2 scallions, thinly sliced
¼ cup chopped fresh flat-leaf parsley

1 Heat oil in medium saucepan over medium heat. Add mushrooms, onion, celery, and bell pepper; cook, stirring occasionally, until vegetables are softened, 6–8 minutes. Add garlic, Cajun seasoning, and oregano and cook, stirring constantly, until fragrant, 30 seconds.

2 Stir in rice and broth; bring to boil. Reduce heat, cover, and simmer until liquid is absorbed and rice is tender, 10–12 minutes. Remove from heat; stir in scallions and parsley.

PER SERVING (⅔ cup): 101 Cal, 2 g Total Fat, 0 g Sat Fat, 0 g Trans Fat, 0 mg Chol, 255 mg Sod, 18 g Carb, 3 g Fib, 4 g Prot, 37 mg Calc.

PointsPlus value: *3.*

cook's note

To make it a meal, stir a 15½-ounce can small red beans, rinsed and drained into the pilaf and cook an additional 2 minutes until heated through for a filling and flavorful vegetarian meal (the per serving *PointsPlus* value will increase by *2*).

spicy coconut basmati rice with black-eyed peas

Serves 8

2 teaspoons olive oil
1 onion, thinly sliced
2 garlic cloves, minced
1 Scotch bonnet or other very hot pepper, seeded and minced
1¾ cups brown basmati rice

4 cups reduced-sodium chicken broth
½ cup light coconut milk
1 (15½-ounce) can black-eyed peas, rinsed and drained
2 scallions, thinly sliced

1 Heat oil in large saucepan over medium-high heat. Add onion, garlic, and pepper; cook, stirring often, until vegetables are softened, about 5 minutes. Add rice and stir to coat.

2 Stir in broth and coconut milk; bring to boil. Reduce heat and simmer, covered, until liquid is absorbed and rice is tender, 45–50 minutes. Stir in peas and cook until heated through, 2 minutes. Stir in scallions.

PER SERVING (¾ cup): 208 Cal, 4 g Total Fat, 2 g Sat Fat, 0 g Trans Fat, 2 mg Chol, 172 mg Sod, 38 g Carb, 3 g Fib, 7 g Prot, 21 mg Calc.

PointsPlus value: **6.**

cook's note

If you can't find a Scotch bonnet pepper, you can use an ordinary jalapeño in this recipe. Leave some of the seeds in when you mince the jalapeño for added spice.

pear and apple haroset with walnuts

Serves 12 • Vegetarian

2 small pears, peeled, cored, and
   finely chopped
2 small apples, peeled, cored, and finely
   chopped
½ cup pitted dates, finely chopped

3 tablespoons golden raisins, chopped
⅓ cup walnut halves, toasted and
   finely chopped
¼ cup sweet Malaga wine or grape juice
¼ teaspoon cinnamon

Combine all the ingredients in medium bowl. Cover with plastic wrap and refrigerate at least 1 hour or up to 24 hours to allow fruits to soften.

PER SERVING (¼ cup): 71 Cal, 2 g Total Fat, 0 g Sat Fat, 0 g Trans Fat, 0 mg Chol, 2 mg Sod, 12 g Carb, 1 g Fib, 1 g Prot, 9 mg Calc.

PointsPlus value: **2.**

cook's note

Haroset is most often eaten in a "sandwich" with horseradish between pieces of matzo. But it's also delicious to serve as a sweet accompaniment to roast turkey or lamb.

fresh cranberry sauce with dried apricots

Serves 24 • Vegetarian

2 (12-ounce) bags fresh or frozen
 cranberries
1½ cups cranberry juice cocktail
1¼ cups sugar

¾ cup dried apricots, chopped
2 tablespoons minced peeled fresh ginger
1 cinnamon stick

1 Combine all the ingredients in large saucepan; bring to boil. Reduce heat and simmer, stirring occasionally, until most cranberries pop open and sauce thickens, about 10 minutes.

2 Pour sauce into medium bowl and let cool. Remove and discard cinnamon stick. Cover and refrigerate until chilled, at least 3 hours.

PER SERVING (3 tablespoons): 79 Cal, 0 g Total Fat, 0 g Sat Fat, 0 g Trans Fat, 0 mg Chol, 1 mg Sod, 20 g Carb, 1 g Fib, 0 g Prot, 3 mg Calc.
PointsPlus value: *2.*

cook's note

You can store any leftover sauce in the refrigerator for up to 4 days to enjoy alongside roast chicken or turkey, as a sandwich spread, in a fruit smoothie, or on top of vanilla ice cream.

sweets

Sweet Potato Pie
with Pumpkinseed
Brittle, page 335

apricot-raisin spice cake

Serves 20

TOPPING

¼ cup chopped walnuts
3 tablespoons all-purpose flour
3 tablespoons packed light brown sugar
2 tablespoons canola oil
½ teaspoon cinnamon

CAKE

2 cups all-purpose flour
2 teaspoons baking powder
1 teaspoon cinnamon
½ teaspoon baking soda
¼ teaspoon ground cloves
3 large eggs
1 cup packed light brown sugar
1 cup apple butter
⅓ cup canola oil
1 teaspoon vanilla extract
½ cup dried apricots, finely chopped
½ cup golden raisins

1 Preheat oven to 350°F. Line an 8-inch square baking pan with foil, allowing foil to extend over rim of pan by 2 inches. Spray with nonstick spray.

2 To make topping, stir together topping ingredients in small bowl until moistened.

3 To make cake, whisk together flour, baking powder, cinnamon, baking soda, and cloves in medium bowl. With an electric mixer on high speed, beat eggs in large bowl until thickened, about 2 minutes. Gradually add brown sugar, beating until light and fluffy, about 3 minutes. Reduce speed to low. Beat in apple butter, oil, and vanilla until combined. Add flour mixture and beat just until blended. Stir in apricots and raisins.

4 Pour batter into pan; sprinkle evenly with topping. Bake until toothpick inserted into center comes out clean, 35–40 minutes. Let cool completely in pan on wire rack. Lift cake out using foil as handles.

PER SERVING (1/20 of cake): 213 Cal, 7 g Total Fat, 1 g Sat Fat, 0 g Trans Fat, 32 mg Chol, 95 mg Sod, 36 g Carb, 1 g Fib, 3 g Prot, 53 mg Calc.

PointsPlus value: **6.**

Apricot-Raisin Spice Cake

banana-spice cake with cream cheese frosting

Serves 24

CAKE

2 cups all-purpose flour
¾ cup granulated sugar
2 teaspoons baking powder
¾ teaspoon cinnamon
½ teaspoon baking soda
½ teaspoon salt
¼ teaspoon ground nutmeg
¾ cup low-fat buttermilk
2 ripe medium bananas, mashed (1 cup)
2 large eggs
1 large egg white
⅓ cup canola oil
1 teaspoon vanilla extract

FROSTING

1 (8-ounce) package light cream cheese (Neufchâtel), at room temperature
½ cup confectioners' sugar
3 tablespoons low-fat (1 percent) milk
1 teaspoon vanilla extract

1 Preheat oven to 350°F. Spray 9 × 13-inch baking pan with nonstick spray.

2 To make cake, whisk together flour, granulated sugar, baking powder, cinnamon, baking soda, salt, and nutmeg in medium bowl. Whisk together buttermilk, bananas, eggs, egg white, oil, and vanilla in separate medium bowl. Gradually add buttermilk mixture to flour mixture, stirring just until blended.

3 Pour batter into pan. Bake until toothpick inserted into center comes out clean, 30–35 minutes. Let cool in pan on wire rack 10 minutes. Run thin knife around the edge of cake to loosen it from pan. Remove cake from pan and let cool completely on rack.

4 Meanwhile, to make frosting, with an electric mixer on high speed, beat all frosting ingredients in medium bowl until smooth, about 1 minute. With narrow metal spatula, spread frosting over top of cake. Cut into 24 squares.

PER SERVING (1 square): 144 Cal, 6 g Total Fat, 2 g Sat Fat, 0 g Trans Fat, 25 mg Chol, 197 mg Sod, 20 g Carb, 1 g Fib, 3 g Prot, 45 mg Calc.
PointsPlus value: *4.*

chocolate-chip layer cake with ricotta frosting

Serves 20

CAKE

2 cups cake flour
2 teaspoons baking powder
½ teaspoon baking soda
½ teaspoon salt
2 large eggs, at room temperature
2 large egg whites, at room temperature
½ cup granulated sugar
½ cup low-fat buttermilk
¼ cup canola oil
½ cup semisweet mini–chocolate chips

FROSTING

1 (15-ounce) container fat-free ricotta cheese
1 (3-ounce) package fat-free cream cheese, at room temperature
¾ cup confectioners' sugar
1½ teaspoons vanilla extract

1 To make cake, preheat oven to 350°F. Spray two 8-inch round cake pans with nonstick spray; line with wax-paper rounds and spray rounds with nonstick spray.

2 Whisk together flour, baking powder, baking soda, and salt in medium bowl. With electric mixer on high speed, beat eggs and egg whites in large bowl until light and thick, about 2 minutes. Gradually beat in granulated sugar, beating until mixture is light and very fluffy, about 3 minutes. Beat in buttermilk and oil on low speed, beating just until blended. Beat in flour mixture, beating just until incorporated. Fold in chocolate chips.

3 Spoon batter evenly into pans and level tops. Bake until toothpick inserted into centers comes out clean, 30–40 minutes. Let cool in pans on racks 10 minutes. Invert layers onto racks; peel off and discard wax paper, and cool layers completely.

4 To make frosting, with electric mixer on high speed, beat ricotta, cream cheese, confectioners' sugar, and vanilla in medium bowl until smooth, about 1 minute.

5 Place 1 cake layer, rounded side down, on serving plate. With narrow metal spatula, spread ½ cup frosting over layer. Top with remaining layer, rounded side up. Spread remaining frosting over top and sides of cake. Cut into 20 slices.

PER SERVING (1 slice): 170 Cal, 5 g Total Fat, 1 g Sat Fat, 0 g Trans Fat, 24 mg Chol, 199 mg Sod, 25 g Carb, 1 g Fib, 6 g Prot, 88 mg Calc.

PointsPlus value: *4.*

Double Chocolate Chiffon Cake

double chocolate chiffon cake

Serves 16

3 ounces bittersweet chocolate, chopped
½ cup Dutch process cocoa powder
1 cup boiling water
2 cups all-purpose flour
2 teaspoons baking powder
¾ teaspoon salt

1½ cups granulated sugar
4 large eggs, separated
⅓ cup canola oil
3 large egg whites
½ teaspoon cream of tartar
1 tablespoon confectioners' sugar

1 Preheat oven to 325°F. Combine chocolate and cocoa in medium bowl; pour in boiling water and let stand 5 minutes. Whisk until chocolate is melted and smooth. Let cool.

2 Whisk together flour, baking powder, salt, and 1 cup granulated sugar in large bowl. Add 4 egg yolks and oil to cooled cocoa mixture and whisk until blended. Stir cocoa mixture into flour mixture.

3 Combine the 7 egg whites and cream of tartar in another large bowl. Beat with electric mixer on medium-high speed until soft peaks form. With mixer on high speed, very gradually add remaining ½ cup granulated sugar, beating until stiff peaks form.

4 Stir one-fourth of egg white–mixture into chocolate batter. Pour batter over whites remaining in bowl and gently fold together with rubber spatula, folding just until no white streaks remain. Pour batter into ungreased 10-inch tube pan with removable bottom; level top. Bake until cake springs back when pressed lightly, about 1 hour 5 minutes. Let cake cool upside down by fitting tube over neck of wine bottle or by resting pan on 4 upturned glasses.

5 Run a long thin knife around inside and outside edges of pan; remove cake. Dust with confectioners' sugar just before serving. Cut into 16 slices.

PER SERVING (1 slice): 227 Cal, 9 g Total Fat, 2 g Sat Fat, 0 g Trans Fat, 53 mg Chol, 184 mg Sod, 36 g Carb, 2 g Fib, 5 g Prot, 22 mg Calc.

PointsPlus value: *7.*

be a better baker

Understand the basic terms used in recipes and you'll soon be baking like a pro.

Beat   To combine ingredients while incorporating air using a wooden spoon, fork, handheld mixer, or stand mixer.

Blend   To combine two or more ingredients.

Caramelize   To heat sugar until it is melted and browned.

Coats Back of Spoon   When a thin layer coats the back of a metal spoon when dipped into a mixture.

Combine   To stir two or more ingredients together until mixed.

Cool   To allow to stand to come to room temperature.

Cream   To beat butter or cream cheese until creamy or butter and sugar until light and fluffy.

Crimp   To create a decorative edge on a pie crust by shaping the raised edge.

Cut In   When making pastry dough, to cut fat into the flour mixture until pea-sized using a pastry blender or two knives used scissor-fashion.

Drizzle   To drip a glaze or icing over a cake or other baked good.

Fold In   To gently combine a light mixture with a heavier one without losing volume.

Knead   To press, fold, and turn dough to achieve a smooth texture.

Mix   To combine two or more ingredients.

Mix Until Moistened   To combine a liquid with dry ingredients just until the dry ingredients are evenly and thoroughly moistened. The mixture is often lumpy.

Slit   To cut partway through a food surface to allow steam to escape while baking.

Soften   Recipes often call for softened butter for easy blending or beating. Leave the butter out at room temperature for about 30 minutes until pliable—not greasy or melting.

Soft Peaks   To beat egg whites until rounded peaks form when the beaters are lifted.

Stiff Peaks   To beat egg whites until pointed peaks form when the beaters are lifted.

Toothpick Comes Out Clean   To determine if a cake is done, insert a wooden toothpick in the center; if no crumbs are attached to the toothpick, the cake is done.

Whisk   To stir ingredients using a wire whisk to create a smooth texture or to incorporate air.

Zest   The flavorful, colorful outer peel of citrus fruit.

sour cream bundt cake with pecan streusel

Serves 16

½ cup pecans, chopped
½ cup packed light brown sugar
1½ teaspoons cinnamon
½ teaspoon ground cloves
¼ teaspoon ground nutmeg
1½ cups whole wheat pastry flour
1 cup all-purpose flour
2 teaspoons baking powder
½ teaspoon baking soda

½ teaspoon salt
4 tablespoons unsalted butter, softened
1⅓ cups granulated sugar
2 large eggs
2 large egg whites
1¼ cups fat-free sour cream
2 teaspoons vanilla extract
1 teaspoon confectioners' sugar

1 Preheat oven to 350°F. Spray 10-inch Bundt pan with nonstick spray.

2 Evenly sprinkle 2 tablespoons pecans in bottom of pan. Combine remaining pecans, brown sugar, cinnamon, cloves, and nutmeg in small bowl. Whisk together pastry flour, all-purpose flour, baking powder, baking soda, and salt in medium bowl.

3 With an electric mixer on medium speed, beat butter and 1/3 cup granulated sugar in large bowl until light and fluffy, about 2 minutes. Gradually beat in remaining 1 cup granulated sugar, then beat 1 minute longer. Beat in eggs and egg whites, one at a time, beating well after each addition. Beat in sour cream and vanilla. Reduce mixer speed to low. Gradually add flour mixture, beating just until blended.

4 Spoon one-third of batter into pan; spread evenly. Sprinkle evenly with half of pecan mixture. Spoon half of remaining batter on top; spread evenly. Sprinkle with remaining pecan mixture. Spoon remaining batter on top; spread evenly. Bake until toothpick inserted into center comes out clean, 40–45 minutes. Let cool in pan on wire rack 10 minutes. Remove cake from pan and let cool completely on rack. Dust with confectioners' sugar.

PER SERVING (⅟₁₆ of cake): 233 Cal, 6 g Total Fat, 2 g Sat Fat, 0 g Trans Fat, 36 mg Chol, 219 mg Sod, 42 g Carb, 2 g Fib, 5 g Prot, 78 mg Calc.

PointsPlus value: **6.**

cook's note

Whole wheat pastry flour is made from very finely ground soft white wheat. It gives a lighter texture and a more tender crumb in baked goods than regular whole wheat flour, even though it contains almost the same amount of fiber and other nutrients. Look for it in a natural-food store or a well-stocked supermarket.

strawberry-lemon cake roll

Serves 12

5 large eggs, separated
½ cup granulated sugar
1 teaspoon pure lemon extract
½ cup all-purpose flour
3 tablespoons plus ⅓ cup confectioners' sugar

¼ pound light cream cheese (Neufchâtel)
½ cup fat-free ricotta cheese
1½ teaspoons grated lemon zest
1 (1-pound) container strawberries
⅓ cup no-sugar-added strawberry preserves

1 Preheat oven to 350°F. Spray 15 × 10 × 1-inch jelly-roll pan with nonstick spray. Line with wax paper and spray paper with nonstick spray.

2 Beat egg whites in large bowl with electric mixer on medium-high speed until soft peaks form. With mixer on high speed, gradually add ¼ cup granulated sugar, beating until stiff peaks form. Set aside.

3 Add lemon extract and remaining ¼ cup granulated sugar to egg yolks in medium bowl; beat with electric mixer on high speed until thickened and pale yellow, about 4 minutes. Fold in flour with rubber spatula. Pour yolk mixture over beaten egg whites; gently fold together with spatula just until no white streaks remain. Scrape batter into prepared pan and spread evenly with spatula. Bake until top springs back when pressed lightly with your fingertip, 12–15 minutes.

4 While cake bakes, sift 2 tablespoons confectioners' sugar onto clean kitchen towel. When cake is done, immediately invert onto towel. Carefully peel off wax paper from bottom of cake and discard. Starting from a long side, roll cake jelly-roll-style in towel. Completely cool rolled cake on rack.

5 Meanwhile, combine cream cheese, ricotta, lemon zest, and remaining 1/3 cup confectioners' sugar in small bowl. Beat with electric mixer until very smooth. Cover and refrigerate. Hull and slice enough strawberries to measure 1 cup.

6 Unroll cake so that a long side is in front of you. Spread preserves over cake, leaving ½-inch border along opposite long side. Arrange sliced strawberries over closer half of cake. Spread cake with ricotta mixture, leaving 1-inch border on opposite long side. Roll cake, starting from closer long side. With serrated knife, trim ends of cake; place cake seam side down on platter. Sift remaining 1 tablespoon confectioners' sugar over cake and arrange whole strawberries around it. To serve, cut cake on slight diagonal into 12 slices with serrated knife. Serve with whole berries.

PER SERVING (1 slice cake and 1 strawberry): 145 Cal, 4 g Total Fat, 2 g Sat Fat, 0 g Trans Fat, 97 mg Chol, 75 mg Sod, 22 g Carb, 1 g Fib, 5 g Prot, 40 mg Calc.

PointsPlus value: **4.**

honey-glazed autumn apple cake

Serves 20

3 cups all-purpose flour
1½ cups packed light brown sugar
2 teaspoons baking powder
1 teaspoon cinnamon
½ teaspoon baking soda
½ teaspoon ground nutmeg
¼ teaspoon salt

3 large eggs
¾ cup apple cider
6 tablespoons canola oil
1 teaspoon vanilla extract
2 large Golden Delicious apples, peeled,
　cored, and chopped
¼ cup honey, warmed

1　Preheat oven to 375°F. Spray 10-inch tube pan with nonstick spray and dust with flour.

2　Whisk together flour, brown sugar, baking powder, cinnamon, baking soda, nutmeg, and salt in large bowl. Whisk together eggs, cider, oil, and vanilla in medium bowl. Add egg mixture to flour mixture and beat with electric mixer on low speed until well combined, about 3 minutes. Stir in apples.

3　Pour batter into pan. Bake until toothpick inserted into center of cake comes out clean, about 45 minutes. Cool in pan on rack 15 minutes. Remove cake from pan and cool completely on rack. Drizzle with honey just before serving and cut into 20 slices.

PER SERVING (1 slice): 206 Cal, 6 g Total Fat, 1 g Sat Fat, 0 g Trans Fat, 32 mg Chol, 116 mg Sod, 38 g Carb, 1 g Fib, 3 g Prot, 31 mg Calc.

PointsPlus value: *6.*

ginger-pumpkin cheesecake

Serves 16

18 gingersnaps, broken in half
2 tablespoons unsalted butter, melted
2 tablespoons plus ½ cup granulated sugar
1 (15-ounce) container fat-free ricotta cheese
1 (8-ounce) package light cream cheese (Neufchâtel)
½ cup packed light brown sugar

2 tablespoons cornstarch
2 teaspoons pumpkin pie spice
1 (15 ½-ounce) can pumpkin puree
1 cup fat-free egg substitute
1 cup thawed frozen fat-free whipped topping
Grated nutmeg (optional)

1 Preheat oven to 350°F. Put gingersnaps in food processor and pulse to make fine crumbs. Add melted butter and 2 tablespoons granulated sugar; pulse until blended. Spoon crumb mixture into 9-inch springform pan; press evenly onto bottom and up sides of pan. Bake until set, 8 minutes; cool completely on rack.

2 Put ricotta in food processor (bowl need not be washed out first) and pulse until smooth. Add cream cheese, brown sugar, cornstarch, pumpkin pie spice, and remaining ½ cup granulated sugar; process until blended and smooth, stopping to scrape down sides of bowl a few times. Add pumpkin puree and egg substitute; pulse until mixed. Pour filling over crust and level top. Bake until filling is set and no longer jiggles in center, about 1 hour 10 minutes.

3 Cool cheesecake in pan on rack. Cover pan with plastic wrap; refrigerate until chilled, 4 hours or overnight. To serve, release and remove sides of pan. Spread top of cheesecake evenly with whipped topping and sprinkle with nutmeg (if using). Cut into 16 slices.

PER SERVING (1 slice): 191 Cal, 6 g Total Fat, 3 g Sat Fat, 0 g Trans Fat, 19 mg Chol, 177 mg Sod, 29 g Carb, 2 g Fib, 6 g Prot, 86 mg Calc.

PointsPlus value: *5.*

Ginger-Pumpkin Cheesecake

pomegranate-glazed cheesecake

Serves 16

12 low-fat graham crackers
8 tablespoons plus 1 cup sugar
2 tablespoons unsalted butter, melted
1 (8-ounce) package light cream cheese
   (Neufchâtel)
1 (8-ounce) package fat-free cream cheese

1 (16-ounce) container fat-free sour cream
2 large eggs
2 large egg whites
1 teaspoon vanilla extract
2 cups pomegranate juice

1. Preheat oven to 350°F. Spray bottom and sides of 9-inch springform pan lightly with nonstick spray.

2. Combine graham crackers and 2 tablespoons sugar in food processor; pulse to make fine crumbs. Transfer to small bowl and stir in melted butter. Press crumb mixture evenly onto bottom and halfway up sides of springform pan. Bake until golden, 8–10 minutes; cool completely on rack. Reduce oven temperature to 325°F.

3. Combine light cream cheese, fat-free cream cheese, and sour cream in large bowl; beat with electric mixer on medium speed until smooth. Add eggs, egg whites, vanilla, and 1 cup sugar; beat just until combined, stopping once or twice to scrape down sides of bowl. Pour mixture over crust in pan and transfer to oven. Bake until cake is set around edges but still jiggles slightly in center when shaken, about 1 hour. Turn off oven and let cake sit in oven 1 hour longer. Refrigerate until chilled, at least 3 hours.

4. Meanwhile, combine remaining 6 tablespoons sugar and pomegranate juice in small saucepan; bring to boil over medium-high heat. Reduce heat to medium and simmer until liquid is thick enough to coat back of spoon, about 30 minutes. Transfer to small bowl and refrigerate until chilled.

5. Remove cheesecake from springform pan and place on platter. Pour half of pomegranate syrup over top. Cut cake into 16 slices. Spoon small amount of remaining syrup over each slice.

PER SERVING (1 slice cheesecake and 2 teaspoons syrup): 215 Cal, 6 g Total Fat, 4 g Sat Fat, 0 g Trans Fat, 45 mg Chol, 192 mg Sod, 34 g Carb, 0 g Fib, 6 g Prot, 83 mg Calc.

PointsPlus value: **6.**

cook's note

To seed a pomegranate for garnishing the cake, cut off the top, slicing through the white pith, but not into the seed cavity. Score the pomegranate into quarters, avoiding the seed cavity. Place in a bowl of cold water and gently pry the seeds out with your fingers; the seeds will sink to the bottom.

sweet potato pie with pumpkinseed brittle

Serves 12

1 cup all-purpose flour
¼ cup whole wheat pastry flour
1 tablespoon granulated sugar
¾ teaspoon salt
3 tablespoons canola oil
2–3 tablespoons water
1 (15½-ounce) can cut sweet yams in light
    syrup, drained
¾ cup packed dark brown sugar

1 (12-ounce) can fat-free evaporated milk
¼ cup orange juice
2 tablespoons molasses or sorghum
2 large eggs
1 large egg white
1½ teaspoons pumpkin pie spice
½ cup raw shelled green pumpkin seeds
2 tablespoons maple syrup

1 To make crust, put all-purpose flour, pastry flour, sugar, and ¼ teaspoon salt in food processor; pulse until blended. Pour oil through feed tube and pulse until mixture resembles coarse crumbs. Add water, 1 tablespoon at a time, and pulse until dough forms. Flatten dough into disk; wrap in plastic wrap and refrigerate at least 1 hour or up to 3 days.

2 Preheat oven to 375°F. On lightly floured surface, roll dough out to 12-inch circle; ease it into 10-inch deep-dish pie pan, pressing evenly onto bottom and up sides of pan. Prick dough all over with fork. Crimp edges.

3 Line pie crust with foil; fill with pie weights or dried beans. Bake until dough looks dried around edges, about 20 minutes; remove foil and weights. Return crust to oven and bake just until golden, 10–12 minutes longer. Cool crust in pan on rack 10 minutes. Maintain oven temperature.

4 Meanwhile, to make filling, combine yams and brown sugar in food processor and pulse until smooth. Add evaporated milk, orange juice, molasses, eggs, egg white, spice, and remaining ½ teaspoon salt; pulse until blended. Pour filling into crust. Bake just until center is set, 40–45 minutes. Cool completely on rack.

5 To make topping, spray 12-inch square of aluminum foil with nonstick spray and set aside. Place pumpkinseeds in small nonstick skillet over medium heat and toast, stirring often, until seeds are golden, about 2 minutes. Add maple syrup; cook, stirring constantly, until syrup has reduced to glaze, about 2 minutes. Spread pumpkinseed mixture onto foil and cool. Just before serving, break brittle into pieces and sprinkle over pie. Cut pie into 12 wedges.

PER SERVING (1 wedge): 249 Cal, 7 g Total Fat, 1 g Sat Fat, 0 g Trans Fat, 32 mg Chol, 212 mg Sod, 41 g Carb, 2 g Fib, 7 g Prot, 120 mg Calc.
PointsPlus value: 7.

Chocolate Cupcakes with Peanut Butter Frosting

chocolate cupcakes with peanut butter frosting

Serves 24

CUPCAKES

1 cup cake flour
1 cup granulated sugar
½ cup unsweetened cocoa powder
1 teaspoon baking powder
¼ teaspoon baking soda
¼ teaspoon salt
½ cup low-fat buttermilk
⅓ cup canola oil
1 large egg
1 large egg white
1 teaspoon vanilla extract
1 ounce semisweet chocolate, melted
    and cooled

FROSTING

½ cup light cream cheese (Neufchâtel),
    softened
¼ cup reduced-fat creamy peanut butter
¼ cup confectioners' sugar
¼ cup unsalted roasted peanuts, chopped

1. Preheat oven to 350°F. Spray 24-cup mini-muffin pan with nonstick spray.

2. To make cupcakes, whisk together cake flour, granulated sugar, cocoa, baking powder, baking soda, and salt in medium bowl. Whisk together buttermilk, oil, egg, egg white, and vanilla in large bowl. Whisk melted chocolate into buttermilk mixture. Add flour mixture, stirring just until blended.

3. Fill each muffin cup two-thirds full with batter. Bake until toothpick inserted into center comes out clean, about 25 minutes. Let cool in pan on wire rack 10 minutes. Remove cupcakes from pan and let cool completely on rack.

4. Meanwhile, to make frosting, with an electric mixer on low speed, beat cream cheese, peanut butter, and confectioners' sugar in small bowl until smooth, about 2 minutes.

5. With small spatula, spread frosting over tops of cupcakes; sprinkle with peanuts.

PER SERVING (1 cupcake): 138 Cal, 7 g Total Fat, 2 g Sat Fat, 0 g Trans Fat, 13 mg Chol, 105 mg Sod, 18 g Carb, 1 g Fib, 4 g Prot, 28 mg Calc.

PointsPlus value: *4.*

coconut cream pie with gingersnap crust

Serves 8

CRUST

15 reduced-fat gingersnap cookies,
    crumbled
1 tablespoon plus 2 teaspoons canola oil
1 tablespoon chopped almonds

FILLING

1 envelope unflavored gelatin
¼ cup cold water
¼ cup sugar
3 tablespoons all-purpose flour
1 cup low-fat (1 percent) milk
½ cup light coconut milk
1 large egg
Pinch salt
1 teaspoon coconut extract
½ cup thawed frozen light whipped topping
2 tablespoons flaked sweetened
    coconut, toasted

1 Preheat oven to 375°F. Spray 9-inch pie plate with nonstick spray.

2 To make crust, put gingersnaps in food processor and pulse until finely ground. Add oil and almonds; process until crumbly. Press crumb mixture evenly onto bottom and up side of pie plate. Bake until set, 8–10 minutes. Let cool completely on wire rack.

3 To make filling, sprinkle gelatin over water in microwavable cup. Let stand until softened, about 5 minutes. Microwave on High until gelatin is completely dissolved, about 15 seconds.

4 Whisk together sugar and flour in medium saucepan. Whisk in milk, coconut milk, egg, and salt and set over medium-high heat. Cook, stirring constantly, until mixture thickens, about 4 minutes (do not let boil). Remove saucepan from heat. Stir in gelatin mixture and coconut extract. Pour into medium bowl; refrigerate until filling begins to set, about 30 minutes. Whisk until smooth and creamy. With rubber spatula, gently fold in whipped topping. Pour into crust and sprinkle with toasted coconut. Refrigerate until firm, at least 2 hours or up to 6 hours.

PER SERVING (⅛ of pie): 168 Cal, 7 g Total Fat, 2 g Sat Fat, 0 g Trans Fat, 28 mg Chol, 150 mg Sod, 23 g Carb, 1 g Fib, 4 g Prot, 58 mg Calc.
PointsPlus value: **5.**

chocolate-almond meringue pie

Serves 12

FILLING

1½ cups low-fat (1 percent) milk
1 large egg
½ cup sugar
¼ cup all-purpose flour
¼ teaspoon salt
¼ cup semisweet chocolate chips
½ teaspoon almond extract
1 (6-ounce) prepared chocolate cookie crust

MERINGUE

4 large egg whites
½ teaspoon cream of tartar
½ cup sugar
¼ teaspoon almond extract
1 tablespoon chopped almonds, toasted

1 Preheat oven to 375°F.

2 To make filling, whisk together milk, egg, sugar, flour, and salt in medium saucepan, then set over medium-high heat. Cook, stirring constantly, until mixture thickens and coats back of spoon, about 4 minutes (do not let boil or mixture may curdle). Remove saucepan from heat; stir in chocolate chips and almond extract until chocolate is melted and mixture is smooth. Pour into crust.

3 To make meringue, with an electric mixer on medium speed, beat egg whites and cream of tartar in large bowl until soft peaks form. Increase speed to medium-high. Sprinkle in sugar, 1 tablespoon at a time, beating until stiff, glossy peaks form. Beat in almond extract.

4 Spoon meringue over filling, spreading it to edge of crust to completely enclose filling; sprinkle with almonds. Bake until meringue is golden brown, about 15 minutes. Let cool on wire rack about 1 hour. Refrigerate at least 3 hours or up to 6 hours. This pie is best eaten the day it is prepared.

PER SERVING (1⁄12 of pie): 195 Cal, 7 g Total Fat, 2 g Sat Fat, 0 g Trans Fat, 21 mg Chol, 163 mg Sod, 31 g Carb, 1 g Fib, 4 g Prot, 46 mg Calc.
PointsPlus value: **5.**

summer fruit tart with phyllo crust

Serves 10

¼ cup packed light brown sugar
1 tablespoon all-purpose flour
¼ teaspoon cinnamon
Pinch salt
4 ripe medium nectarines, halved, pitted, and sliced

1 cup blueberries
1 tablespoon grated lemon zest (about 2 lemons)
6 (12 × 17-inch) sheets frozen phyllo dough, thawed
1 tablespoon unsalted butter, melted

1. Preheat oven to 375°F. Spray 10-inch pizza pan or large baking sheet with nonstick spray.

2. Combine brown sugar, flour, cinnamon, and salt in large bowl. Add nectarines, blueberries, and lemon zest; toss to mix well.

3. Lay 1 phyllo sheet in pan; lightly spray with nonstick spray. Keep remaining phyllo covered with damp paper towel and plastic wrap to keep it from drying out. Working quickly, repeat with remaining 5 phyllo sheets, placing corners at different angles and lightly spraying each sheet with nonstick spray. Roll up edges of phyllo to form 1½-inch-wide rim.

4. Spoon nectarine mixture evenly on top of phyllo and drizzle with melted butter. Bake until edges of phyllo are golden brown and nectarines are tender, about 45 minutes. Let cool on wire rack about 1 hour before serving.

PER SERVING (¹⁄₁₀ of tart): 102 Cal, 1 g Total Fat, 1 g Sat Fat, 0 g Trans Fat, 3 mg Chol, 81 mg Sod, 21 g Carb, 1 g Fib, 2 g Prot, 13 mg Calc.

PointsPlus value: **3.**

cook's note

Ripe fruit will give the best flavor when making this tart. To choose the most flavorful nectarines, select those that are yellow with a blush of pink and that give slightly to palm pressure.

Summer Fruit Tart with Phyllo Crust

Almond-Pear Linzer Tart

almond-pear linzer tart

Serves 16

1½ cups white whole wheat flour
1 teaspoon baking powder
½ teaspoon cinnamon
⅓ cup toasted blanched almonds
5 tablespoons light stick butter
¾ cup packed light brown sugar
2 large egg whites

⅓ cup seedless raspberry preserves
½ cup dried cranberries
1 tablespoon granulated sugar
2 teaspoons cornstarch
2 ripe large pears, cored and cut into
  ½-inch slices

1 Preheat oven to 350°F. Spray 10-inch removable-bottom tart pan with nonstick spray and dust with flour.

2 In medium bowl, whisk together flour, baking powder, and cinnamon. Put almonds in food processor and pulse until finely chopped; measure out 1 tablespoon almonds and set aside. Add butter and brown sugar to remaining almonds; pulse until blended. Add egg whites and pulse until blended. Add flour mixture and pulse until combined. Spoon mixture into tart pan and press evenly onto bottom of pan. Spread evenly with preserves, leaving a ½-inch border. Set aside 1 tablespoon cranberries and sprinkle remaining cranberries over preserves.

3 Stir together granulated sugar and cornstarch in medium bowl; add pears and toss to coat. Arrange pear slices in pan in concentric circle. Sprinkle with reserved 1 tablespoon almonds and 1 tablespoon cranberries. Bake tart until toothpick inserted into center comes out with a few moist crumbs, about 50 minutes. Cool completely on wire rack. To serve, remove tart ring and cut tart into 16 slices.

PER SERVING (1 slice): 150 Cal, 4 g Total Fat, 1 g Sat Fat, 0 g Trans Fat, 6 mg Chol, 37 mg Sod, 29 g Carb, 2 g Fib, 3 g Prot, 26 mg Calc.

PointsPlus value: *4.*

lemon-yogurt tart

Serves 10

7 low-fat honey graham crackers
3 tablespoons unsalted butter, melted
1 tablespoon light brown sugar
⅓ cup water
1 envelope unflavored gelatin
1 (14-ounce) can fat-free sweetened
    condensed milk

1¼ cups plain fat-free yogurt
2 teaspoons finely grated lemon zest
½ cup lemon juice
Lemon slices and mint leaves (optional)

1 Preheat oven to 375°F. Put crackers in food processor and pulse to make fine crumbs. Transfer to small bowl and stir in melted butter and brown sugar. Press crumb mixture evenly onto bottom and up sides of 9-inch tart pan with removable bottom, making sure to push mixture all the way to rim. Bake crust until golden, 10–12 minutes. Cool on rack.

2 Meanwhile, pour water into small saucepan; sprinkle gelatin over water and let stand 2 minutes to soften. Set over low heat and cook, stirring frequently, until gelatin dissolves. Remove from heat.

3 Whisk together condensed milk, yogurt, and lemon zest and juice in medium bowl. Gradually whisk in gelatin mixture. Pour mixture into cooled crust. Refrigerate until set, at least 3 hours or up to 1 day. Decorate tart with lemon slices and mint (if using) and cut into 10 wedges.

PER SERVING (1 wedge): 184 Cal, 4 g Total Fat, 2 g Sat Fat, 0 g Trans Fat, 12 mg Chol, 81 mg Sod, 33 g Carb, 0 g Fib, 6 g Prot, 155 mg Calc.

PointsPlus value: **5.**

Lemon-Yogurt Tart and
Chocolate-Cranberry
Oatmeal Cookies, page 370

bake

To cook food in the dry heat of the oven.

what you need

For making baked goods and desserts, shiny metal pans are best because they reflect heat and create a light brown crust. For baking meats, poultry, seafood, and casseroles, use ovenproof glass, enamel-coated cast iron, and porcelain baking dishes.

how it's done

Unless otherwise specified in the recipe, place the oven rack in the center of the oven. Preheat the oven. Spray the pan or baking dish with nonstick spray. Spoon cake batters into the pans evenly; spread thick batters evenly. For muffins, fill the pan two-thirds full.

Season meats, poultry, and seafood and place in a single layer in a baking dish.

Bake casseroles in a baking dish that holds the food with room to spare so that liquids do not bubble over in the oven. Follow the instructions in the recipe to determine doneness.

apple-cranberry crisp

Serves 8

½ cup plus 2 tablespoons all-purpose flour
½ cup quick-cooking (not instant) or old-fashioned oats
½ cup sugar
¼ teaspoon cinnamon
⅛ teaspoon salt
3 tablespoons cold unsalted butter, diced

1 teaspoon water
3 pounds apples, peeled and thinly sliced
¾ cup fresh or frozen cranberries
1 teaspoon grated peeled fresh ginger
1 teaspoon vanilla extract

1 Preheat oven to 375°F. Spray 7 × 11-inch baking dish with nonstick spray.

2 To make topping, combine ½ cup flour, oats, ¼ cup sugar, cinnamon, and salt in medium bowl. Add butter and pinch with your fingers to form coarse crumbs. Add water and firmly press mixture to form clumps.

3 Combine apples, cranberries, remaining ¼ cup sugar and 2 tablespoons flour, ginger, and vanilla in large bowl; mix well. Transfer to baking dish. Sprinkle topping over fruit. Bake until filling is bubbly and topping is golden, 55 minutes–1 hour. Serve warm or at room temperature.

PER SERVING (about ¾ cup): 239 Cal, 5 g Total Fat, 3 g Sat Fat, 0 g Trans Fat, 11 mg Chol, 38 mg Sod, 49 g Carb, 6 g Fib, 2 g Prot, 21 mg Calc.

PointsPlus value: *6.*

spiced peach crisp

Serves 12

3 (20-ounce) bags frozen unsweetened
   sliced peaches
1 cup sugar
2 tablespoons plus ½ cup all-purpose flour
2 teaspoons vanilla extract
¼ teaspoon almond extract

½ teaspoon ground ginger
1 cup old-fashioned oats
½ teaspoon cinnamon
¼ teaspoon salt
¼ cup unsalted butter, cut into small pieces
1 tablespoon water

1 Preheat oven to 375°F. Spray 3-quart baking dish with nonstick spray.

2 Combine peaches, ½ cup sugar, 2 tablespoons flour, vanilla extract, almond extract, and ¼ teaspoon ginger in large bowl; mix well, transfer to baking dish and level top.

3 Combine oats, cinnamon, salt, and remaining ½ cup sugar, ½ cup flour, and ¼ teaspoon ginger in medium bowl. Add butter and rub into mixture with your fingertips, or cut it in with pastry cutter. Stir in water; with your hands, press mixture into clumps. Break clumps into smaller pieces and scatter over top of peach mixture.

4 Bake until filling bubbles and top is golden, 45–50 minutes. Serve warm or at room temperature.

PER SERVING (about 1 cup): 210 Cal, 4 g Total Fat, 2 g Sat Fat, 0 g Trans Fat, 10 mg Chol, 50 mg Sod, 39 g Carb, 3 g Fib, 3 g Prot, 7 mg Calc.
PointsPlus value: **5.**

cook's note

To reheat, place crisp in 300°F oven until heated through, 20–30 minutes.

harvest fruit strudels with pecans

Serves 12

3 tablespoons all-purpose flour
½ cup plus 2 teaspoons granulated sugar
2½ teaspoons cinnamon
½ teaspoon salt
2 red plums, pitted and sliced
1 Granny Smith apple, peeled, cored, and thinly sliced
1 Anjou pear, peeled, cored, and thinly sliced

½ cup dried cranberries
2 tablespoons lemon juice
2 tablespoons finely chopped pecans
14 (9 × 14-inch) sheets frozen phyllo dough, thawed
2 tablespoons confectioners' sugar

1 To make fruit filling, combine flour, ½ cup granulated sugar, 2 teaspoons cinnamon, and salt in large bowl. Add plums, apple, pear, cranberries, and lemon juice; toss well.

2 Combine pecans and remaining 2 teaspoons granulated sugar and ½ teaspoon cinnamon in small bowl.

3 Preheat oven to 400°F. Lay 1 sheet of phyllo dough on work surface with a long side facing you. Cover remaining phyllo with damp towel and plastic wrap to prevent it from drying out. Lightly spray phyllo sheet with nonstick spray. Continue layering with 6 more sheets, lightly spraying each sheet with nonstick spray.

4 Spoon half of fruit filling over phyllo, leaving 2-inch border all around. Fold 2-inch borders on short sides of phyllo over filling, then roll up jelly-roll style, starting with the long side near you and making sure not to make roll too tight and tear phyllo. Repeat with remaining phyllo and fruit mixture, making 2 strudels.

5 Place strudels, seam side down, on large baking sheet. Lightly spray strudels with nonstick spray. Cut four 1-inch slits in top of each strudel to allow steam to escape. Sprinkle strudels evenly with pecan mixture. Bake until filling is hot and phyllo is golden, 25–30 minutes. Cool on baking sheet at least 45 minutes. Just before serving, dust with confectioners' sugar and slice each strudel on diagonal into 6 slices.

PER SERVING (1 slice): 142 Cal, 1 g Total Fat, 0 g Sat Fat, 0 g Trans Fat, 0 mg Chol, 226 mg Sod, 32 g Carb, 2 g Fib, 2 g Prot, 9 mg Calc.

PointsPlus value: *4.*

coconut-cardamom rice pudding

Serves 8

2½ cups water
Pinch salt
1 cup long-grain white rice, preferably
   jasmine or basmati
2 cups low-fat (1 percent) milk
1 (14-ounce) can light coconut milk

¼ cup packed light brown sugar
¼ cup granulated sugar
1 teaspoon ground cardamom
¼ cup shredded sweetened coconut,
   toasted

1   Bring water and salt to boil in heavy medium saucepan over high heat. Add rice and reduce heat to low. Cook, covered, 20 minutes. Remove saucepan from heat and let stand, covered, about 10 minutes.

2   Stir milk, coconut milk, brown sugar, granulated sugar, and cardamom into rice and set over medium heat; bring just to boil. Reduce heat to low and simmer, stirring frequently, until mixture is thick and creamy and rice is very soft, about 30 minutes, stirring constantly during last 5 minutes of cooking.

3   Spoon rice pudding into medium bowl and let cool to room temperature, stirring occasionally. Refrigerate, covered, until chilled, at least 4 hours or overnight.

4   Spoon pudding evenly into 8 dessert dishes. Top evenly with coconut.

PER SERVING (½ cup pudding with ½ tablespoon coconut): 202 Cal, 4 g Total Fat, 3 g Sat Fat, 0 g Trans Fat, 3 mg Chol, 88 mg Sod, 38 g Carb, 1 g Fib, 4 g Prot, 86 mg Calc.

PointsPlus value: *5.*

Ready, Set, Bake

There's no secret to creating bake shop worthy desserts—all it takes is a little smart preparation. Here are the steps to take before you bake.

Equip yourself. Before you begin, make sure you have the right pans or dishes for the dessert you're making. Most recipes call for standard cake and baking pans, but some call for specialty items like tart pans and ramekins that you may need to borrow or shop for.

Read the recipe. Read through the entire recipe so you will be familiar with the ingredients and the steps required. Seemingly simple recipes can call for unusual spices that you'll need to buy or require or long chilling or freezing times that you may not have time for.

Softening equals success. To incorporate smoothly into a batter, recipes often call for butter and cream cheese to be "softened" or "at room temperature." Give yourself time for this important step. If you do forget, you can cut butter or cream cheese into small pieces to soften faster, or you can microwave them on the defrost setting in 10 second increments until softened.

Preheat the oven. To achieve optimal volume, it is vital for most cakes and quick breads to go into the oven as soon as the batter is mixed. If they stand on the counter while the oven is heating, the sweets may not rise properly.

Measure Up

If you measure carefully and correctly, you will get consistent results each time you bake.

Brown Sugar Firmly pack the sugar into a dry measuring cup, then level it off with the straight edge of a knife.

Butter The wrapper that a stick of butter comes in is premarked for tablespoons, ¼ cup, ⅓ cup, and ½ cup, so there is no need to measure it.

Dry Ingredients Use standard dry measuring cups that come in nesting sets of ¼, ⅓, ½, and 1 cup. To measure flour, first stir it to aerate, then lightly spoon into the desired size cup to overflowing. Level it off with the straight edge of a knife.

Liquids Place a glass measuring cup with a spout on the counter and add the desired amount of liquid. Bend down to check the amount at eye level.

Sour Cream and Yogurt Use standard dry measuring cups. Spoon the ingredient into a cup, and level it off with a rubber spatula.

Spices, Herbs, and Citrus Zest Use standard measuring spoons that come in nesting sets of ⅛, ¼, ½, and 1 teaspoon and 1 tablespoon. Fill the spoon with the ingredient, then level it off with the straight edge of a knife.

lemon custards with raspberry sauce

Serves 4

6 ounces fat-free cream cheese
1 cup fat-free ricotta cheese
8 tablespoons confectioners' sugar
½ cup fat-free plain Greek yogurt
¼ cup thawed frozen fat-free whipped
    topping

2 teaspoons grated lemon zest
½ cup fresh or frozen unsweetened
    raspberries, thawed
2 tablespoons seedless raspberry jam

1 Beat cream cheese with electric mixer on high speed in medium bowl until smooth. Beat in ricotta and 6 tablespoons confectioners' sugar. Gently fold in yogurt, whipped topping, and lemon zest with rubber spatula.

2 Cut out 4 (8-inch) squares cheesecloth; dampen slightly with cold water. Line 4 (6-ounce) ramekins or custard cups with cheesecloth, allowing excess to hang over edges. Spoon cream cheese mixture into ramekins. Fold excess cheesecloth over tops. Refrigerate until set, about 4 hours or overnight.

3 Meanwhile, combine raspberries, jam, and remaining 2 tablespoons confectioners' sugar in food processor and puree. Pour mixture through sieve set over bowl, pressing on solids with spoon to extract as much liquid as possible; discard solids. Cover sauce and refrigerate.

4 Pour off any liquid that has collected inside ramekins. Invert ramekins on dessert plates; peel off cheesecloth. Spoon or drizzle sauce around plates.

PER SERVING (1 custard with 2 tablespoons sauce): 208 Cal, 1 g Total Fat, 0 g Sat Fat, 0 g Trans Fat, 13 mg Chol, 310 mg Sod, 33 g Carb, 1 g Fib, 14 g Prot, 201 mg Calc.

PointsPlus value: **5.**

double chocolate puddings

Serves 4

¼ cup sugar
2 tablespoons cornstarch
2 cups fat-free half-and-half
2 ounces semisweet chocolate, finely chopped
1 ounce bittersweet chocolate, finely chopped

1 large egg yolk
1 tablespoon almond liqueur, such as Amaretto
1 teaspoon vanilla extract
Pinch salt

1 Whisk together sugar and cornstarch in medium saucepan. Slowly whisk in half-and-half, whisking until smooth. Set pan over medium heat; cook, whisking constantly, until mixture thickens and bubbles, 6–8 minutes. Immediately remove saucepan from heat. Stir in semisweet and bittersweet chocolate, stirring until chocolate is melted and smooth.

2 Whisk together egg yolk, liqueur, vanilla, and salt in medium bowl. Slowly whisk half of hot half-and-half mixture into yolk mixture. Add yolk mixture to saucepan and cook over low heat, stirring constantly with wooden spoon, just until mixture thickens, 1–2 minutes.

3 Immediately divide pudding evenly among four (5-ounce) ramekins; let cool to room temperature. Refrigerate, covered, until thoroughly chilled and set, at least 3 hours or up to 3 days.

PER SERVING (1 ramekin): 277 Cal, 9 g Total Fat, 4 g Sat Fat, 0 g Trans Fat, 56 mg Chol, 139 mg Sod, 43 g Carb, 1 g Fib, 6 g Prot, 171 mg Calc.

PointsPlus value: **8.**

raspberry tiramisu

Serves 12

½ cup boiling water
1 tablespoon plus 1 teaspoon instant
  espresso powder
1 tablespoon granulated sugar
3 tablespoons coffee-flavored liqueur
1 cup plain fat-free Greek yogurt
½ cup plus 2 teaspoons confectioners'
  sugar

1 tablespoon grated orange zest
1 teaspoon vanilla extract
1 cup thawed frozen fat-free whipped
  topping
2 (3-ounce) packages ladyfingers
  (48 ladyfingers)
2 cups fresh raspberries

1 Combine boiling water, espresso powder, and granulated sugar in medium bowl; stir until espresso powder and sugar have dissolved. Stir in liqueur; let cool slightly.

2 Combine yogurt, ½ cup confectioners' sugar, orange zest, and vanilla in large bowl. Gently fold in whipped topping.

3 Line bottom of 3-quart baking dish with half of ladyfingers. Brush with half of espresso mixture. Top with half of yogurt mixture. Repeat with remaining ladyfingers, espresso mixture, and yogurt mixture. Cover with plastic wrap, being careful not to let wrap touch surface of tiramisu; refrigerate until chilled, at least 4 hours or up to 3 days.

4 Just before serving, sprinkle tiramisu with raspberries and dust with remaining 2 teaspoons confectioners' sugar. Cut into 12 squares.

PER SERVING (1 square): 122 Cal, 1 g Total Fat, 1 g Sat Fat, 0 g Trans Fat, 52 mg Chol, 32 mg Sod, 22 g Carb, 1 g Fib, 3 g Prot, 24 mg Calc.

PointsPlus value: **3.**

strawberry-chocolate ice-cream cake

Serves 12

1 cup cake flour
1½ teaspoons baking powder
¼ teaspoon salt
½ cup fat-free egg substitute
¾ cup sugar
¼ cup hot water
2 tablespoons unsalted butter, melted
1 teaspoon vanilla extract

2 pints fat-free strawberry ice cream, slightly softened
1 pint fat-free chocolate ice cream, slightly softened
12 large fresh strawberries
12 tablespoons purchased strawberry topping

1. Preheat oven to 350°F. Spray 9-inch square baking pan with nonstick spray. Line with wax paper; spray with nonstick spray.

2. Whisk together cake flour, baking powder, and salt in medium bowl. With an electric mixer on high speed, beat egg substitute in large bowl until thickened, about 3 minutes. Gradually add sugar, beating until fluffy, about 3 minutes. Reduce speed to low. Beat in water, butter, and vanilla until combined. Add flour mixture and beat just until blended.

3. Pour batter into pan. Bake until toothpick inserted into center comes out clean, 20–25 minutes. Let cool completely in pan on wire rack. Run thin knife around edge of cake to loosen it from pan. Invert onto rack; remove wax paper.

4. With serrated knife, cut cake horizontally in half. Place 1 layer, cut side up, on serving plate. With narrow metal spatula, spread 2 cups strawberry ice cream over cake in an even layer, spreading it all the way to edges. Freeze until firm, about 30 minutes. Spread chocolate ice cream over strawberry ice cream in an even layer; freeze until firm, about 30 minutes. Spread remaining strawberry ice cream on top of chocolate ice cream; top with remaining cake layer, cut side down. Wrap tightly in heavy-duty foil; freeze until completely frozen, at least 3 hours or up to 1 week.

5. Let cake stand at room temperature 10 minutes. With serrated knife, cut cake in half, then cut each half crosswise into 6 slices. Place a cake slice and a strawberry on each of 12 chilled plates, drizzle cake evenly with sauce, and serve at once.

PER SERVING (¹⁄₁₂ of cake with 1 tablespoon sauce): 225 Cal, 2 g Total Fat, 1 g Sat Fat, 0 g Trans Fat, 5 mg Chol, 193 mg Sod, 47 g Carb, 1 g Fib, 5 g Prot, 154 mg Calc.

PointsPlus value: **6.**

chocolate-cherry ice-cream loaf

Serves 12

1 (1½-quart) container no-sugar-added light
    vanilla ice cream
12 small chocolate wafer cookies
1 tablespoon unsalted butter, melted

⅛ teaspoon almond extract
1 (15-ounce) can dark sweet cherries
    (packed in water), well drained

1. Spoon 2 cups ice cream into medium bowl; set aside to soften slightly and return remaining ice cream to freezer. Line 8½ × 4½-inch metal loaf pan with plastic wrap, allowing wrap to extend over rim by several inches.

2. Put cookies in food processor and pulse to make crumbs. Transfer crumbs to small bowl and stir in melted butter.

3. Stir almond extract into softened ice cream in bowl; fold in cherries. Spoon ice-cream mixture into lined pan and smooth top; sprinkle with 1/3 cup crumb mixture and press down gently. Freeze until firm, about 2 hours.

4. Remove remaining ice cream from freezer and leave at room temperature just until softened. Remove loaf pan from freezer and gently spread softened ice cream on frozen ice-cream mixture, being careful not to disturb crumbs. Sprinkle with remaining crumb mixture; press crumbs into ice cream. Fold excess plastic wrap over top of loaf to cover and freeze until firm enough to slice, at least 8 hours.

5. To serve, unwrap plastic at top of loaf. Invert loaf on platter and remove and discard plastic wrap. Cut loaf into 12 slices, rinsing knife with hot water after cutting each slice.

PER SERVING (1 slice): 153 Cal, 6 g Total Fat, 3 g Sat Fat, 0 g Trans Fat, 14 mg Chol, 93 mg Sod, 22 g Carb, 0 g Fib, 4 g Prot, 133 mg Calc.

PointsPlus* value: *4.

cook's note

This is a perfect make-ahead dessert for summer entertaining. You can store it in the freezer up to 2 weeks.

ruby grapefruit–lime granita

Serves 6

3 cups pink or ruby red grapefruit juice
1 cup boiling water
½ cup superfine sugar

1 tablespoon grated lime zest
2 tablespoons Campari
Fresh mint leaves

① Whisk grapefruit juice, water, sugar, and lime zest in large bowl until sugar dissolves. Pour mixture into 9 × 13-inch baking dish. Cover and freeze until partially frozen, about 2 hours. Remove from freezer and stir with fork, breaking up ice crystals. Cover pan again and return to freezer. Continue to freeze, stirring mixture with fork every 30 minutes, until completely icy, about 3 hours longer.

② Scoop granita loosely into airtight container and store in freezer up to 1 month. To serve, scoop into glasses. Drizzle each serving with 1 teaspoon Campari and garnish with mint leaves.

PER SERVING (¾ cup): 127 Cal, 0 g Total Fat, 0 g Sat Fat, 0 g Trans Fat, 0 mg Chol, 2 mg Sod, 30 g Carb, 0 g Fib, 1 g Prot, 15 mg Calc.

PointsPlus value: *3.*

cook's note

Campari is a dark red herb- and fruit-infused apéritif. If you prefer, you can drizzle the granita with raspberry liqueur, or for an alcohol-free option, use red grape juice.

Ruby Grapefruit–Lime Granita

melon wedges with raspberry-yogurt drizzle

Serves 6

2 cups frozen unsweetened raspberries, thawed
¼ cup plain fat-free Greek yogurt
3 tablespoons honey

1 cantaloupe, peeled, seeded, and cut into 12 wedges
1 honeydew melon, peeled, seeded, and cut into 12 wedges

1 To make sauce, pulse raspberries in food processor until pureed. Strain puree through sieve set over bowl; discard seeds. Stir yogurt and honey into puree. Cover and refrigerate.

2 Arrange cantaloupe and honeydew wedges alternately on large serving platter. Serve with sauce on the side.

PER SERVING (4 melon wedges and 2½ tablespoons sauce): 190 Cal, 1 g Total Fat, 0 g Sat Fat, 0 g Trans Fat, 0 mg Chol, 59 mg Sod, 46 g Carb, 5 g Fib, 4 g Prot, 55 mg Calc.

PointsPlus value: *5.*

caramel apples

Serves 6

6 small Gala apples
6 ice-pop sticks
¾ (14-ounce) bag traditional caramels, such
as Kraft's

2 tablespoons orange juice
1 teaspoon vanilla extract
⅛ teaspoon cinnamon

① Remove stems from apples; rinse and dry apples completely. Insert 1 ice-pop stick into stem end of each apple. Line baking sheet with parchment paper or wax paper and spray lightly with canola oil nonstick spray.

② Unwrap caramels if necessary. Combine caramels, orange juice, vanilla, and cinnamon in a medium saucepan over medium heat. Cook, stirring constantly, until caramels melt and mixture is smooth, about 5 minutes. Remove from heat.

③ Working with one apple at a time, tilt saucepan to one side and dip apple three-quarters of the way into caramel mixture; twirl to coat. Let excess caramel drip back into pan. Scrape off any excess caramel from bottom of apple with table knife. Turn apple right side up and allow caramel to settle. Transfer to baking sheet, stick side up. Repeat with remaining apples.

④ Refrigerate apples until caramel is firm, 30 minutes or up to 2 days.

PER SERVING (1 caramel apple without decorations): 256 Cal, 4 g Total Fat, 3 g Sat Fat, 0 g Trans Fat, 4 mg Chol, 122 mg Sod, 55 g Carb, 4 g Fib, 3 g Prot, 77 mg Calc.
PointsPlus* value: *7.

cook's note

To give these apples a festive touch for a Halloween celebration, dip the apples in the caramel, then dip the tops of the apples into mini marshmallows, candy corn, or mini chocolate chips.

Chocolate Brownie Ice-
Cream Sandwiches

chocolate brownie ice-cream sandwiches

Serves 15

¾ cup white whole wheat flour
3 tablespoons unsweetened cocoa
½ teaspoon baking soda
¾ cup sugar
5 tablespoons light stick butter
2 tablespoons water

2 ounces unsweetened chocolate,
  finely chopped
1 large egg
1½ cups vanilla fat-free ice cream
1½ cups coffee fat-free frozen yogurt
¼ cup sliced almonds, toasted

1 Preheat oven to 350°F. Spray 15 × 10-inch jelly-roll pan with nonstick spray. Line pan with foil, spray again with nonstick spray, and dust lightly with flour.

2 Whisk together flour, cocoa, and baking soda in small bowl. In medium saucepan, combine sugar, butter, and water; bring to boil over medium heat, stirring occasionally. Remove saucepan from heat and stir in chocolate, stirring until chocolate melts; let cool 10 minutes. Whisk in egg; stir in flour mixture. Scrape batter into prepared pan and spread thinly and evenly. Bake until toothpick inserted into center comes out clean, about 12 minutes. Cool in pan on rack, then refrigerate 10 minutes.

3 While brownie layer chills, let ice cream and frozen yogurt sit at room temperature to soften slightly. Turn brownie layer onto cutting board and carefully peel off foil. Cut brownie in half lengthwise, forming 2 rectangles, each 5 × 15 inches. Spread one half with vanilla ice cream and other half with coffee frozen yogurt. Sprinkle ice cream and yogurt evenly with almonds. Sandwich layers together, brownie layers on outside. Cover with plastic wrap and freeze until firm, about 3 hours.

4 Remove plastic wrap and place frozen sandwich on cutting board. With a heavy knife, cut into thirds lengthwise. Slice each third into 5 small rectangular sandwiches. Wrap each sandwich in plastic wrap, place sandwiches in large zip-close plastic freezer bag, and freeze up to 1 week.

PER SERVING (1 sandwich): 151 Cal, 6 g Total Fat, 3 g Sat Fat, 0 g Trans Fat, 21 mg Chol, 69 mg Sod, 24 g Carb, 2 g Fib, 4 g Prot, 53 mg Calc.

PointsPlus* value: *4.

roasted pineapple and raspberries with lemon sorbet

Serves 6

3 tablespoons packed light brown sugar
½ teaspoon cinnamon
1 small ripe pineapple, peeled, cored, and
    cut into ¾-inch chunks

1½ cups fresh raspberries
1 pint lemon sorbet

1 Preheat oven to 425°F. Spray 15 × 10-inch jelly-roll pan with nonstick spray.

2 Stir brown sugar and cinnamon together in small bowl. Spread pineapple chunks on pan and sprinkle with brown sugar mixture. Roast, stirring once halfway through cooking time, until pineapple softens and browns in a few spots, about 12 minutes. Let cool.

3 Spoon pineapple into 6 dessert dishes; top evenly with raspberries. Top each with 1/3-cup scoop lemon sorbet.

PER SERVING (¾ cup fruit and ⅓ cup sorbet): 197 Cal, 0 g Total Fat, 0 g Sat Fat, 0 g Trans Fat, 0 mg Chol, 10 mg Sod, 51 g Carb, 4 g Fib, 1 g Prot, 36 mg Calc.
PointsPlus value: **5.**

cook's note

If you're intimidated by peeling and coring a pineapple, you can buy one already prepped in the produce department of most supermarkets.

oranges with fresh raspberry sauce and chocolate

Serves 4

1 cup fresh or thawed frozen raspberries
¼ cup confectioners' sugar
1½ teaspoons lemon juice

4 large navel oranges
4 tablespoons shaved bittersweet chocolate

1   To make sauce, puree raspberries, sugar, and lemon juice in food processor until smooth. Push puree through a strainer; discard seeds.

2   With knife, cut away peel and white pith from oranges; cut into thick slices. Arrange slices evenly on 4 serving plates. Drizzle oranges with raspberry sauce and sprinkle with chocolate.

PER SERVING (1 orange, 2 tablespoons sauce, and 1 tablespoon chocolate): 160 Cal, 2 g Total Fat, 1 g Sat Fat, 0 g Trans Fat, 0 mg Chol, 1 mg Sod, 36 g Carb, 6 g Fib, 2 g Prot, 83 mg Calc.

PointsPlus value: *4.*

cook's note

Make a double batch of the raspberry sauce and use it to dress up angel food cake, pound cake, or vanilla ice cream. It will keep, refrigerated, for up to 1 week.

chocolate-coffee ice-cream pie

Serves 12

CRUST

9 whole (2½ × 5-inch) chocolate graham
    crackers, crumbled
2 tablespoons honey
1 tablespoon canola oil
1 tablespoon low-fat (1 percent) milk

FILLING

2 pints fat-free chocolate ice cream, slightly
    softened
1 pint fat-free coffee ice cream, slightly
    softened
¾ cup light chocolate syrup
2 ounces semisweet chocolate, chopped
3 cups fresh raspberries

1. Preheat oven to 375°F. Spray 9-inch pie plate with nonstick spray.

2. To make crust, put graham crackers in food processor and pulse until finely ground. Add honey, oil, and milk; process until moist and crumbly. Press crumb mixture evenly onto bottom and up side of pie plate. Bake until firm, 8–10 minutes. Let cool completely on wire rack, then freeze until firm, about 30 minutes.

3. To make filling, with narrow metal spatula, spread 2 cups chocolate ice cream in crust in an even layer; freeze until firm, about 30 minutes. Spread coffee ice cream on top of chocolate ice cream; freeze until firm, about 30 minutes. Spread remaining chocolate ice cream on top of coffee ice cream. Loosely wrap pie in wax paper and then in heavy-duty foil. Freeze until completely frozen, at least 4 hours or up to 1 week.

4. Let pie soften slightly in refrigerator about 15 minutes. Cut pie into 12 wedges and place on plates. Drizzle each serving with 1 tablespoon sauce and sprinkle evenly with chocolate. Serve at once with raspberries.

PER SERVING (1/12 of pie, 1 tablespoon sauce, and ¼ cup raspberries): 215 Cal, 5 g Total Fat, 2 g Sat Fat, 0 g Trans Fat, 2 mg Chol, 157 mg Sod, 41 g Carb, 2 g Fib, 5 g Prot, 125 mg Calc.

PointsPlus value: **6.**

cook's note

For a different version of this pie, use fat-free vanilla and strawberry ice cream and serve it with fresh strawberries.

Chocolate-Coffee Ice-Cream Pie

warm berry ice-cream sundaes with pistachios

Serves 6 • Ready in 20 minutes or less

1 tablespoon unsalted butter
4 cups fresh strawberries, hulled and sliced
1 cup fresh blueberries
1 cup fresh raspberries
3 tablespoons sugar

2 tablespoons orange juice
1 teaspoon grated lemon zest
3 cups vanilla fat-free ice cream
3 tablespoons pistachios, toasted and chopped

① Melt butter in large nonstick skillet over medium-high heat. Add strawberries, blueberries, raspberries, sugar, and orange juice. Cook, stirring occasionally, until berries are softened and juicy, 3–4 minutes. Remove from heat and stir in zest.

② Spoon ½ cup ice cream into each of 6 dessert bowls; top evenly with berry mixture and pistachios and serve at once.

PER SERVING (1 sundae): 215 Cal, 5 g Total Fat, 1 g Sat Fat, 0 g Trans Fat, 5 mg Chol, 68 mg Sod, 40 g Carb, 6 g Fib, 5 g Prot, 127 mg Calc.

PointsPlus value: *6.*

toasted pound cake ice-cream sundaes

Serves 6

½ cup fat-free milk
⅓ cup sugar
¼ cup unsweetened cocoa powder
Pinch salt
1 tablespoon semisweet chocolate chips
2 teaspoons unsalted butter

½ teaspoon vanilla extract
2 (½-inch-thick) slices reduced-fat pound cake, toasted
3 cups fat-free vanilla ice cream
3 cups sliced fresh strawberries

1 To make chocolate sauce, whisk together milk, sugar, cocoa, and salt in small heavy-bottomed saucepan. Set over medium heat; bring just to simmer, whisking frequently.

2 Remove from heat; add chocolate chips, butter, and vanilla and whisk until smooth. Let cool, cover, and refrigerate up to 1 week. (Stir before serving.)

3 Cut pound cake slices into ½-inch cubes. Spoon ½ cup ice cream into each of 6 dessert bowls; top evenly with pound cake cubes and strawberries. Drizzle with chocolate sauce and serve at once.

PER SERVING (1 sundae): 237 Cal, 3 g Total Fat, 2 g Sat Fat, 0 g Trans Fat, 4 mg Chol, 151 mg Sod, 49 g Carb, 4 g Fib, 6 g Prot, 162 mg Calc.

PointsPlus value: **6.**

easy white chocolate drop cookies

Serves 24

½ cup quick-cooking (not instant) oats
1 cup all-purpose flour
½ teaspoon baking soda
¼ teaspoon salt
4 tablespoons unsalted butter, melted
   and cooled

¾ cup packed light brown sugar
1 large egg
1 teaspoon vanilla extract
4 ounces white chocolate, cut into
   ¼-inch pieces

1 Place oven racks in upper and lower thirds of oven and preheat oven to 350°F. Spray 2 large baking sheets with nonstick spray.

2 Put oats in blender and process until finely ground. Combine oats, flour, baking soda, and salt in small bowl. With an electric mixer on low speed, beat butter, brown sugar, egg, and vanilla in large bowl until well blended. Add flour mixture and beat until blended. Stir chocolate into dough.

3 Drop dough by level tablespoonfuls onto baking sheets 2 inches apart. With glass dipped in flour, or with your fingers, press each mound to make 2-inch rounds. Bake until lightly browned along edges, 9–11 minutes, rotating baking sheets halfway through baking. Let cool on baking sheets on wire racks about 1 minute. With spatula, transfer cookies to racks and let cool completely.

PER SERVING (1 cookie): 98 Cal, 4 g Total Fat, 2 g Sat Fat, 0 g Trans Fat, 15 mg Chol, 60 mg Sod, 15 g Carb, 0 g Fib, 1 g Prot, 18 mg Calc.

PointsPlus value: *3.*

flourless chocolate-walnut cookies

Serves 24

2⅓ cups confectioners' sugar
¾ cup Dutch-process cocoa powder
⅛ teaspoon salt

3 large egg whites, at room temperature
2 teaspoons chocolate extract
1 cup walnuts, chopped

1 Place oven racks in upper and lower thirds of oven; preheat oven to 350°F. Line 2 large baking sheets with parchment paper.

2 Sift confectioners' sugar, cocoa, and salt into medium bowl. With electric mixer on low speed, beat egg whites into cocoa mixture until blended. Increase speed to high and continue beating 1 minute. Beat in chocolate extract. Fold in walnuts.

3 Drop dough by level tablespoonfuls onto baking sheets, making 24 cookies and leaving 2 inches between them. Bake until shiny, cracked, and firm to the touch, 13–15 minutes. Cool on baking sheets. Store in airtight container up to 3 days.

PER SERVING (1 cookie): 82 Cal, 3 g Total Fat, 0 g Sat Fat, 0 g Trans Fat, 0 mg Chol, 20 mg Sod, 14 g Carb, 1 g Fib, 2 g Prot, 8 mg Calc.

PointsPlus value: *2.*

chocolate-cranberry oatmeal cookies

Serves 12

½ cup all-purpose flour
¼ cup quick-cooking oats
½ teaspoon baking soda
⅛ teaspoon salt
2 tablespoons unsalted butter, melted and cooled

⅓ cup packed light brown sugar
1 large egg
1 teaspoon vanilla extract
2 ounces semisweet chocolate, cut into ¼-inch pieces
⅓ cup dried cranberries

1 Preheat oven to 350°F. Spray large baking sheet with nonstick spray.

2 Combine flour, oats, baking soda, and salt in small bowl; set aside. With electric mixer on low speed, beat melted butter, brown sugar, egg, and vanilla in medium bowl until well blended. Add flour mixture and stir just until combined. Fold in chocolate and cranberries.

3 Drop dough by level tablespoonfuls onto baking sheet, making 12 mounds and leaving 2 inches between them. With bottom of glass dipped in flour or with your fingers, press each mound to make 2-inch rounds. Bake until edges are lightly browned, 9–11 minutes. Cool cookies on baking sheet for 1 minute, then transfer with spatula to rack to cool completely. Store in airtight container up to 2 days.

PER SERVING (1 cookie): 104 Cal, 4 g Total Fat, 2 g Sat Fat, 0 g Trans Fat, 23 mg Chol, 85 mg Sod, 16 g Carb, 1 g Fib, 2 g Prot, 12 mg Calc.

PointsPlus value: *3.*

coconut-almond macaroons

Serves 24

4 large egg whites, at room temperature
½ teaspoon cream of tartar
¼ teaspoon salt
¾ cup sugar

¼ teaspoon coconut extract
¼ teaspoon almond extract
1 cup sweetened flaked coconut
¼ cup sliced almonds, chopped

1 Place oven racks in upper and lower thirds of oven. Preheat oven to 250°F. Line 2 large baking sheets with parchment paper.

2 Combine egg whites, cream of tartar, and salt in large bowl. Beat with electric mixer on high speed until soft peaks form. With mixer running, add sugar, 1 tablespoon at a time. Beat until stiff peaks form. Beat in coconut extract and almond extract. Fold in coconut flakes and sliced almonds with rubber spatula.

3 Drop batter by level tablespoonfuls onto baking sheets. Bake until macaroons are dried, about 1 hour, rotating baking sheets top to bottom after 30 minutes. Cool on baking sheets. With a spatula, gently lift macaroons from paper; store in airtight container up to 3 days.

PER SERVING (3 macaroons): 48 Cal, 2 g Total Fat, 1 g Sat Fat, 0 g Trans Fat, 0 mg Chol, 41 mg Sod, 8 g Carb, 0 g Fib, 1 g Prot, 3 mg Calc.

PointsPlus value: *1.*

benne wafers

Serves 24

¼ cup honey
¼ cup sugar
2 tablespoons unsalted butter
¼ cup all-purpose flour

¼ teaspoon baking powder
⅛ teaspoon baking soda
3 tablespoons toasted sesame seeds

1. Preheat oven to 350°F. Line large baking sheet with parchment paper.

2. Combine honey, sugar, and butter in medium saucepan; bring to boil over medium heat. Boil, stirring often, 1 minute. Remove pan from heat and gradually stir in flour. Stir in baking powder and baking soda (the mixture will foam). Stir in sesame seeds. Set saucepan over pan of barely simmering water to keep batter warm (it will become too thick to work with if allowed to cool).

3. Drop batter by level teaspoonfuls onto baking sheet, making batch of 8 cookies and leaving 3 inches between each (batter will spread considerably during baking). Bake until cookies are lacy and lightly browned, 4–5 minutes; cookies can burn quickly, so watch them carefully.

4. Cool cookies on sheet just until they begin to set, about 1 minute. With wide metal spatula, immediately transfer cookies to rack to cool completely. Repeat with remaining batter, making about 5 more batches and reusing same sheet of parchment.

PER SERVING (2 cookies): 38 Cal, 1 g Total Fat, 1 g Sat Fat, 0 g Trans Fat, 3 mg Chol, 11 mg Sod, 6 g Carb, 0 g Fib, 0 g Prot, 3 mg Calc.

PointsPlus value: *1.*

cook's note

Benne wafers have been a sweet Southern tradition since Colonial times when Africans brought sesame seeds, which they called benne seeds, to America. These cookies are good keepers; you can store them in an airtight container at room temperature for up to a week.

chocolate-drizzled cranberry-chocolate biscotti

Serves 10

1½ cups all-purpose flour	2 large eggs
½ cup unsweetened cocoa powder	2 tablespoons unsalted butter, melted
2 teaspoons baking powder	1 teaspoon vanilla extract
½ teaspoon baking soda	¾ cup dried cranberries
¼ teaspoon salt	1 ounce semisweet chocolate
¾ cup sugar	

1. Preheat oven to 350°F. Spray large baking sheet with nonstick spray.

2. Combine flour, cocoa, baking powder, baking soda, and salt in large bowl. With an electric mixer on medium speed, beat sugar, eggs, butter, and vanilla in medium bowl. Reduce speed to low. Add flour mixture to egg mixture; beat until well combined (the dough will be fairly dry). Add cranberries, kneading dough a few times in bowl if necessary.

3. Sprinkle work surface lightly with flour. Turn dough onto surface and divide in half. With floured hands, working one piece at a time, roll dough with palms of your hands into 15 × 1½-inch log. Place log on baking sheet. Repeat with remaining dough, placing logs 2 inches apart. Bake until firm and toothpick inserted into center of each log comes out clean, about 15 minutes. With wide spatula, carefully transfer logs to cutting board; let cool 10 minutes.

4. Meanwhile, reduce oven temperature to 300°F. With serrated knife, slice each log crosswise into thirty (½-inch-thick) slices. Place slices 1 inch apart on baking sheet. Bake until fairly dry, turning over once, about 10 minutes per side. Cool completely on wire rack.

5. Place chocolate in small microwavable bowl and microwave on High, stirring every 15 seconds, until melted and smooth, 45 seconds–1 minute. Transfer chocolate to small zip-close plastic bag. Cut off tiny corner of bag and decoratively drizzle chocolate over cookies. Refrigerate or let stand in cool place until chocolate is firm.

PER SERVING (3 cookies): 102 Cal, 3 g Total Fat, 0 g Sat Fat, 0 g Trans Fat, 24 mg Chol, 64 mg Sod, 18 g Carb, 3 g Fib, 3 g Prot, 18 mg Calc.

PointsPlus value: **3.**

spiced brown butter cookies

Serves 36

4 tablespoons unsalted butter
1½ cups all-purpose flour
½ teaspoon cinnamon
¼ teaspoon ground cloves
¼ teaspoon ground allspice
½ teaspoon baking soda

½ teaspoon salt
¾ cup packed dark brown sugar
¼ cup honey
1 large egg white
2 teaspoons vanilla extract
⅓ cup fat-free sour cream

1 Place oven racks in upper and lower thirds of oven and preheat oven to 350°F. Spray 2 large baking sheets with nonstick spray.

2 Melt butter in small saucepan over low heat. Continue to cook, swirling pan occasionally, until butter turns nut brown, about 2 minutes. Pour butter into small bowl and let cool to room temperature.

3 Whisk together flour, cinnamon, cloves, allspice, baking soda, and salt in small bowl. Stir together brown sugar, honey, egg white, and vanilla in large bowl until blended. Stir browned butter, then sour cream into brown sugar mixture. Add flour mixture and stir until blended. Drop dough by teaspoonfuls onto baking sheets about 2 inches apart. Bake until cookies spring back when lightly pressed, 8–10 minutes, rotating baking sheets halfway through baking. Let cool on baking sheets on wire racks about 2 minutes. With spatula, transfer cookies to racks and let cool completely.

PER SERVING (1 cookie): 58 Cal, 1 g Total Fat, 1 g Sat Fat, 0 g Trans Fat, 4 mg Chol, 57 mg Sod, 10 g Carb, 0 g Fib, 1 g Prot, 9 mg Calc.

PointsPlus value: *1.*

From top, clockwise:
Spiced Brown Butter
Cookies, Chocolate Drizzled
Cranberry-Chocolate Biscotti,
page 373, and Apricot-
Oat Squares, page 376

apricot-oat squares

Serves 16

1 cup whole wheat pastry flour
¾ cup quick-cooking (not instant) oats
½ cup packed light brown sugar
¼ cup slivered almonds, finely chopped
½ teaspoon cinnamon
½ teaspoon baking soda

¼ teaspoon salt
1 large egg white
2 tablespoons canola oil
1 tablespoon fat-free milk
1 (10-ounce) jar apricot fruit spread
½ cup chopped dried apricots

1. Preheat oven to 350°F. Line 9-inch square baking pan with foil, allowing foil to extend over rim of pan by 2 inches. Spray foil with nonstick spray.

2. Combine pastry flour, oats, brown sugar, almonds, cinnamon, baking soda, and salt in large bowl. With fork, beat together egg white, oil, and milk in small bowl. Add egg mixture to flour mixture, stirring until well blended. With your fingers, blend mixture until moist crumbs form. Reserve 2/3 cup. Transfer remaining oat mixture to pan, pressing firmly to form an even layer. Bake until set and lightly browned along edges, about 10 minutes.

3. Stir together fruit spread and apricots in small bowl; spread evenly over hot crust. Crumble reserved oat mixture on top. Bake until fruit spread is bubbly at edges and top is browned, 15–20 minutes. Let cool completely in pan on wire rack. Lift out using foil as handles; cut into 16 squares.

PER SERVING (1 square): 146 Cal, 3 g Total Fat, 0 g Sat Fat, 0 g Trans Fat, 0 mg Chol, 85 mg Sod, 29 g Carb, 3 g Fib, 3 g Prot, 25 mg Calc.

PointsPlus value: **4.**

fudgy walnut brownies

Serves 16

3 tablespoons unsalted butter
½ cup unsweetened cocoa
1½ teaspoons instant espresso powder
1 teaspoon vanilla extract
¾ cup packed light brown sugar

2 large eggs
¾ cup all-purpose flour
½ teaspoon baking powder
¼ teaspoon salt
¾ cup coarsely chopped walnuts

1 Preheat oven to 350°F. Line 8-inch square baking pan with foil, allowing foil to extend over rim of pan by 2 inches. Spray foil with nonstick spray.

2 Melt butter in medium saucepan over low heat. Remove saucepan from heat and whisk in cocoa, espresso powder, and vanilla. Let cool 5 minutes, then whisk in brown sugar and eggs.

3 Whisk together flour, baking powder, and salt in small bowl. Add flour mixture to cocoa mixture, stirring just until blended. Scrape batter into baking pan and level top. Sprinkle with walnuts. Bake until toothpick inserted into center comes out with moist crumbs clinging to it, 20–25 minutes.

4 Cool brownies completely in pan on rack. When cool, lift brownies from pan using overhanging foil as handles; cut into 16 squares. Store in airtight container up to 1 day.

PER SERVING (1 square): 134 Cal, 7 g Total Fat, 2 g Sat Fat, 0 g Trans Fat, 32 mg Chol, 61 mg Sod, 17 g Carb, 2 g Fib, 3 g Prot, 23 mg Calc.

PointsPlus value: *4.*

menus for every day and special days

Family Weekend Breakfast

SERVES 4

Cremini, Spinach, and Goat Cheese
Frittata, 3
Coriander-Lime Roasted Pineapple, 24
Raspberry-Orange Corn Muffins, 23

Weekend Brunch with Friends

SERVES 6

Smoky Sweet Potato, Canadian Bacon, and
Corn Hash, 5
Poached eggs
Melon Wedges with Raspberry-Yogurt
Drizzle, 358
Maple–Raisin Bran Muffins, 20

Saturday Night Steak Dinner

SERVES 6

Shrimp with Tomato-Chipotle Relish, 84
Hearts of Romaine with Creamy Lime
Dressing, 65
Grilled Sirloin with Coffee-Molasses Barbecue
Sauce, 111
Chili-Lime Corn on the Cob, 299
Coconut Cream Pie with Gingersnap
Crust, 338

Pack a Picnic

SERVES 4

Southwestern Tuna Wraps, 33
Hoppin' John Salad, 53
Apricot-Oat Squares, 376

Burger Night Menu

SERVES 4

Green Salad with Roasted Corn and Cumin
Vinaigrette, 62
Southwestern Salsa Burgers, 31
Honey-Glazed Sweet Potato Fries, 306
Spiced Brown Butter Cookies, 374

Backyard Cookout

SERVES 6

Chopped Salad with Feta Cheese, 58
Grilled Pork Tenderloin with Pineapple-Basil
Relish, 125
Green Beans with Feta and Mint, 289
Toasted Pound Cake–Ice Cream Sundaes, 367

Laid-Back Summer Get Together

SERVES 4

Heirloom Tomato Salad with Feta and
Capers, 69
Chicken and Vegetable Kebabs with Minted
Rice Pilaf, 149
Balsamic Marinated Roasted Peppers with
Basil, 286
Summer Fruit Tart with Phyllo Crust, 340

Comforting Autumn Dinner

SERVES 4

Bratwursts and Sauerkraut Braised in Beer, 133
Warm Potato Salad with Mustard Dressing, 301
Honey-Glazed Autumn Apple Cake, 331

Snow Day at Home

SERVES 4

Roasted Red Pepper Beef Stew, 115

Mashed Potatoes with Leeks and Garlic, 302

Oranges with Fresh Raspberry Sauce and
Chocolate, 363

Casual Asian Dinner

SERVES 6

Steamed Shrimp Dumplings with Soy Dipping
Sauce, 88

Orange-Basil Beef and Broccoli Stir-Fry, 114

Roasted Pineapple and Raspberries with Lemon
Sorbet, 362

Dinner for Two

SERVES 2

Honeydew and Prosciutto Skewers, 72

Honey Roasted Carrots, 290

Spice-Rubbed Lamb Chops with Grape
Tomato–Couscous, 137

Double Chocolate Puddings, 352

Come for Cocktails

SERVES 12

Italian Sausage and Spinach-Stuffed
Mushrooms, 77

Bacon–Cheddar Cheese Tarts, 73

Roasted Potato Slices with Smoked Salmon
Spread, 78

Chickpea and Tomato Pita Pizzas, 99

Curry Roasted Cauliflower and Broccoli with
Yogurt-Mint Sauce, 100

Chocolate Drizzled Cranberry-Chocolate
Biscotti, 373

Game Time Party

SERVES 6

Toasted Snack Mix, 101

Apple, Celery, and Walnut Salad with Dijon
Dressing, 67

Chicken Chili with Black Beans and Sweet
Potato, 155

Easy White Chocolate Drop Cookies, 368

Southern Supper

SERVES 4

Artichoke–White Bean Dip with Veggies and
Pita Chips, 93

Blackened Cajun Catfish, 186

Louisiana Rice Pilaf, 316

Celery Root Salad, 309

Benne Wafers, 372

Easter Dinner

SERVES 6

Red Pepper–Basil Dip with Spring
Vegetables, 94

Spinach and Endive Salad with Walnut
Vinaigrette, 51

Grilled Rack of Lamb with Lemon-Mint
Crust, 135

Asparagus with Chopped Egg and Dill, 284

Lemon-Yogurt Tart, 344

Passover Dinner

SERVES 12

Matzo Ball Soup with Homemade Chicken
Broth, 37

Wine-Braised Beef Brisket, 105

Asparagus-Mushroom Matzo Farfel, 311

Lemon Green Beans with Pine Nuts, 288

Coconut-Almond Macaroons, 371

Rosh Hashanah Menu

SERVES 6

Roasted Beet and Fresh Plum Salad, 68
Orange-Rosemary Glazed Turkey Breast, 166
Oven Roasted Kale with Caramelized
    Onions, 297
Apricot-Raisin Spice Cake, 322

Hanukkah Buffet

SERVES 6

Potato-Turnip Latkes, 304
Mustard and Herb-Crusted Salmon, 174
Chopped Salad with Feta Cheese, 58
Roasted Ratatouille, 293
Harvest Fruit Strudels with Pecans, 348

Children's Halloween Party

SERVES 6

Creamy Salsa Dip with Vegetables, 91
Crispy Chicken Strips with Buttermilk Dipping
    Sauce, 150
Caramel Apples, 359

Thanksgiving Dinner

SERVES 12

Honey-Brined Turkey with Homemade
    Gravy, 164
Pear and Sage Stuffing, 310
Green Beans and Mushrooms with Walnuts, 287
Maple-Orange Mashed Sweet Potatoes, 307
Fresh Cranberry Sauce with Dried Apricots, 319
Ginger-Pumpkin Cheesecake, 332

Christmas Dinner

SERVES 12

Crabmeat and Avocado Salad in Endive, 89
Crown Roast of Pork with Cranberry-Rice
    Pilaf, 120
Parsnip and Potato Mash with Chives, 303
Rosemary-Roasted Brussels Sprouts and
    Carrots, 291
Almond-Pear Linzer Tart, 343

recipes by *PointsPlus* value

Chickpea, Watercress, and Pear Salad, 60

Chickpeas with Swiss Chard and Grape Tomatoes, 216

Chocolate-Coffee Ice-Cream Pie, 364

Coconut-Almond French Toast with Tropical Fruit, 11

Five-Spice Catfish with Pineapple-Pepper Stir Fry, 185

Garlicky Spinach and Fontina Pizza, 281

Gingery Chicken and Vegetable Stir-Fry, 263

Green Lentils and Rice with Caramelized Onions, 211

Grilled T-Bone Steak with Portuguese Piri-Piri Sauce, 109

Grilled Zucchini and Couscous with Fresh Herb Sauce, 313

Honey-Glazed Autumn Apple Cake, 331

Indian Chicken with Cucumber-Mango Sauce, 257

Italian Beef and Mushroom Meat Loaf, 119

Linguine with Stir-Fried Vegetables, 229

Orange-Basil Beef and Broccoli Stir-Fry, 114

Orange-Basil Chicken, 260

Poached Eggs with Green Chile–Tomato Sauce, 2

Pomegranate-Glazed Cheesecake, 334

Pork and Pepper Stir-Fry, 253

Quick Moo Shu Pork, 245

Rosemary-Balsamic Pork Chops, 252

Rosemary-Lemon Roasted Chicken with Sweet Potatoes, 140

Salmon and White Bean Salad, 54

Shrimp, Pineapple, and Avocado Salad, 56

Smoky Sweet "Baked" Beans, 217

Sour Cream Bundt Cake with Pecan Streusel, 329

Southwestern Salsa Burgers, 31

Spice-Rubbed Chicken with Cucumber-Fennel Sauce, 259

Spicy Coconut Basmati Rice with Black-Eyed Peas, 317

Steamed Mussels with Oven Frites, 200

Strawberry-Chocolate Ice-Cream Cake, 354

Thai Tofu and Edamame Stir-Fry, 205

Toasted Pound Cake Ice-Cream Sundaes, 367

Tofu-Soba Noodle Salad with Napa Cabbage, 204

Turkey Sloppy Joes, 170

Walnut-Pear Coffeecake, 19

Warm Berry Ice-Cream Sundaes with Pistachios, 366

White Bean Soup with Cabbage, 44

7 PointsPlus value

Basil Basmati with Green Beans and Blue Cheese, 223

Braised Chicken with White Beans and Tomatoes, 152

Bratwursts and Sauerkraut Braised in Beer, 133

Bulgur Pilaf with Apricots and Feta, 224

Caramel Apples, 359

Cinnamon-Raisin Granola with Sunflower Seeds, 17

Cornish Hens with Spinach-Apple Stuffing, 171

Crispy Chicken Strips with Buttermilk Dipping Sauce, 150

Curried Pork Chops with Chutney Sauce, 247

Double Chocolate Chiffon Cake, 327

Easy Homemade Gnocchi with Asparagus and Tomatoes, 226

Gingery Scallop and Snap Pea Stir-Fry, 196

Grilled Salmon with Honey-Lime Fruit Salad, 176

Herb Roasted Beef Tenderloin and Root Vegetables, 104

Honey-Glazed Pork Chops, 249

Lemon Cod and Potato Casserole, 188

Lemongrass-Scallion Burgers, 29

Middle Eastern Chicken and Pita Salad, 143

Moroccan Chickpea and Lentil Stew, 210

Orange-Rosemary Glazed Turkey Breast, 166

Pan-Seared Tuna with Citrus-Avocado Salsa, 182

Pasta with Roasted Tomatoes and Basil, 232

Penne with Vegetable Bolognese, 230

Pork Chops and Rice with Mole Sauce, 128

Pork Chops with Dried Cherry Sauce, 248

Quick Chicken Fried Rice with Tomatoes and Cilantro, 266

Quinoa and Butternut Squash Pilaf with Goat Cheese, 225

Red Curry Beef, Napa Cabbage, and Noodle Salad, 113

Roasted Pork Tenderloin with Apple-Raisin Sauce, 121

Shiitake and Barley–Stuffed Cabbage, 221

Shrimp and Pasta with Spicy Marinara Sauce, 272

Shrimp, Chorizo, and Rice Stew, 191

Spaghetti with Mussels, Clams, and Shrimp, 201

Sweet Potato Pie with Pumpkinseed Brittle, 335

Thyme-Crusted Roast Pork Loin with Apricot-Port Sauce, 122

Tuna and Black Bean Cheeseburgers, 278

Tunisian Chickpea and Wheat Berry Stew, 222

White Beans and Mustard Greens with Parmesan, 215

8 PointsPlus value

Asian Chicken Noodle Soup, 144

Baked Skillet Pancake with Peach-Blueberry Compote, 13

Crown Roast of Pork with Cranberry-Rice Pilaf, 120

Double Chocolate Puddings, 352

Easy Pantry Minestrone, 208

Gnocchi and Squash with Red Pepper–Basil Sauce, 279

Lemon-Pepper Shrimp and Pasta, 273

Merlot-Braised Beef Roast and Vegetables, 106

Noodle Kugel with Dates and Apricots, 312

Pasta with Spinach Pesto and Feta, 231

Prosciutto and Arugula Pizza, 132

Quick Beef and Vegetable Chili, 242

Quick Pork Chops Parmesan, 250

Roasted Red Pepper Beef Stew, 115

Sausage and Pepper Breakfast Wraps, 4

Shrimp and Pasta with Rosemary-Lemon Tomato Sauce, 275

index